SIMPLIFYING
FINANCE
FOR EVERYONE

Essential concepts to nurture
your financial growth

CHETAN PATEL

INDIA · SINGAPORE · MALAYSIA

Notion Press

Old No. 38, New No. 6
McNichols Road, Chetpet
Chennai - 600 031

First Published by Notion Press 2019
Copyright © Chetan Patel 2019
All Rights Reserved.

ISBN 978-1-68466-469-6

Dedicating this to the young and vibrant enterprising world.

Contents

Part B

Preface

Finance has a significant influence on any individual's life. From a person with modest income sources to a high net worth individual, finance touches everyone. Managing it becomes critical for both individuals and businesses. It is with this motive, I tried writing a book in simple language, which touches financial management for both businesses and individuals. Proper management of finances leads to prosperity and the ability to take some bold decisions with proper calculated risks.

While managing the finances for individuals is pretty simple and straightforward, with ever-growing credit and electronic payment platforms, personal financial management has taken a new dimension. Things must be seen holistically. These need proper consideration while planning and controlling funds. Also, managing expenditure is just one part, but the most important part of personal financial management is earning income. An individual should be motivated to explore and lay down a proper career roadmap. They should be encouraged to envisage the financial implications of choosing those paths. They should be able to assess the different means through which they can earn income during their lifetime. Such exercises can facilitate in taking the right steps and the requisite decisions to grow and thrive.

When individuals collaborate or come on their own to start a business venture, this requires even more exhaustive management of finances, which is many times a painstaking exercise. With more liberalisation given to businesses and technology touching everyone's life, the barriers to enter businesses have significantly reduced, and this has resulted in a higher growth in startups. Businesses today are more competitive than ever, and this will only increase with the passage of time. All this requires better management of money which is a scarce resource. This entails proper record keeping in the form of accounting and taking proper decisions with regards to earning money. Proper accounting and funds management is possible only when businesses have sound planning and controlling processes in place. All of this is covered in this book along with two comprehensive case studies that cover the essential elements of any business and finance. Understanding business finance is not only important for business people but investors as well, who invest in businesses or companies.

Various concepts and tools that are used in finance are placed properly in different sections to enable the reader to appreciate their importance and enable them to apply them judiciously. A simple and powerful understanding of finance should touch upon every individual and help them to plan things around money and control it to realise their dreams and ambitions and uncover their full potential. Thus, this book is primarily meant for all individuals. This can be used by a student as a stepping stone to understand finance which eventually will touch them. This can be used by a person in their personal capacity to manage their funds and create a long-term plan for their career and financial goals. This can be used by new and existing businesses to better manage their businesses and finances. This can be used by potential and present investors who are always tempted to invest in companies but have little understanding of business finance. This is Finance for Everyone.

Acknowledgments

This book is a product of my experience as a finance professional for many years now. This wouldn't have been possible without the collaboration and support from my previous and present managers, stakeholders, my team members and business partners, who have enriched my experience and guided me in understanding business and finance comprehensively.

Equally important is to acknowledge the support that I received from my family. They have always stood beside me, motivated and inspired me to write. I'd like to deeply thank my wife Sneha, my daughter Nishka, my parents Mrs. Nirmala Patel and Mr. Kantilal Patel, and my in-laws Mr. Navinbhai Patel, Mrs. Bhavna Patel, Dr. Swapnil Patel and Dr. Shivani Patel.

Much of my thought process have been shaped by my cousin Mr. Chirag Contractor, who is also my mentor. I wish to thank him for providing me with a proper direction in my chosen career path and actively supporting me in my project.

Mr. Bhupesh Bhatt deserves a special mention. I'm thankful to him for helping me build a theme for this book. My friend Mr. Rajesh Udeshi has been very instrumental in making me realise the importance of keeping the complex world of finance, simple. I was introduced to the world of value investing by Mr. Sunil Paleja. Personal branding, which is incorporated in this book, was introduced to me by Ravi Chatterjee. There are a couple of people whom I'll like to acknowledge for their constructive feedback, who include Dr. Minal Contractor, Mr. Sanjay Pancholi, Sweta Contractor and Shraddha Contractor Patel.

Last but not the least, I would like to thank Notion Press who supported me and agreed to publish this book.

Section 1

Introduction

One of the most important inventions of mankind is money. It is at the centre of any commercial or business activity. Everyone requires money, be it an individual, a business or a government. Activities come to a halt in the absence of money. Much of the massive growth or progress in mankind, over centuries, has been possible with money acting as a medium of exchange. Money these days can be in different forms or currencies. It can be in the form of cash or bank balance, and in different currencies in which the value of it can be expressed. Some major currencies of the world include the United States Dollar (USD), Euro, Pound Sterling, Japanese Yen, Swiss Francs, Indian Rupee (INR), Chinese Yuan and many more.

Cash is king, irrespective of whether it is in hard cash or as a deposit in a bank. Whether we crave for it or curse it, much of what we aspire for has a monetary value. It becomes important for any individual, business or government to better manage their money. Government finances are outside the scope of this book; this book deals primarily with individuals and businesses.

Any individual has basic needs. When this is met, there is a need for a better lifestyle. When you get a better lifestyle, one aspires for more luxury, and many times, this is a continuous cycle. All this depends on the quantum of money that an individual has. Typically for any individual, salary, business, or investments are the source of obtaining money. This is also referred to as income. Most individuals rely on a salary, which has the least risk of earning. The probability of getting a fixed sum of money every month is always very high. The income earned by the individual goes into fulfilling the basic needs firstly.

These are related to food, clothing, shelter, education and health. For this, a certain amount of money is required. If there is a significant balance left after this, an individual always upgrade themselves to a better lifestyle and better products and services. At end of all this, there is either a surplus or a deficit which is left. Surplus would typically occur when there is judicious spending versus income. Deficit, on the contrary, occurs when there is extravagant expenditure versus the income earned.

The surplus earned can be kept in the form of cash or in a bank as a fixed deposit or a savings deposit or it can be invested somewhere. Depending on your risk profile or how much risk you can take, you can decide to park your savings in safe investments like bank fixed deposits or bonds or company debentures. Or you can decide to take a risk and invest in adventurous assets like shares and mutual funds or even start your own business. Returns on investments are typically proportional to the risk taken. A higher risk could probably fetch higher returns, but there's a risk of losing the money invested. On the other hand, a lower risk will have the least probability of losing the invested money. However, it will give lower returns. It's up to an individual to decide where she or he plans to invest. It is at the sole discretion of any individual. A proper balance can facilitate minimising risks and provide better returns.

If an individual decides to start a business, expand the existing business or invest in someone's business, then separate management of finances needs to be done for the same. Even if an individual is investing in shares (which gives ownership rights to an individual to publicly listed companies), an understanding of finances related to business is important to make investment decisions. This should be of real interest to potential or existing shareholders who plan to invest in companies for a longer duration. It helps in assessing the price they are paying to get part ownership in such companies.

Any enterprise or business activity requires an entrepreneur, people, place and equipment. These can be referred to as the four elements required for running the business. If you take any one of these elements out of the equation, the activity will cease to exist. Money brings all the four elements together. Money is the motivating force for the entrepreneur to step in and the source to balance the three elements. A multitude of activities or transactions is carried on by the entrepreneur, involving people, equipment, and other resources to generate income from an enterprising activity.

In business, money is a catalytic force which is supposed to ensure that all the business activities move on seamlessly. The management of money, therefore, forms the basis of financial management. Financial management is often viewed as a complex subject involving a lot of numbers. Many times, debits and credits are viewed as an alien concept. The aim here is to provide a simplified view of finance to the readers. Finance consists of a wide range of activities, which needs to be understood well in a logical form. An understanding of finance is required for better planning and thoughtful spending, smooth running of business operations, and making sound decisions. The aim is not to make the reader a financial wizard. It only tries to provide a common and simplified view which can facilitate the reader to encounter this subject that touches her/him on a regular basis. Ignoring financial management is like digging the grave for oneself, be it in an individual capacity or a business.

This book is meant for all individuals, entrepreneurs and investors, both existing or potential ones and students from a non-finance background (I would say this could be a good book for students from the finance background as well). To anyone who has a keen interest to know the subject but is scared away by complex financial jargons, this book should prove to be useful.

This book does not intend to go by the strict definitions of finance, but I wish to provide my worldview of this subject. This is my perception of the subject which is based on my experiences as a finance professional. The book is broken down into two parts.

Financial management starts with accounting and bookkeeping and funds management. This will be covered in the first part of the book.

As mentioned earlier, any individual or business enters into a multitude of commercial activities to generate income, and this must be recorded on a regular basis. There are certain principles that are developed, over a period of time, to ensure records are maintained in a standardised form. In accounting parlance, they are referred to as concepts and conventions of accounting. Accounting standards are developed to facilitate and provide a standard approach for recording transactions related to a wide range of economic activities that a business undergoes.

Accounting must be maintained in a particular way. There's a format in which the recording takes place, and it is supposed to be maintained in a set of books. (Of course, these days there are many accounting packages, software, and applications available which have replaced physical books.) The books in which transactions are originally recorded is referred to as a journal. From journals, these transactions are systematically transferred and recorded in another set of books which are specific to a certain set of people or firms or companies which the business deals with. Or these are related to expenses incurred by the business or they pertain to cash which flows in and out of the business. Journals transfer records related to these individuals, expenses, income or assets in a separate record referred to as ledgers.

Each transaction involves receiving something and giving away something in return. These are represented in the form of debits and credits. Debits and credits govern the overall recording process.

At the end of every quarter, month or year, the above records are summarised in statements called profit and loss statements and balance sheets. They provide an assessment about the financial performance and the health of a business.

While the above may be relevant for the business, the same can be replicated for individuals as well, albeit in a simple format. However, if one understands the principles of accounting related to business, it can help them in maintaining their personal records related to earnings and spending in a much better way. This can be a powerful tool that can be employed to maintain a consistent lifestyle.

I have tried to simplify accounting by taking a hypothetical case study which reflects real-life business activities that any business might encounter on a regular basis. Many people confuse accounting with financial management. For many people, an accountant is the finance guy, which is not correct. While accounting is a quintessential element of finance, there are a whole lot of things associated with this subject. Accounting helps you in painting the true picture of your business in monetary terms. This further helps you to take appropriate decisions. But it's not an end.

As I said in the beginning, a business needs money to get all the requisite resources to run the business. It is important that this scarce resource is managed properly to ensure that the operations run smoothly. So, funds management or cash management is another element of financial management. Money can be brought by the entrepreneur by themselves, which is also called the **capital,** or it can be borrowed from outside through banks or financial institutions. People providing funds from outside can be referred to as the vendors providing money for a short period, medium-term period, or long period depending on the requirements of the business and, in return, they charge interests and fees.

For every possible activity you can imagine, business requires money. It starts as soon as you conceptualise an idea and want to bring it to reality. In the beginning, you need money to invest in plant or machinery, build inventories, hire people, and purchase or rent facilities. This varies depending on the type of business you plan to operate. Then, for running the daily operations of the business, money is needed. It is needed to pay off the obligation to the state in the form of taxes. All these activities, in turn, bring in income for the business. There's a time lag between earning income and spending money associated with the above activities. Sufficient funds must be maintained always. Also, care must be taken to ensure that a proper balance is maintained between the funds brought by the entrepreneur and the borrowings from outside. The funds borrowed from outside have a fixed obligation and need to be repaid. Any mismanagement of funds can spell troubles for the business and put it in jeopardy. That makes managing funds a critical part of financial management.

Needless to say, similar activities, maybe at a much smaller scale, impact individuals as well. Cash flow management and maintaining a proper balance of funds from internal sources (own funds) and external sources (predominantly banks) are very critical. For society at large, proper discipline maintained by the majority of individuals can help in sustainable growth. At the personal level, this type of exercise helps in planning expenses, especially potential big expenses like buying a house or car or making any other big investments like a lavish holiday abroad. For any aspiring entrepreneur, this can provide an understanding on the timing when she/he can go ahead and start their venture. Care should be taken to incorporate any potential contingencies.

All the things mentioned above require proper planning, regular monitoring, and controlling and that is another topic associated with finance. This will be covered in the second part of the book. A good business or personal practice would be to plan things and anticipate potential earnings in advance, based on your personal experience, or in case of a business, the market in which you're operating.

In business, relevant people and resources must be obtained or sourced in advance to be present in the market and grow your business. This would require creating future projections which again can be for a short period, like a quarterly plan or a yearly plan or it can be a medium-term plan for two to five years, or it can be for a longer duration, like more than a five-year plan. One can have their own view of a short-term or long-term plan, but the essence remains the same.

For individuals, strategic planning is required to invest in themselves, and this is where an individual needs to have an assessment about herself or himself. This is a topic of personal brand management. An individual's earning potential depends on how they develop themselves and what they aspire to do in the long-term. Such an exercise facilitates in undertaking appropriate investments in oneself, and it further helps in getting visibility on earnings in the long-term.

Business Plans

In simple terms, a plan provides an estimate of the income likely to be earned and the expenditure likely to be incurred to earn income, for a specific period. This exercise has to be done with the utmost honesty by considering all the possible factors impacting the business in order to sustain and grow the business. To a great extent, it requires common sense and a good deal of understanding of your business. Each and every element that drives business has to be properly evaluated as they are the building blocks of the entire planning exercise. It shouldn't be a number-crunching exercise, as it often ends up being in many cases.

For medium and big businesses, the people managing the regular affairs of the business need to be involved and provide their view of the market. They need to provide an assessment of people and resources required to run the business. This is the essence of business planning. However, a small entrepreneur can do this exercise on his own, maybe with the help of financial or business consultants. Business plans have to be translated into monetary terms where a proper assessment needs to be made of the costs likely to be incurred and the revenue likely to come from different business activities. Care must be taken to assign proper rates at which resources will be procured and a price at which offerings will be sold by taking a realistic view of the market.

Successful businesses monitor and evaluate the above financial and business plans on a regular basis. They also monitor their transactions properly. Similarly, a person maintaining good discipline about her/his money will monitor spends against the plan.

The difference between the plans and the actual results are called **variances**, which need to be tracked by the business. Variance acts as a friend for individuals and business as it gives a true story of the financial impact of planned activities. In business, an entrepreneur or management should be accountable to these variances. Variance reflects how well or bad you did things versus how you planned it. When you try to deep dive into these variances, it can throw some interesting insights. It can help you to either gain confidence in your decision-making process or take corrective actions.

For a business to be monitored properly, it needs regular reporting. Reporting can be as simple and small as evaluating revenues or income that the entrepreneur earns during the day or assessing the quantum of stock being used during a day or week by the business. Large and mid-corporations have their own systems and processes to take care of this, but it's not that difficult to have a simple and effective reporting structure for a small business. These days, there are many software available that can be subscribed and used to track inventory, collections and sales for small businesses. There are many business intelligence tools available in the market that can cater to the needs of different businesses. But even without them, this exercise requires just some amount of discipline to maintain it.

Reporting is the fundamental building block of a good controls process. It further helps in performance analysis and profitability management. It helps you assess your performance against your plans. Certain products, services or customers tend to give you more profits than others. A reporting system tracks all of this.

A business can have a great product, a strong demand, and a market, but if it doesn't have a good monitoring process, and if it does not assign accountability to the people managing it, it can lead to troubled times.

I personally have witnessed a rock-solid business run by a small entrepreneur shut down due to lack of better controls. It failed to keep some basic controls like keeping a track of utilisation of its inventory and keeping a track of collections managed by the people it had employed. While trust is important, there needs to be a proper account of all the scarce resources that business owns. There's a saying which applies aptly to controlling: 'In God we trust, for the rest we need data' (a phrase often used by my erstwhile manager). It is therefore important to have a proper monitoring mechanism in place. You need to identify the critical components to track and apply common sense. In the above case, it was the inventory that had to be controlled, as it's used to generate cash for the business. The entrepreneur should have assigned accountability to the managers. They should have been accountable for the variances between consumption and availability. This could have avoided a lot of leakages, and the business would have continued successfully.

On the other hand, I am really impressed with my local grocery vendor who has a good knowledge of all products on his shelf. He's not formally well educated but uses his common sense to ensure that he's not over- or under-delivering to his customers. He tracks his performance and keeps a track of the stock on a daily basis. This further helps in ensuring that he doesn't block his money on piling up huge stock and at the same time this ensures that he has sufficient stock to meet the demand of his customers. This helps him to avoid or minimise leakages. If there are variances still occurring, he would reconcile with the basic records which he maintains and can take corrective action if needed.

Reporting and proper monitoring form the basis for better controlling practices. The principles apply to all businesses. It further helps in developing processes or policies pertaining to invoicing or pricing or credit or inventory control or procurement or hiring. It can facilitate in determining the terms and conditions with which you deal with others. Sound and standard commercial processes can help you to focus your energies where it's required the most, which is growing your business more profitably. Also, it is important that a business gets its affairs and processes audited either internally or with the help of expert auditors. Certain legislations make it mandatory to have statutory audits done by professionally qualified accountants, if the business reaches a specific threshold or is operating in a specific industry.

For individuals, it's always advisable to maintain a diary which I'll be covering in the bookkeeping and accounting section. Variances should be evaluated against the plan, and, if required, plans should be revised to consider some changing dynamics. An individual too maintains inventory of her/his requirement. For high value items, it is more important to have proper control over its consumption. This can avoid some unnecessary expenditure and money can be used for something better. This is all up to an individual's discretion. No proper definitions can be assigned related to extravagance. But a judicious call can really help you in avoiding waste and further facilitate in leading a much better lifestyle.

All what I have said so far, mainly related to accounting, funds management, planning and controlling, are the elements of financial management. To me, financial management is proper accounting and funds management through proper planning and control practices. The same can be explored further in the book.

PART A

Section 2

Bookkeeping and Accounting – Backbone of Finance

I. Abbreviations Often Used in This Book

During the course of reading this book, you'll find the usage of letters like **k** applied after any number or **Mn** and **Bn** applied after numbers. Similarly, the currency is expressed in INR (Indian Rupee) as against Rs. or the rupee symbol (₹). To make things clear, let me give a few instances

INR 1,000 is expressed as INR 1k in this book. This means INR 1k stands for one thousand Indian rupees.
INR 1,000,000 is expressed as INR 1 Mn. This means INR 1Mn stands for one million Indian rupees.
INR 1,000,000,000 is expressed as INR 1 Bn. This means INR 1Bn stands for one billion Indian rupees.

Let me further clarify this so as to correlate to the terms like lakhs or crores that we often use instead of millions and billions.

INR 100k = INR 1 lakh
INR 1 Mn = INR 10 lakhs
INR 10 Mn = INR 1 crore
INR 1 Bn = INR 100 crores

Familiarising yourself with these will help in better understanding the examples given in this book and also the case studies.

II. Basics of Bookkeeping and Accounting

A business, whether small or big, or an individual has to deal with numerous commercial activities or transactions. It's humanly impossible to keep a track of them unless they are recorded somewhere in a systematic and standardised manner. This systematic approach followed to record these activities or transactions is referred to as bookkeeping and accounting. Bookkeeping helps in tracking day-to-day activities and at the end of period facilitates in assessing how you've performed financially with all your dealings. We'll first cover how bookkeeping and accounting can be maintained for business and then move to record keeping that will prove useful for individuals. If one understands the principles of bookkeeping as outlined below for business, then it'll be easy to understand how it can apply to individuals. We'll cover this before concluding this section.

In business, if you're unable to keep track of your activities, you're running in deep trouble. It may happen that you'll not be able to understand where your finances are going and very soon you might run short of funds.

It's always advisable to hire the services of accountants to cater to maintaining books of accounts. However, if you can apply common sense and understand the basic principles of accounting and if you do not have a high volume of transactions, this activity can be done by an individual themselves.

Every business person and investor needs to understand accounting. Without this, they can't assess how businesses are performing and whether it's worthwhile to keep investing or spending time on them. Therefore, it's imperative to have an understanding of the basic principles on which accounting is based. The idea is not to go into technical details, but the aim is to explain the basic principles in the simplest possible way. Without understanding accounting, it's difficult to understand other elements of finance which are related to funds management, planning and controlling.

So now the question is what should be recorded?

A person with a sound financial acumen and discipline would always record all activities where money is involved. She/he might maintain a diary for the same. This would include all her/his earnings and spends. Similarly, every activity related to business has to be recorded where money is involved. It starts right from the time the entrepreneur brings in funds to start the business, which is also called **capital**.

There is one important point that I would like to highlight before moving ahead. In accounting, a business is always considered to be different from the entrepreneur who started it. Accounting treats business as a different entity or person altogether. Business owes money to the entrepreneur in the form of capital. Business doesn't own anything by itself. It gets the funds from the entrepreneur or from a third party, also referred to as borrowed funds. This is used to generate assets and earn income.

An entrepreneur can give away her/his right of ownership to someone else, but the business will continue to go on. We have many business houses which were started some 100–150 years ago. Their original promoters had already passed their ownership to their heirs. But the companies are still existent. Change of guard does not impact the existence of business.

Tata Group of companies, one of the leading business houses in India, has been managed under the leadership of different business leaders. There has been multiple changes in leadership in the last 150 years of its existence, but this change doesn't impact Tata Group in any way. It continues to exist as a separate business entity, different from the owners who own and manage it.

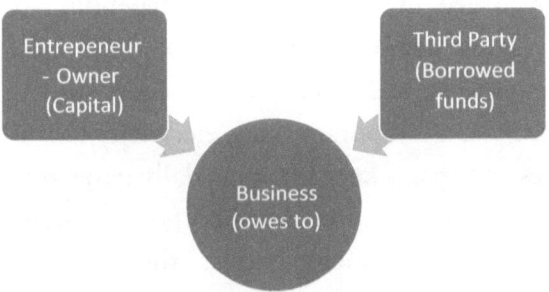

Coming back to what should be recorded. Every business transaction involves giving away either goods or services or any other material and receiving money in return. Alternatively, it can also include receiving goods or services or any other material and giving away money in return. For example, if you hire an assistant to help you with your task, it involves receiving his services and giving him money at the end of the month. The service that you receive here is expressed in financial terms as salary. This is paid either through cash, bank transfers via cheque, or direct transfer in bank. Similarly, you may sell your services or goods to someone and receive money in return. This is expressed as a sales transaction and is the income of the business. Every business transaction involves giving away something and taking something in return.

> Give and Take is the essence of any Business Transaction

Any service or goods or materials sold by the business for which it receives money is the **income** or **revenue** of any business. This income or revenue are earned when a business has produced any product or is giving away any service. To produce a product or deliver a service, there are numerous costs which a business must incur. These costs are related to purchase of goods or raw materials to produce a finished product. These costs can be related to hiring people, agencies or others to conduct different business activities. Thus, a business receives different materials or goods or services to generate income.

All the services and goods/materials **received** by the business are expressed and recorded in different forms depending on the nature of the transaction. These services and goods received can be expressed as salaries or wages paid to staff and workers. Rent paid to a landlord for taking their facility on a temporary basis, electricity bills paid to electricity companies, stores and spares kept for some daily usage by the business, raw material procured for production, finished goods purchased for trading, machinery purchased for producing goods…the list is huge. In accounting terminology, these are referred to as **expenses**.

As mentioned earlier, the expenses are incurred to generate revenue or income. Revenue or income is generated through sale of goods or providing services. These goods and services are **given** away by the business to its customers who procure them, or, in other words, the customers receive these goods or services from the business.

Anything that the business receives as services or goods must be paid for. This is normally settled through cash or bank transfers. Similarly, anything that the business gives in the form of goods and services that represents the income of the business is received in the form of cash or bank transfers. Thus, whenever a business is receiving something, it pays in cash or does a bank transfer and similarly whenever it is giving something to earn income, it gets cash or bank transfers in return. This explains that **every transaction has two elements**. It is in the form of **receipt**, which can be services, goods or cash, and in the form of **payment**, which again are services, goods or cash.

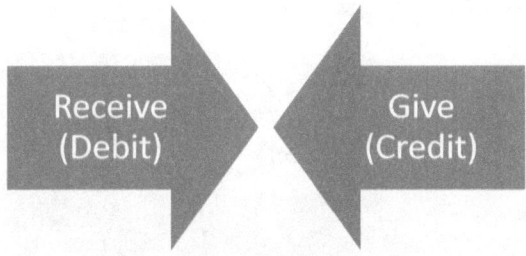

Receive (Debit) — Give (Credit)

All transactions are not always settled immediately in cash or bank transfers. In many transactions, business gives time to pay money or takes time to pay money. These are transactions on **credit**. After the specific period as agreed by both the seller and the buyer, the payment must be made. But a transaction should be recorded when the activity or an event takes place. So, as soon as a purchasing or selling activity takes place, it must be recorded, even if the cash is coming or going to be paid at a later stage. The person receiving something from the business but pays later is referred to as a **debtor.** The time given to the debtor to make a payment to the business is referred to as credit period. Similarly, business needs to pay something at a later stage to the person who provided services or goods and that person is referred to as a **creditor**. These debtors and creditors are as good as cash owned or owed by the business, if they have a good financial standing and have good integrity. Most of the businesses run on this trust. So, if you give away your goods or services without receiving cash immediately, then your transaction is with debtors. The business has to receive money from the debtors at a later stage. The same applies to creditors from whom you have received services or goods and you are paying them at a later stage.

The act of receiving or giving goods, services or cash or even creating debtors and creditors is the essence of debits and credits, on which the entire book keeping and accounting is based. Debits and credits govern the process of recording transaction. **Anything that you receive is debited, and anything that you give away is credited**. Thus, if you receive cash, goods or services or if someone owes you something, it gets debited, and if you're giving away your goods or services to generate income or paying cash or if you owe money to someone, it gets credited. That brings me to the golden rules of accounting.

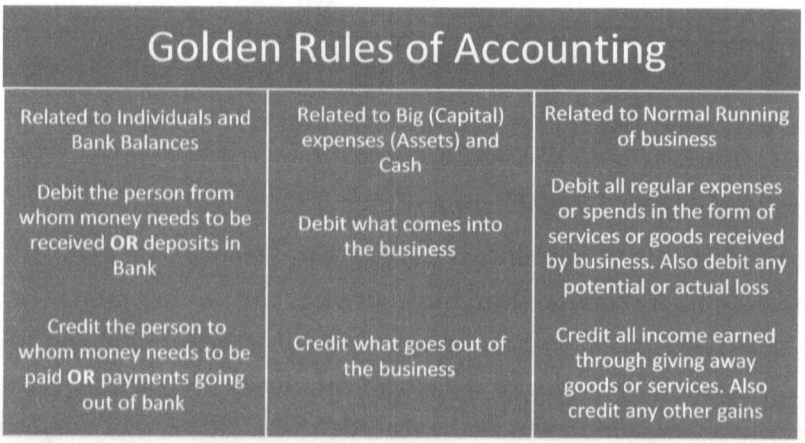

Golden Rules of Accounting		
Related to Individuals and Bank Balances	Related to Big (Capital) expenses (Assets) and Cash	Related to Normal Running of business
Debit the person from whom money needs to be received **OR** deposits in Bank	Debit what comes into the business	Debit all regular expenses or spends in the form of services or goods received by business. Also debit any potential or actual loss
Credit the person to whom money needs to be paid **OR** payments going out of bank	Credit what goes out of the business	Credit all income earned through giving away goods or services. Also credit any other gains

III. Type of Expenses

I've introduced the term 'expenses' in the above paragraph. Now let's understand more a it. The expenses that a business incurs can be for the short term or the long term. Short-term expenses are the ones which give benefit for a shorter duration. They're incurred to get services or goods for a limited time frame, which normally can last for a few days or months or maximum a year. These can be considered as day-to-day expenditure which the business incurs on getting either electricity, getting a facility on rent, getting services from someone in return for salaries, wages or commission, procuring raw material to produce goods, or procuring finished goods for trading. The crux out here is that they are incurred on a regular day-to-day basis and their impact is immediate to revenue- or income-generating activities. Once they are incurred to generate any income, they have to be repeated again to get the requisite turnover or to drive the income again. They act as a fuel for the business, without which the business cannot run or generate revenues. As they are directly related to generating revenues, they are referred to as **revenue expenditure.**

Imagine, you've the best machinery in the world, but there's no one to operate it for you and generate goods from the machinery, or imagine you don't have raw materials to get the final output or imagine you have everything but don't have electricity or fuel to run the machine. In such cases, it's impossible to make the best use of that machine and you can hardly generate any revenue or income from producing goods. Similarly, if you've the best of facilities in the heart of the city and you wish to provide software services to your clients, but you don't have people who can give you those services required for meeting customer's requirement, then again you can't generate revenues. People who work for you, raw materials, fuel and electricity are examples of revenue expenditure. They are incurred most probably every month to earn income.

Sometimes, even after incurring such expenses, they do not yield any result. In such cases, they act as losses as no revenue is generated from the same.

As important as revenue expenditure, there are certain expenses incurred for the long term. Sometimes the business feels that it needs to have control over the infrastructure or it needs to incur expenditure on some key assets, without which it can't function. These expenses once made tend to give benefits for a much longer duration. They can be two years, five years, fifteen years, twenty years and so on. These expenses can be referred to as strategic in nature. There is a huge spending in the beginning and it tends to give benefits over a period of time. Any wrong decision out here could put the business in jeopardy.

Most of these expenses are quite huge and are funded either by the entrepreneur's capital if there is huge capital available with the entrepreneur or at times it's borrowed from outside, which can be banks or financial institutions. A wise decision incurred on these expenses normally tends to give returns for a longer duration and improves the entrepreneur's ability to make more profit and thereby improve capital. A miscalculation would mean that the capital gets eroded and the entrepreneur might not have capital left for doing any further activity. As these expenses normally tend to have a direct impact on the capital of the business, they are referred to as **capital expenditure** and involve buying land for building a facility or a plant, machinery or other equipment, and all these things that will remain for a longer duration in the business.

They enhance the capacity of the business to generate more income. Such capital expenditures are also referred to as **assets** or **investments**.

(However, even revenue expenditure is an investment. It's an investment done to earn returns in the short term or near future. Certain revenue expenses are strategic in nature like headcount related costs or marketing costs. Without a proper balanced headcount, or marketing investments, it's not possible to earn revenues, for many businesses.)

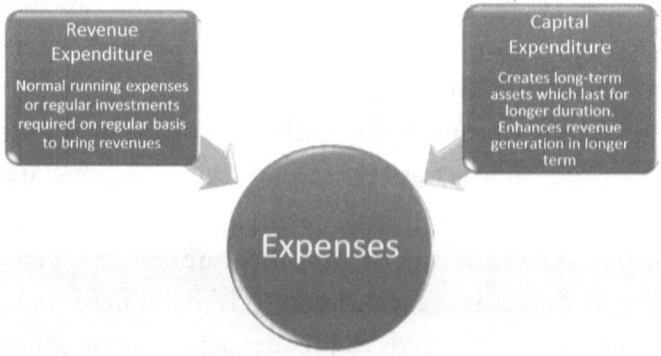

IV. Depreciation and Its Impact on Financial Statement

The financial performance of a business has to be assessed periodically, which can be a year, a quarter or a month. This is determined by deducting all expenses from the income earned. It either results in profits, which is when income is higher than expenses, or loss when expenses are higher than income. Not all expenses are considered while doing a financial performance assessment. Only revenue expenditure is considered while evaluating the financial performance of a business. Thus, the moment you incur revenue expenses, they must be recognised and reflected in the records for assessing the financial performance. This does not hold true for capital expenditure. With respect to capital expenses, once they are incurred, they last for a long duration and so they are not taken into consideration for assessing financial performance for a specific period. But it's important to note that these capital expenses too have a finite life.

As I mentioned earlier, it can be 2 years, 5 years or 20 years. This is like expenditure incurred to purchase a car by an individual, which will typically last for 5 to 7 years on an average. So every year, there is some provision that needs to be kept for its wear and tear or obsolescence, because in future it will have to be replaced. This provision amount is also called as **depreciation**. Depreciation reduces the value of the capital expenditure to reflect the utilised part of the asset (capital expenditure). So, while you're not writing down the entire capital expenditure, what you're doing is writing off a part of it, which was utilised, and assessing your financial performance accordingly to reflect the utilised portion of the asset. This is the essence of prudent accounting.

For example, if you buy a car, and you expect it will last for an average of 5 to 7 years after which you don't expect it to function properly and you expect to sell it off as scrap or to a second hand dealer. Thus, every year, there will be some wear and tear or depreciation with your car. This is determined by dividing the cost of the asset with the expected useful life of the asset. If the car was bought for INR 500k, it is expected to last for 7 years, after which you expect to sell it as a scrap. You expect the scrap value as INR 10k. In that case, the depreciation value of your asset should be INR 490k (INR 500k minus INR 10k for scrap) divided by 7 years. Thus, every year, you need to provide INR 70k for depreciation.

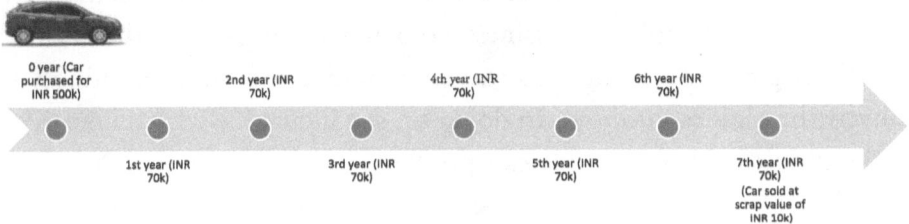

As you'll see in the image above, INR 70k provision every year for 7 years will cover the cost of the vehicle over its expected useful life and will properly reflect the utilised portion of the car every year.

If due to some unforeseen circumstances, the car is beyond any repair and gets damaged, then in that case, the balance useful life of the car should be written off in the period when the incident takes place. For example, if the car gets damaged in the 3rd year and is irreparable and can't be put to use, then in the 3rd year, the balance amount should be considered as a loss and recorded appropriately. Any loss incurred during the normal running of the business should be recorded in the period in which it was incurred. Similarly, here the balance value of the car is a loss and should be recorded in the 3rd year. It impacts the amount of income generated either in individual capacity or business. Now, if the individual was a cab driver, it will impact his ability to generate money henceforth. He might have to pull out money from his resources or through a bank to obtain a new car and after that he can start making money.

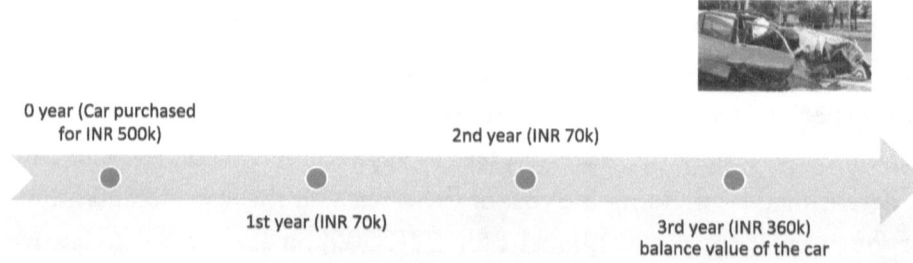

Now, let's understand how a financial performance is assessed and the treatment of all expenses for assessing financial performance during a specific period. This specific period can be a month, a quarter or a year. Technically speaking, it can be on a daily basis, but no one tracks like that. Let me take an example of a business woman who's engaged in the business of making plastic toys. She requires some moulds and other machinery to convert the plastics into toys. In doing so, she incurs INR 1 Million (Mn) in the moulds. These moulds can produce, on an average, 10,000 units in a year. The useful life of the asset as called out by a technical expert is 5 years. The entrepreneur makes full utilisation of these moulds and makes 10,000 toys during the year and sells it in the market. She generates INR 250 on selling each toy. The raw material cost is INR 100 for each toy and she incurs some cost towards hiring people to manufacture those toys, pays rent for her facility, and incurs maintenance costs and others which amount to INR 500,000 during the year. In this case, the expenses incurred on raw material, people, renting a facility and maintenance are revenue expenditure and they have to be recognised in the period in which they are incurred as an expense for evaluating the financial performance. These expenses help the business to generate the sales of 10000 units for which it receives INR 2.5 M as revenue or income. This is how the financial performance would look like:

> Total revenue generated during the year (10,000 units *INR 250 per unit) = INR 2,500,000 (cash received/goods given)
> Less: Cost of raw materials (10,000 units * INR 100 per unit) = INR 1,000,000 (goods received/cash given)
> Other expenses like wages, rent, maintenance = INR 500,000 (services received/cash given)
> Total surplus over expenditure or Profit = INR 1,000,000

The entrepreneur incurred INR 1 Mn on moulds, which have a useful life of 5 years. These moulds also have helped in generating sales of 10k units, and they will continue to provide benefit for a much longer duration. It is expected that they will continue to give this benefit for 5 years. That basically would mean that one fifth of this expenditure should be provided for depreciation. Depreciation value in this case will be INR 1 Mn divided by 5 years. This will work out to INR 200k. So now the revised statement will be as follows:

> Total surplus over expenditure after considering all normal/ revenue expenses = INR 1,000,000
> Less: Depreciation = INR 200,000
> Net profit or surplus during the year = INR 800,000

The above part now gives us a holistic view of financial performance during the year.

Irrespective of whether you're able to generate revenue or not, once you've incurred an expenditure, whether revenue expenditure or capital expenditure, it will impact the money that you've brought into the business. Unless you're efficient enough to generate revenues out of it, it will only drain your limited resources. The risk taken by you by incurring those expenses will not yield the right dividends, if sufficient revenue is not generated from the same. So always ensure to take everything into consideration while incurring these expenses. This is discussed in greater depths in the subsequent sections of this book.

While assessing the financial performance for a particular period is one part, a business should also maintain a record of all the assets that it owns and also all the payments that it is liable to pay. In the above case, machinery and cash are the assets owned by the business. The value of machine is the cost price of the machine reduced by depreciation every year.

V. Timing of the Transaction

While I had mentioned that a transaction has to be recorded when an event or activity or transaction occurs, it needs to be understood when we can consider an event to have actually occurred. An income is considered to have been earned when there is a transfer in the ownership of goods or services from the seller to the buyer. Thus, in the above example, when the toy gets transferred from the entrepreneur to any consumer who has paid for that toy, the transaction is considered a sales transaction. If there is a mere intention to buy goods or services, it means that someone has just expressed her/his interest to buy the toys in the above case, without committing to buy it. Though there might be a strong interest, with no commitment to buy and no willingness to pay in return for the toy, the sales transaction is not considered to have taken place.

When goods or services are transferred from a seller to a buyer for a certain amount of money that is agreed by both of them, only then is the activity considered a sales transaction. Many a time, businesses offer goods on credit. In such cases, if there is probability of receiving money, then the transaction can be considered good for recognition of revenues.

The concept of revenue recognition is explained in more depth in the case study.

With respect to expenses, they need to be recognised as soon as you incur them. Even if you've not earned any income from incurring these expenses, then also you need to record these expenses while evaluating your financial performance for a specific period. For example, you're in the business of manufacturing toys and you take a facility on rent. Now, if you manufacture one unit of a toy or 10 units or 10,000 units, you need to pay rent. The landlord will not forgo your rent just because of your inability to manufacture your products and be efficient. The same applies for depreciation as well. If you have installed machinery or built a facility which has a finite life, then you need to provide for wear and tear, irrespective of your efficiency to manufacture sub-optimal units or more-than-optimal units.

Also, if you anticipate any loss, make a proper provision for it. For example, you anticipate that one of your customers, who bought 100 units from you, might not be able to pay as he's running into financial difficulties. You realised this after the transaction had occurred and the goods were already with him. In that case, even if the loss has not occurred, it is better to make a provision of INR 25,000 (INR 100*INR 250), as the payment from customer has been delayed for a long time and the probability of receiving the money is very less. It is more appropriate to reflect loss in the period when the revenue was recognised rather than at a later stage, especially when you know the probability of recovering is very low.

If the loss materialises say the next year, you do not have to take the financial impact for the same in the next year. Also, as you would have provided for the amount earlier in your financial performance assessment, you save yourself from taking the real financial impact when it eventually occurs.

Provisions like these will always take care of potential financial impact pertaining to a specific period and help in reflecting the true picture of financial performance. Provisions can be related to possible inability to pay money by customer, after making a sales transaction with them (also referred to as bad debts in financial terms). Another provision can be related to inventory which has become obsolete.

A manufacturing or a trading business maintains an inventory of goods. Any material which is bought for production or other business use or for trading, but is not consumed and is likely to be consumed and provide benefits in future is called **Inventory** or **Stocks**. These stocks of goods are normally recorded at the cost of manufacturing them or procuring them. Sometimes, due to a sudden change in market conditions or due to huge volume of production in the past, the selling price of the stocks might be below the cost of manufacturing or procuring them. In such a case, the value of inventory should be assessed at market price. The value of inventory should be assessed at either the cost value or market value, whichever is lower.

Sometimes, in certain transactional business, a business is obliged to take returns and can't put any terms or conditions for taking goods back due to some legislation that protect consumers. In such a case, it's always advisable to check how many returns took place historically and accordingly a provision should be done for returns after assessing the ratio of historical returns to sales.

Thus, in a nutshell, a business should recognise revenues only when ownership in goods or services is transferred and there is reasonable certainty of obtaining money. However, while recording expenses, the business should not only recognise all the spends incurred, but should also recognise all the provisions and potential losses related to that particular period, even if they will be paid or impact later. By doing this, a prudent approach towards assessing the financial health of business is taken into consideration.

It's often said that once money is invested or spent, it takes a good amount of time to bring it back with higher value. So spend your money judiciously.

> Record benefits only when realised, but provide for all spends and losses, even if not materialised.
> (governing principle of Accounting)

A typical business cycle is represented below. It helps in understanding the timing of recording any business transaction.

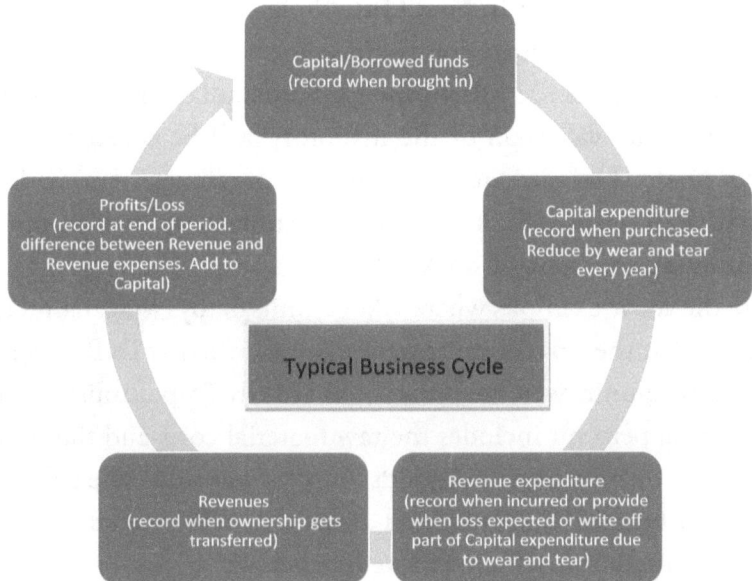

Prudence can be further strengthened through maintaining a consistent approach. This can be done by ensuring that you are recording the transactions in a manner that is consistent throughout the life of the business.

In the above example of moulds, if at the time of buying the moulds, you assess the useful life of the asset to be 5 years and you provide depreciation for INR 200k each year, you can't change it abruptly to INR 300k the next year, if the above assumptions still hold good. You should ensure consistency in your records.

Apart from depreciation, there is another topic which always needs to be consistently recorded period after period. This relates to the inventory which is bought or manufactured by the business but is not consumed during the period. We do not consider inventory while assessing the financial performance of the business for a specific period. But this remains as an asset for the business and will provide returns in future.

While it's straightforward to assess the value for most of the assets, proper care has to be taken to assess value of inventory just like depreciation. Inventory value can be assessed either using FIFO basis or LIFO basis.

FIFO stands for First In First Out. Under this approach, the business would maintain an inventory control in such a way that the stocks coming first are consumed first. Similarly, the stocks manufactured or bought first are sold first. The valuation of the inventory will be based on the latest purchases made. The rates at which the last purchases were made or the cost at which the last batch of goods were manufactured will be considered for determining the value of stocks.

From the above example, where 10,000 units of toys were manufactured, let's assume that the first 5k units were manufactured at INR 125 per unit and the balance units were manufactured at INR 75 per unit. The cost of manufacturing per unit includes the raw material costs and the processing costs. Of the 10k manufactured goods, only 9k was sold. The balance units remaining to be sold are considered assets that will generate revenues in future. The situation looks something like below:

Total units of toys sold – 9,000 units
Total units of toys manufactured – 10,000 units
Balance units left – 1,000 units

In this case, the cost incurred for selling goods was as follows:

Cost of first 5,000 toys – INR 125 * 5000 units = INR 625,000
Cost of next 4000 toys – INR 75 * 5000 units = INR 300,000

Thus, the cost incurred to sell 9k units was INR 625k and INR 300k which works out to INR 925,000.

1000 units are left and in this case, the valuation of inventory will be based on the last batch manufactured which was done at a cost of INR 75 per unit. So the valuation of inventory will be INR 75k (INR 75 * 1k units).

LIFO is completely the opposite of FIFO. LIFO stands for **Last in and First out**. Here the stocks that are consumed first are the ones that are bought or manufactured last. Thus taking the above example, the cost incurred to sell goods is as follows:

Cost of first 5,000 toys – INR 75 * 5000 units = INR 375,000
Cost of next 4000 toys – INR 125 * 4000 units = INR 500,000

Cost incurred to sell 9k units in this case will be INR 375k and INR 500k or INR 875k.

The value of inventory that will be taken forward in this case will be based on the cost of the first batch which is INR 125,000 (INR 125 per unit * 1000 units).

Apart from FIFO and LIFO, businesses can use **weighted average cost method** to value inventory. Here the average price of all goods in the stock are considered irrespective of their purchase date. Thus, in the above example, the value of inventory for 1000 units will be as follows:

Cost of manufacturing first batch of 5000 units – INR 125* 5000 units = INR 625,000
Cost of manufacturing second batch of 5000 units – INR 75* 5000 units = INR 375,000
Total cost of manufacturing 10,000 units = INR 1,000,000

Thus, the cost of one unit works out to INR 100 per unit which is calculated by dividing INR 1 Mn by 10k units manufactured. Thus, the inventory value will be INR 100,000 in this case.

Cost of goods sold will be INR 9k * 1000 units or INR 900k.

In all the cases, the cost of selling 9k units and inventory value in total will remain at INR 1 Mn as that is the cost of manufacturing 10k units. The method of the inventory valuation might change, but the overall cost of manufacturing will remain the same. Inventory value will vary depending on the method used for assessing inventory. Once a particular method for inventory valuation is fixed, say FIFO, LIFO or weighted average method, the same should be consistently applied throughout the life of the business to maintain a prudential approach on valuation. Only under rare exceptional circumstances, it can be changed and the resultant impact should be clearly provided to all relevant stakeholders.

VI.   Where are the records created?

After having dealt a fair bit of the principles governing the accounting process, it is now important to understand where to record these transactions and the format in which records needs to be maintained. Transactions are typically recorded in journals and then transferred to ledgers. A lot of accounting packages and ERPs (enterprise resource planning) are available that manage record keeping.

Journal

As soon as any transaction is concluded, it is supposed to be recorded somewhere and a journal serves that purpose. Journals are also referred to as the books of original entry. By this, I mean it's the first point where transaction or business activity is first registered. Every transaction has two parts and the same must be reflected in journals. As we've seen above, anything that is received is debited and anything that is given away is credited.

A typical journal maintained in manual form would look something like this.

| | | | | Amt in INR |
Date	Account Title or Description	Ref	Debit	Credit
5-Aug-18	Cash Account Dr.		10000	
	To Sales Account			10000
	Towards Cash Received from Sales of Goods			

The account which is getting debited is always reflected by 'Dr' and the account getting credited is referred by writing 'To' before mentioning the account for which it was credited for. This is just to show how records are maintained.

The amount by which the transaction is debited and credited must be the same. If we recollect the principles of debit and credit, which was covered before, we will understand that every transaction consists of giving something and receiving something in return for a certain monetary value.

In the above case, goods were sold to a customer for cash for INR 10k. In this scenario, goods worth INR 10k were given away by the business, which is credited. Against this was cash received by the business, and the same is debited. So, goods worth INR 10k went out of the business and cash of INR 10k came into the business.

A record is complete only when both the elements are recorded. Also, all these records should be backed up or substantiated with proper evidence. There must be vouchers, receipts, work documents or contracts supporting any transaction. This also helps when you try to tie the physical assets with what you record. This process is called **reconciliation** in accounting. This also keeps a check on the person maintaining these records. As money is involved, it should always be ensured that all records are validated or corroborated with relevant supporting documents to avoid any leakages.

This systematic recording with relevant supporting documents makes the record keeping or book keeping more credible.

There are different types of journals serving different purposes. They are also referred to as subsidiary books. We'll cover it in the case study section.

Ledgers

The journal by itself will not tell anything. Records will have more meaning if they are classified properly and summarised. At end of the period, the records must be summarised to assess the financial health of the business. Every aspect, whether related to giving or receiving, must be represented by an account. The accounts can be related to sales done by the business, cash, purchases made, individuals or businesses with whom the business deals with, and assets of the business or capital. Remember the golden rules. We have three golden rules touching individuals and business (including bank), assets and investments (including cash) and running or revenue expenses and income. Broadly speaking, the golden rules cover the different types of accounts that a business deals with and it needs to maintain. In the above example, we had two accounts viz. cash and sales accounts. These accounts form the basis for classification and summarisation.

So once the records are recorded in journals, they are then transferred to ledgers for systematic classification and recording at account level.

Let's take the above example of a journal and create ledgers related to two accounts. They will appear like below. The debit side of the transactions appear on the left-hand side and the credit side of the transactions appear on the right hand side of the ledgers.

Dr			Cash Account				Cr
Date	Particulars	JF	Amount	Date	Particulars	JF	Amount
5-Aug-18	To Sales		10,000	5-Aug-18	By Bal c/f		10,000
Total			10,000				10,000

Dr			Sales Account				Cr
Date	Particulars	JF	Amount	Date	Particulars	JF	Amount
5-Aug-18	To Bal c/f		10,000	5-Aug-18	By Cash		10,000
Total			10,000				10,000

In the above case for a cash account, you'll notice that in the journal cash account was debited against the sales account. The debit portion of the cash account will show 'sales' account in the ledger. This implies that cash is being received by the business on account of sales and with that, the balance that is available in the cash account is INR 10k. As the amount of debit is higher than the credit, it implies that the business owns INR 10k of cash, or it also implies that the cash received is higher than the cash paid out. The same is reflected by balancing the credit side of the cash account with the balance amount that is carried forward (c/f) by the business during the period, which is INR 10k in this case. This also represents the cash available with the business during the particular period, which was INR 10k. Cash is an asset for the business. Anything that comes in is debited and anything that goes out is credited. Cash should always have the debit balance as the amount of cash going out cannot be greater than the amount available.

Similar to the cash account, there is a sales account. Here, we're crediting it against the cash we received of INR 10k. The goods given out against cash reflect the income generated during the period. The total income generated during the period is reflected by the balance amount c/f during the period, which is INR 10k in the above case. The sales account is related to the normal running of the business. All incomes and gains have to be credited. Sales are an income and should be credited. Unless the transaction is reversed due to returns taken by the customers, this should never be debited.

Journals and ledgers together form the **books of accounts** for the business.

How does one determine if the account has a debit or credit balance?

In the above case, the debits in cash account were higher than the credits. The amount by which the credit side was short from the debit side must be incorporated by a balancing entry on the credit side. This will make the debits and credits equal. The amount by which the credit side is balanced to reflect the amount on the debit side is referred to as **debit balance**. A debit balance in a cash account represents that a net cash of INR 10k is available with the businss.

For sales, the credit is higher than debit; so the balancing amount in this case will be a **credit balance**. This represents the total income generated during the period as INR 10k.

The balances communicate the health of the business. In the above case, they communicate that the business has net cash of INR 10k and net sales of INR 10k was done during the period. When all the balances are combined together, they will take the shape of the profit and loss statement and balance sheet.

VII. Profit and Loss Statements and Balance Sheets

A **Profit and Loss (P&L)** statement and balance sheet are nothing but the summary of all transactions that occur during the period. A profit and loss statement summarises all transactions related to a specific period. It summarises the income and expenditure occurred during the period. The expenditure referred to out here is revenue expenditure and provisions.

The difference between the income and expenditure is classified as profit or loss depending on whether revenue is higher than expenses and vice versa.

As mentioned earlier, the business gets money from either the entrepreneur or from borrowings from outside parties. These funds are then utilised to earn income and create assets that in turn provide income. The **Balance Sheet** provides a summary of all sources from which the business gets funds and how it has utilised those funds. The profits arising in a business during a period help in strengthening the business to get more funds through its regular operations. This belongs to the entrepreneur for the risk she/he takes for undertaking the enterprising activity. Similarly, any loss goes to reduce entrepreneur's capital. Again, this represents the risk the entrepreneur took, which didn't materialise in gains. These profits or loss are therefore either added or deducted from the capital in balance sheet.

The profit and loss statement or balance sheet is summarised from the balances available in the ledgers. The balances related to the normal running of the business, as appearing in the ledger, are reflected in the profit and loss statement (P&L). The resultant profit or loss from the P&L statement is added or deducted from the capital. All balances related to individuals, capital or bank accounts or balances related to cash and capital expenditures (assets and investments) appear in the balance sheet. The profit and loss statement and balance sheet provide an assessment of the financial health of any business during a specific period.

As mentioned earlier, give and take is the essence of any transaction and that's why every transaction has two aspects. When a balance sheet is prepared, the sources of funds always tie up with the amount applicable to utilisation of funds. This, in a way, reflects the two aspects of any transaction. All funds procured or sourced by the business through capital or borrowed sources must be put to specific use by building assets or creating investments or at least there must be cash or bank balance. Thus, sources of funds or liabilities in balance sheet of the business are equal to the utilisation of funds which are invested in different forms of assets.

Assets of business = Capital + Borrowed funds
(Utilisation of funds = Source of funds)

A profit and loss statement and balance sheet can be created for a specific period. Now this can be on monthly basis, quarterly basis, half-yearly basis or yearly basis. Stock markets require listed companies to provide their financial performance on quarterly basis.

The chart below helps in understanding how records flow from one set of books to other and how profit and loss (P&L) and balance sheet is made.

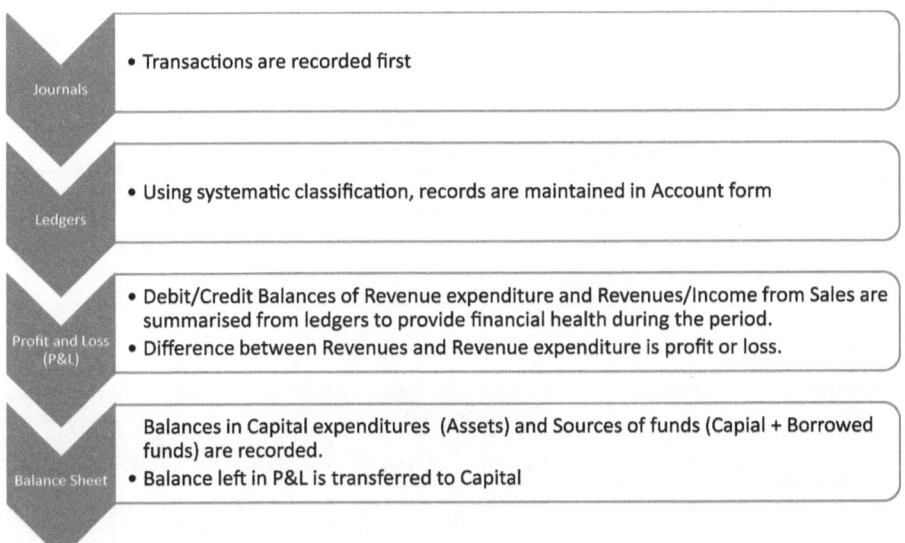

Journals
- Transactions are recorded first

Ledgers
- Using systematic classification, records are maintained in Account form

Profit and Loss (P&L)
- Debit/Credit Balances of Revenue expenditure and Revenues/Income from Sales are summarised from ledgers to provide financial health during the period.
- Difference between Revenues and Revenue expenditure is profit or loss.

Balance Sheet
- Balances in Capital expenditures (Assets) and Sources of funds (Capial + Borrowed funds) are recorded.
- Balance left in P&L is transferred to Capital

As you'll see from the above, journals form the basis for all recording. They are transferred into proper accounts called ledgers. The balance of these ledgers summarises all the business activities and provides a view of the balance sheet and the profit and loss statement which provides an assessment of financial health of the business.

Let me take a very small example to explain the profit and loss statement and balance sheet. Mr. X begins as a fruit vendor on 1st Jan 2018. He invests INR 2k to buy fruits from the market. He brings in INR 1k into the business and INR 1k is borrowed from a local vendor for one month. He purchases INR 2k worth of fruits and sells at a profit of INR 20%. So now, let's determine the impact of these transactions on his ability to create assets during the day.

Let's put the transactions in a journal, translate them into ledgers and create a profit and loss statement and balance sheet.

The journals will have the following entries:

Date	Account Title or Description	Ref	Debit	Credit
1-Jan-18	Cash Account Dr.		2000	
	To Capital Account			1000
	To Borrowings Account			1000
	Towards Cash Introduced in the Business			
1-Jan-18	Purchase Account Dr.		2000	
	To Cash Account			2000
	Goods Brought by the Business for Trading			
1-Jan-18	Cash Account Dr.		2400	
	To Sales Account			2400
	Total Cash Sales for the Period			

These journals when translated into ledgers will be as follows:

Dr	Capital Account							Cr
Date	Particulars	JF	Amount	Date	Particulars	JF	Amount
1-Jan-18	To Balance c/f		1,000	1-Jan-18	By Cash Account		1,000
Total			1,000				1,000

Dr	Borrowings (Local Vendor) Account							Cr
Date	Particulars	JF	Amount	Date	Particulars	JF	Amount
1-Jan-18	To Balance c/f		1,000	1-Jan-18	By Cash Account		1,000
Total			1,000				1,000

Dr	Cash Account							Cr
Date	Particulars	JF	Amount	Date	Particulars	JF	Amount
1-Jan-18	To Capital Account		1,000	1-Jan-18	By Purchases Account		2,000
1-Jan-18	To Borrowings Account		1,000	1-Jan-18	By Balance c/f		2,400
1-Jan-18	To Sales Account		2,400				
Total			4,400				4,400

Dr			Purchases Account				Cr	
Date	Particulars	JF	Amount	Date	Particulars	JF	Amount
1-Jan-18	To Cash Account		2,000	1-Jan-18	By Balance c/f		2,000
					(Transferred to P&L A/c)		
Total			2,000				2,000

Dr			Sales Account				Cr	
Date	Particulars	JF	Amount	Date	Particulars	JF	Amount
1-Jan-18	To Balance c/f		2,400	1-Jan-18	By Cash Account		2,400
	(Transferred to P&L A/c)						
Total			2,400				2,400

Let's summarise the balances of the ledgers into either a profit and loss statement (P&L A/c) or a balance sheet.

Sales and purchases are related to a specific period and are regular transactions of the business. They are related to the normal running of the business and are transferred to P&L.

However, balances in capital, borrowings represent what a business owes to its owner and other parties. Cash represents the asset created by the business. These balances will get transferred to the balance sheet.

Profit and Loss Statement (P&L Account)			
Dr			Cr
Particulars	Amount	Particulars	Amount
Purchases Account	2,000	Sales Account	2400
Balance (Profit)	400		
(Carried to Balance Sheet. It's a Credit Balance)			
Total	2,400	Total	2,400

Balance Sheet			
Assets (Utilisation of Funds)	Amount	Liabilities (Sources of Funds)	Amount
Cash Account	2,400	Capital Account	1000
		Add: Profit	400
		Total in Capital Account	1400
		Borrowings	1000
Total	2,400	Total	2,400

In the above example, you'll notice that INR 2k introduced in the business gives a return of INR 400 during the day. That is the value addition. Cash has increased from INR 2k to INR 2.4k. Of this, the business owes INR 1k to outside party viz. a local vendor. The profit is a credit balance and goes to increase capital. A loss will be a debit balance and will go to reduce the capital.

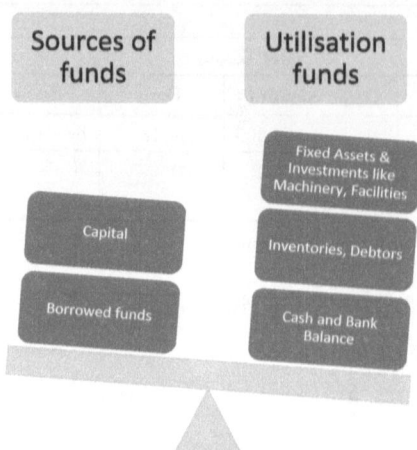

Profit or loss is a balancing figure. In the above example, INR 2k of funds brought in, generated INR 2.4k of cash and thereby facilitated in earning INR 400 of profit which is the balancing figure. Profit is an incentive for the entrepreneur to take risks and provide value additions.

If I get too much into details, this will start tilting towards a technical discussion, which I want to avoid. So I'll try to explain accounting with a case study. This will cover the principles that I had called out earlier in the book. The case study will reflect a real-life scenario. The case presented to you is pertaining to a small business with relatively few transactions. However, it captures all the nuances of business and trade that an entrepreneur goes through on daily basis. I'll try to give the background of each transaction as it might help you to connect and correlate with real-life situations that you or any entrepreneur goes through on daily basis. It should also help you in appreciating the principles on which all of bookkeeping and accounting is built. I have tried to make this case study as exhaustive to cover all possible transactions, while trying to maintain simplicity. This case study can also be taken as a reference material in case you wish to personally maintain your own business records.

VIII. Case Study

Let's take our example of a toy manufacturer and let me try to get into more details about her business.

Ms. Sneha Patel starts her venture as a businesswoman and establishes her own firm on 1st January 2017. The firm's name is Nishka Toys. Sneha brings INR 500k into the business and a computer she had purchased recently for INR 20k. Of the cash she brings, she deposits INR 490k in the bank account, which is opened for business activities and balance is kept as cash. She pays INR 120k as a deposit to a landlord who owns a factory shed. The monthly rent is INR 10k per month starting from 1st January 2018 and is subject to revision every two years. It is to be paid at end of every month as per the rent agreement. Before starting the business, she was already in talks with a local vendor to purchase the machinery and moulds to manufacture the toys. She is successful in procuring them for INR 950k on 20th January 2018. She is able to arrange funds for the same from a bank which offers to give INR 800k as loan and balance INR 150k is funded by her business viz. Nishka Toys. There is installation cost of INR 50k which is borne directly by Nishka Toys. Both the installation cost and balance amount for the machinery are not funded by a bank loan, but are paid through a cheque. It takes another 10 days for her to install the machinery and start manufacturing. The machine is expected to have a life of 5 years. The maximum capacity of the machine is 15000 units. The interest on the loan of INR 800k for the first year works out to INR 72,295. The business needs to pay the loan in 4 years with an EMI (equated monthly installment) of INR 20,290 per month. This will automatically get deducted from the bank account at end of every month.

The payment schedule for the loan is provided by the bank, which is given below. The EMI starts from 31st Jan 2017. The amount to be paid as principal and interest is provided below for the calendar year 2017.

Due Date for Payment	EMI to Be Paid Each Month	Interest Paid Each Month	Principal Amount of Loan Paid Each Month	Closing Balance of Loan
31-Jan-17	20,290	6,667	13,623	786,377
28-Feb-17	20,290	6,553	13,737	772,640
31-Mar-17	20,290	6,439	13,851	758,789
30-Apr-17	20,290	6,323	13,967	744,822
31-May-17	20,290	6,207	14,083	730,739
30-Jun-17	20,290	6,089	14,201	716,538
31-Jul-17	20,290	5,971	14,319	702,219
31-Aug-17	20,290	5,852	14,438	687,781
30-Sep-17	20,290	5,731	14,559	673,222
31-Oct-17	20,290	5,610	14,680	658,542
30-Nov-17	20,290	5,488	14,802	643,740
31-Dec-17	20,290	5,364	14,926	628,814
Total	243,481	72,294	171,186	

In this case study, I'm not covering indirect taxes viz. GST (Goods and Services Tax) as I wish to keep it simple for readers to comprehend the subject.

Let me pause here before getting into the regular day-to-day transactions that occurred during the year. What are the things to note out here? The businesswoman who runs the business is different from her firm. As called out earlier, the owners are different from the business they establish. The owners can come and go, but the business will continue for a much longer duration. This is important to understand because it helps in maintaining proper accounts of the owner and keeps it separate from the business that they own. It helps in understanding the profits and loss that are attributable to the owner based on the investment or the capital brought by them.

All activities are expressed in monetary terms. Any activity that fails to qualify this criteria, however important it maybe, will get excluded. This can be called a drawback of accounting and it's therefore important that other business factors must be taken into consideration along with accounting statements when making some important decisions.

Another point to understand is that the first paragraph is talking only about the capital expenditure incurred by Nishka Toys, which is mostly funded by a third party viz. a bank. This amount is owed by the business to the bank and represents the borrowings done by the business.

Let's put all the activities in a journal.

The records for Nishka Toys starts from the time Sneha brings in capital of INR 520k. The journal will reflect as follows:

				Amt in INR
Date	Account Title or Description	Ref	Debit	Credit
1-Jan-17	Cash Account Dr.		500,000	
	Computer Account Dr.		20,000	
	To Capital Account			520,000
	Towards Cash and Computer Received from the Entrepreneur as Capital			

Here, the business receives cash and a computer from the entrepreneur. So, it gets debited. As I mentioned the owner is different from the Nishka Toys, which is the business name. So, the business owes Sneha the amount brought by her to the business and is represented as capital account.

Now, in the second activity, the cash is deposited in the bank account. So the next entry will be as follows:

				Amt in INR
Date	Account Title or Description	Ref	Debit	Credit
1-Jan-17	Bank Account Dr.		490,000	
	To Cash Account			490,000
	Cash Deposited in Bank Account			

Here, the bank receives the money owned by Nishka Toys and cash is going out from the business. The bank owes Nishka Toys INR 490k as on 1st Jan 2017 for the deposit it has done.

The transaction with the landlord of the factory shed is represented as follows:

				Amt in INR
Date	Account Title or Description	Ref	Debit	Credit
1-Jan-17	Security Deposit (Landlord) Account Dr.		120,000	
	To Bank Account			120,000
	Security Deposit Paid to Landlord for Factory			

Here, Nishka Toys is paying through bank, which reduces its bank balance by INR 120k. It literally means that the bank is giving away money on behalf of Nishka Toys to the landlord and the landlord is receiving money which needs to be paid whenever Nishka Toys decides to vacate the premises. The landlord owes Nishka Toys because of the security deposit.

The next transaction or activity that needs to be recorded is related to the machinery installed in the factory. The cost of machinery is INR 950k. The installation cost is INR 50k. One thing to note is that all the incidental costs related to bringing the machinery to its usable form should be considered as capital expenditure and is part of the asset costs. So, INR 50k has to be added to asset costs. The total cost is funded by a bank loan of INR 800k and the balance of INR 200k is provided by Nishka Toys. This includes INR 150k for the machinery cost and INR 50k towards installation. The transaction will be represented as follows:

Date	Account Title or Description	Ref	Debit	Credit
20-Jan-17	Machinery Account Dr.		1,000,000	
	To Bank Loan Account			800,000
	To Bank Account			200,000
	Machinery Installed in Factory, Funded by Bank Loan and Owner's Capital			

Machinery is a capital expenditure and any capital expenditure is an asset for the business. When it comes in, it is debited. This is funded by borrowed funds in the form of a bank loan and partly by the business. So, the bank loan account and the bank account (belonging to the business) will get credited. The business owes the bank in the form of a loan of INR 800k and INR 200k will get reduced from the bank balance belonging to the business.

The last transaction for the month relates to the rent paid by Nishka Toys to the landlord.

				Amt in INR
Date	Account Title or Description	Ref	Debit	Credit
31-Jan-17	Rent Account Dr		10,000	
	To Bank Account			10,000
	Rent Paid for Jan 2017			

The shed is taken on rent from day 1 of 2017. Rent must be paid to the landlord at end of the month, even if operations have not started. Rent is a service received by the business from the landlord, who has provided his facility for temporary usage.

In the above, the services received by the business is in the form of rent and will get debited. The bank balance will further get reduced as the rent is paid through cheque.

I hope these preliminary transactions helped you in getting a flavour of typically what needs to be debited and what needs to be credited.

A business does a multitude of activities, especially related to purchases and sales. Cash and cheques or bank transfers are part of every transaction. It would be better if transactions related to these activities are recorded separately. Also, it's not feasible to record everything in one journal.

So, to serve this purpose, there are different types of journals. There are the ones for credit purchases, ones for credit sales, a cash book (including bank deposits and withdrawls), and a journal proper for miscellaneous transactions. Similarly, there are general ledgers which act as a backbone for organisations having large volume of transactions. I'll not cover general ledgers in this book.

Let me now introduce you to the **cash book**, for all the transactions that we have seen so far.

A cash book is similar to a ledger, but in reality it's a subsidiary book and a kind of journal. The best part of maintaining a cash book is that it is possible to segregate the receipts and payments separately. One will find it easy to understand how the receipts are earned and where the payments are going.

If one recollects the golden rule related to cash or bank transactions, anything that is received is debited and anything that goes out must be credited.

The entries of receipts and payments in a cash book are then posted into respective ledgers, which we'll see at the end of the case study before preparing P&L statement.

Cash Book											
Dr											Cr
Receipts						Payment					
Date	Particulars	Ledger folio	Discount	Cash	Bank	Date	Particulars	Ledger folio	Discount	Cash	Bank
1-Jan-17	To Capital Account			500,000		1-Jan-17	By Cash Account	C		450,000	
1-Jan-17	To Bank Account	C			450,000	1-Jan-17	Security Deposit				120,000
						20-Jan-17	By Machinery Account				200,000
						31-Jan-17	By Rent Account				10,000
						31-Jan-17	By Balance c/f			50,000	120,000
				500,000	450,000					500,000	450,000

Cash book includes cash and bank accounts. Normally in business, cash and bank are normally considered the same. Cash and cheques, and these days, online or wire transfers are used interchangeably. But it's still important to keep them separately for record keeping. So, we have two columns to reflect transactions happening via cash and through bank. Any transaction which involves the transfer of cash to a bank or vice versa is termed as a 'contra' entry in accounting terminology and is represented by 'C' in the reference part of the cash book. You'll notice the 'C' in the ledger folio when cash was transferred to the bank. A contra entry typically indicates that no real transaction has taken place but the funds are moving from one form to another.

The EMI paid towards the purchase of machinery will also get recorded each month in a cash book. For the sake of convenience, let me summarise all cash book records related to EMI transactions occurring during the year.

Dr											Cr
	Receipts						Payment				
Date	Particulars	Ledger folio	Discount	Cash	Bank	Date	Particulars	Ledger folio	Discount	Cash	Bank
						31-Jan-17	By Bank Loan Account				13,623
						31-Jan-17	By Bank Interest Account				6,667
						28-Feb-17	By Bank Loan Account				13,737
						28-Feb-17	By Bank Interest Account				6,553
						31-Mar-17	By Bank Loan Account				13,851
						31-Mar-17	By Bank Interest Account				6,439
						30-Apr-17	By Bank Loan Account				13,967
						30-Apr-17	By Bank Interest Account				6,323
						31-May-17	By Bank Loan Account				14,083
						31-May-17	By Bank Interest Account				6,207
						30-Jun-17	By Bank Loan Account				14,201
						30-Jun-17	By Bank Interest Account				6,089
						31-Jul-17	By Bank Loan Account				14,319
						31-Jul-17	By Bank Interest Account				5,971
						31-Aug-17	By Bank Loan Account				14,438

						31-Aug-17	By Bank Interest Account				5,852
						30-Sep-17	By Bank Loan Account				14,559
						30-Sep-17	By Bank Interest Account				5,731
						31-Oct-17	By Bank Loan Account				14,680
						31-Oct-17	By Bank Interest Account				5,610
						30-Nov-17	By Bank Loan Account				14,802
						30-Nov-17	By Bank Interest Account				5,488
						31-Dec-17	By Bank Loan Account				14,926
						31-Dec-17	By Bank Interest Account				5,364

The principal amount and interest amount are going out from the bank account. They represent payments made by the business and will get credited.

The bank that provided the loan will get debited by the principal amount. The debit entry will reduce the amount that the business owes to the bank. Interest is the cost that a business incurs to procure the funds. It's a kind of service fee charged by the bank for borrowing money from them. Interest cost is related to the normal running of the business and can be considered revenue expenditure. So, it must be debited. Thus, the record will have principal and interest getting debited and the bank account getting credited. It will appear as follows:

Bank Loan Account Dr.
Interest on Bank Loan Account Dr
To Bank Account

The total of the bank loan account and the interest on the bank loan account will be equal to the amount going out from the bank account.

In a cash book, the entry on the credit side reflects the above accounting treatment. The principal amount and the interest appear on the credit side. They indicate that the amount from the bank has got reduced due to the principal and interest payments. At the time of preparing the ledger, you'll notice that in the bank loan account and the interest on bank loan account, the bank account appears on the debit side, indicating that part of the bank loan is settled through a cheque and the service, enjoyed in the form of a loan, is also paid through a cheque.

Like bank EMIs, all rent paid during the period from Feb to Dec are summarised in the cash book for the sake of convenience. We already saw the journal entry for the rent earlier. It helps you understand how they are recorded in the cash book.

Dr												Cr
	Receipts						Payment					
Date	Particulars	Ledger folio	Discount	Cash	Bank	Date	Particulars	Ledger folio	Discount	Cash	Bank	
						28-Feb-17	By Rent Account				10,000	
						31-Mar-17	By Rent Account				10,000	
						30-Apr-17	By Rent Account				10,000	
						31-May-17	By Rent Account				10,000	
						30-Jun-17	By Rent Account				10,000	
						31-Jul-17	By Rent Account				10,000	
						31-Aug-17	By Rent Account				10,000	
						30-Sep-17	By Rent Account				10,000	
						31-Oct-17	By Rent Account				10,000	
						30-Nov-17	By Rent Account				10,000	
						31-Dec-17	By Rent Account				10,000	

I'll start introducing you to the other journals one by one in the subsequent part of the case study.

From February to December 2018, Nishka Toys manufactured 10,000 units of toys and was able to get sales orders for 10,000 units, but it was able to invoice 9000 units during this period. There was one batch of 1000 units, which it was not able to invoice. During the February to December period, Nishka Toys hired an unskilled worker and paid him INR 5k per month. It also hired a skilled worker and paid him INR 10k per month. While one was responsible for manufacturing, the other was responsible for assembling and packaging. Sneha did the quality check herself.

In order to manufacture the toys, she needed cotton, cloth, dyes, and some miscellaneous materials. To procure raw materials, Sneha signed a contract with ABC Traders to buy 2500 kg of cotton worth INR 300k over a period of 5 months. She bought 500 kg every month on the 1st of every month starting February. Every time she bought cotton from the vendor, she got 30 days time to pay the dues.

Her other raw materials included cloth, which she procured from a local manufacturer, the XYZ Company, till end of June. She bought three batches, which cost her INR 85k on 1st February, INR 75k on 1st March, and INR 75k on 1st May. The manufacturer gave Nishka Toys 30 days of credit. The details of the purchases of dyes and other materials are provided below.

Dyes – INR 40k till June bought from PQR Limited till June, of which INR 20k was bought on 1st February and another INR 20k was bought on 1st April. The company gave Nishka Toys 15 days of credit. Purchases from the local agency (for other raw materials)– INR 50k- were purchased equally on 1st of every month, starting from February to 1st June, and were settled immediately through cheque. The payment to all vendors was done on time.

Let's record the transactions related to salaries first and then we'll proceed with transactions related to purchases. Salaries were paid at the end of month and were settled through cheque. So it's pretty straightforward to record in the cash book Here, I'll try to record a consolidated entry for the whole year for the convenience of the reader. However, in practice, it must be done separately for each month.

						Cash Book					
Dr											**Cr**
	Receipts						Payment				
Date	Particulars	Ledger folio	Discount	Cash	Bank	Date	Particulars	Ledger folio	Discount	Cash	Bank
						28-Feb-17	By Salaries Account				15,000
						31-Mar-17	By Salaries Account				15,000
						30-Apr-17	By Salaries Account				15,000
						31-May-17	By Salaries Account				15,000
						30-Jun-17	By Salaries Account				15,000
						31-Jul-17	By Salaries Account				15,000
						31-Aug-17	By Salaries Account				15,000
						30-Sep-17	By Salaries Account				15,000
						31-Oct-17	By Salaries Account				15,000
						30-Nov-17	By Salaries Account				15,000
						31-Dec-17	By Salaries Account				15,000

Just to reiterate the point, business is receiving the services for which it's paying money in the form of salaries and wages. The services which are received by business are debited in the form of salaries. The entry for salaries will be as follows:

Salaries Account Dr.
To Cash/Bank Account

The bank balance is getting reduced due to the payment of salaries and so the cash book gets credited. In the salaries account, in the ledger, we'll see that the bank account is debited, indicating that the services brought by the company are paid through cheque.

Now let's introduce another subsidiary book related to purchases. It is called the **purchase book.**

Only credit purchases are recorded in the purchase book. Most of the purchases are always on credit and the volume of purchases is quite significant for any business. So it's always advisable to have a purchase book. Cash purchases are directly recorded in the cash book. The cash book will also record the settlement transactions related to purchases. All of these will be posted in the ledgers. The best part of having a journal specific to purchases and sales is that it gives greater convenience in identifying specific records, which are normally high in volume.

The entries below indicate that the purchases made by the business are done through different vendors, who are also creditors to whom business has a liability to pay in the future. Purchases facilitate in obtaining goods through which business can do manufacturing. It's related to the normal running of the business. So, it will be debited and the person or business providing these goods on credit terms are creditors as mentioned above. The business owes to pay to them and so their accounts will get credited when they give goods on credit. Generally, the entry will be:

Purchase Account Dr.
To Vendor Account

The following is the format in which the purchase book is maintained. This represents the vendors who have provided goods on credit.

Date	Particulars	L.F.	Details	Amount
1-Feb-17	ABC Traders			
	500 kg cotton @ INR 120 per kg			60,000
	XYZ Company			
	Cloth			85,000
	PQR Limited			
	Dyes			20,000
1-Mar-17	ABC Traders			
	500 kg cotton @ INR 120 per kg			60,000
	XYZ Company			
	Cloth			75,000
1-Apr-17	ABC Traders			
	500 kg cotton @ INR 120 per kg			60,000
	PQR Limited			
	Dyes			20,000
1-May-17	ABC Traders			

	500 kg cotton @ INR 120 per kg			60,000
	XYZ Company			
	Cloth			75,000
1-Jun-17	**ABC Traders**			
	500 kg cotton @ INR 120 per kg			60,000

The format is quite self-explanatory. It gives the details of different things purchased from different vendors during the different timeframes on credit.

Now, there are transactions pertaining to the settlement of purchases, as well as cash purchases. Let's cover it through the cash book. The vendor to whom the payment is made will be debited, indicating that payment was made towards dues on purchases. The cash book will have entries in the credit side, indicating payment to the vendors by cheque.

Dr											Cr
	Receipts					Payment					
Date	Particulars	Ledger folio	Discount	Cash	Bank	Date	Particulars	Ledger folio	Discount	Cash	Bank
						1-Feb-17	By Local Agency				10,000
						16-Feb-17	By PQR Limited				20,000
						1-Mar-17	By Local Agency				10,000
						3-Mar-17	By ABC Traders				60,000
						3-Mar-17	By XYZ Company				85,000
						31-Mar-17	By ABC Traders				60,000
						31-Mar-17	By XYZ Company				75,000
						1-Apr-17	By Local Agency				10,000
						16-Apr-17	By PQR Limited				20,000
						1-May-17	By Local Agency				10,000
						1-May-17	By ABC Traders				60,000
						31-May-17	By ABC Traders				60,000
						31-May-17	By XYZ Company				75,000
						1-Jun-17	By Local Agency				10,000
						1-Jul-17	By ABC Traders				60,000

The settlement dates or the dates on which payment for the purchases are done are different from the purchase date. The difference represents the credit period. For example, the dyes purchased on 1st Feb for INR 20k were settled after 15 days on 16th Feb. 15 days was the credit period granted by PQR Limited. The same applies for all other transactions of the purchases and the sales.

However, the settlement of the purchases from the local agency is done on the same date as there is no credit period granted by the local agency. So, nothing will get recorded in the purchase book. For local agency, everything will be recorded in the cash book. In this case, purchases are directly settled through cheque. There are two entries that are made simultaneously at the same time.

Purchases Account Dr
To Vendor Account

And

Vendor Account Dr
To Bank Account

The first entry represents the purchases made from the local agency and the second is towards settling the amount of purchases through cheque. Since it's settled immediately, the two principal accounts that get impacted are the purchases and bank account. But while preparing ledgers, we'll reflect the entries in vendor accounts as well, even though the dues were settled immediately.

During the period, February to June 2017, Nishka Toys was able to manufacture 5000 toys, after running at full capacity. There was a higher utilisation of material due to a different method of manufacturing. However, from the July to December period, production was streamlined, and a new method of manufacturing was adopted with the same machine.

Also, the contracts and vendors were changed. With increasing confidence, the entrepreneur was able to now enter into long-term contracts with the vendors. The revised contract with ABC Traders

was now for 1 ½ years ending on 31ˢᵗ December 2018. General prices for cotton had come down. With the new manufacturing method, the quantum of raw material usage was reduced. Production too was steady and the consumption of cotton now came down from 500 kg to 375 kg per month. The revised rate of buying cotton was INR 80 per kg, which will be subject to review every 6 months. The entrepreneur agreed to buy 500 kg per month. There was a provision to review the purchase commitment every 6 months.

The contract with XYZ Company was now replaced with MNO Company, for buying cloth. The same batch, which was earlier procured at INR 75k, was now available at INR 40k. MNO was one of the leading vendors of cloth. Nishka Toys had committed long-term purchases with the vendor.

Also, due to competitive pressures, PQR Limited was willing to provide dyes at 25% lesser.

The purchases with the local agency continued. On the first of every month, INR 10k of materials were procured.

Cotton was bought on the first of every month. Payment to ABC Traders happened on time, except the last payment that got delayed by 5 days due to some minor dispute over the quality of cotton.

The terms of payment with the MNO company remained the same as was with XYZ Company. The first payment to MNO got delayed by a month and was paid on 1ˢᵗ Sep 2017, due to some small dispute.

Cloth was bought on 1ˢᵗ July for INR 40k. Again, it was bought on 1ˢᵗ Sep for INR 40k and then on 1ˢᵗ Nov for INR 40k.

Dyes were bought on 1ˢᵗ July for INR 15k and again on 1ˢᵗ Oct for INR 15k. The payment was made on time, except the last payment that got delayed by a day.

Most of the materials were consumed and there was no stock of material available, except the materials from the local agency worth INR 5k was not utilised by the end of 2018 and was returned on 31ˢᵗ Dec. This was settled immediately through cash. Also, the quantum of cotton consumption was less, resulting in unused cotton of 750 kg. Dyes were fully consumed by end of the year. The last batch of cloth arriving on 1st Nov was utilised partially. 1/4th of the total cloth was unutilised. If this cloth was sold in the market, the value of this cloth would be INR 12 k. Stocks that arrived first were consumed first. Similarly, stocks that were manufactured first were sold first.

In order to conserve cash in the beginning, the entrepreneur convinced the landlord to bear the electricity cost and the same would be paid by the end of the year along with interest. The amount of electricity bill was INR 28k during the year and INR 2k was charged by the landlord as an interest. Based on the meter readings, 45% of electricity was consumed before 30th June and balance in the second half of the year. Payment for electricity was done to the landlord on 31st Dec. Maintenance cost amounted to INR 50k which was incurred on 26th December and paid through cheque.

This is quite an exhaustive section of the case study, covering different types of transactions related to procurement of materials and services.

This section will cover purchase book, cash book, and some journal entries which do not get covered in any other subsidiary books.

Now, let's start by recording all credit purchases in the purchase journal. It is similar to the transactions that were covered in the previous section.

Purchase Book				
Date	Particulars	L.F.	Details	Amount
1-Jul-17	ABC Traders			
	500 kg cotton @ INR 80 per kg			40,000
	PQR Limited			
	Dyes			15,000
	MNO Company			
	Cloth			40,000
1-Aug-17	ABC Traders			
	500 kg cotton @ INR 80 per kg			40,000
1-Sep-17	ABC Traders			
	500 kg cotton @ INR 80 per kg			40,000
	MNO Company			
	Cloth			40,000

1-Oct-17	**ABC Traders**			
	500 kg cotton @ INR 80 per kg			40,000
	PQR Limited			
	Dyes			15,000
1-Nov-17	**ABC Traders**			
	500 kg cotton @ INR 80 per kg			40,000
	MNO Company			
	Cloth			40,000
1-Dec-17	**ABC Traders**			
	500 kg cotton @ INR 80 per kg			40,000

The quantity of cotton purchased every month was 500 kg. But only 375 kg per month was utilised. This means that from a total quantity of 3000 kg purchased from Jul to Dec, only 2250 kg were consumed. Thus, 750 kg of cotton was unutilised. This forms the inventory for the business. The inventory or stock is owned by the business that will be utilised to earn revenues in the future and so it is to be considered an asset.

The important part is the value at which it needs to be recorded. Based on the situation presented to us, it is clear that the stock that came first was utilised first. The firm was maintaining FIFO basis (First In, First Out) for maintaining its inventory. So, the stock of cotton that had arrived at the last will be retained as inventory. Thus, 250 kg of cotton that came on 1st Nov and the entire 500 kg of cotton that came on 1st Dec remained unutilised. These were purchased at the rate of INR 80 per kg. Thus, the value of the inventory for cotton to be carried in the balance sheet will be 750 kg * INR 80 per kg, which is equal to INR 60k. We'll get into the accounting treatment of stocks in the last part of the case study.

Like cotton, 1/4th of the cloth purchased on 1st Nov was unutilised. The total value of the cloth purchased was INR 40k. Of this, 3/4th was utilised, which is equal to INR 30k. INR 10k of the balance stock will be carried forward in the balance sheet as an inventory. It is retained by the business. The market value of this cloth is expected to be INR 12k. However, it's not sold by the business yet and so the value should not be recorded at INR 12k, unless the estimated market value is lower than the cost price. This is how a business can maintain **prudence** while recording its transactions.

The transaction with the landlord is not a credit purchase. It's a temporary arrangement made to get the funds for paying electricity for which an interest is charged. The transaction should be recorded each month. However, for the sake of simplicity, I'm breaking the transaction into two parts. One part relates to the period 1st Jan to 30th June and another part from 1st Jul to 31st Dec. The same should be credited to the landlord. Services that are in the form of electricity and advance are received by the business for which it will have to pay electricity charges and interest. These will get debited. It's been provided by the landlord, who is the provider of these services for a temporary period. So, his account gets credited. The entry will be as follows. Electricity and interest on the advance are the expenses related to the normal running of the business and will appear in the P&L statement.

			Amt in INR	
Date	Account Title or Description	Ref	Debit	Credit
30-Jun-17	Electricity Account Dr		12600	
	Interest on Advance Dr		900	
	To Landlord Account			13500
	Towards Advance Received for Electricity Costs for First Half of the Year			

31-Dec-17	Electricity Account Dr		15400	
	Interest on Advance Dr		1100	
	To Landlord Account			16500
	Towards Advance Received for Electricity Costs for Second Half of the Year			

Similarly, the services related to maintenance were received and paid through cheque. The typical journal entry is provided below. It will be reflected in the cash book.

Maintenance Account Dr.

To Bank Account

The settlement of all the above transaction, along with cash purchases and the refund from the local agency, is covered in the cash book. The cash book also has an entry for returns settled in cash.

Dr											Cr
		Receipts						Payment			
Date	Particulars	Ledger folio	Discount	Cash	Bank	Date	Particulars	Ledger folio	Discount	Cash	Bank
31-Dec-17	To Local Agency			5,000		1-Jul-17	By Local Agency				10,000
						16-Jul-17	By PQR Limited				15,000
						31-Jul-17	By ABC Traders				40,000
						1-Aug-17	By Local Agency				10,000
						1-Sep-17	By Local Agency				10,000
						1-Sep-17	By ABC Traders				40,000
						1-Sep-17	By MNO Company				40,000
						1-Oct-17	By Local Agency				10,000
						1-Oct-17	By ABC Traders				40,000
						1-Oct-17	By MNO Company				40,000
						17-Oct-17	By PQR Limited				15,000
						31-Oct-17	By ABC Traders				40,000
						1-Nov-17	By Local Agency				10,000
						1-Dec-17	By Local Agency				10,000
						1-Dec-17	By ABC Traders				40,000
						1-Dec-17	By MNO Company				40,000
						26-Dec-17	By Maintenance Account				50,000
						31-Dec-17	By Landlord Account				30,000

The first transaction with the MNO company was settled only on 1st Sep 2017, even though the terms of the payment was 30 days. The payment or receipt entry should be reflected in the books only when cash is paid or received respectively. The last transaction for purchases from ABC Traders was not settled on 31st Dec, but it got settled only in the beginning of January. We are recording transactions occurring from 1st Jan 17 to 31st Dec 17. This means the settlement transaction for the purchases done on 1st Dec for cotton would have to happen on 5th Jan 18, which is not the reporting period. In that case, the firm owes a liability to ABC Traders and it will get reflected in the balance sheet. By not paying on time, the business has created a creditor to the extent of INR 40k, when it closes its books of accounts. The settlement transaction will be reflected in the next accounting period. The small delay of payment to PQR Limited is also reflected properly.

With this, we cover all procurement related transactions. These transactions covered the purchases of raw materials, procurement of services related to people, maintenance and electricity.

Now, let's cover the sales transactions in the last part of our case study. These transactions can also be referred to as revenue generation transactions.

There are certain adjustments, which need to be made, especially for the inventory that is retained by the business for the next financial period. We'll cover that as well in the subsequent section.

Nishka Toys was in talks with certain distributors since January to find a place for itself in the market for its products. It was successful in finding a distributor in the middle of February. The distributor was called RMO Enterprises. A contract was signed with this distributor for a year. As there was only one product manufactured, it was a simple contract. The distributor agreed to purchase stocks at INR 250 per unit. The retail price for the product was INR 360. The following invoices were issued during the period, after receiving purchase orders from RMO. The goods were delivered and invoiced on the same day.

27th February   – 500 Units
15th March 2017 – 1500 Units

25th May 2017	– 1100 Units
1st July	– 1500 Units
1st August	– 1000 Units
1st September	– 2000 Units
1st December	– 900 Units

The distributor agreed to pay in 30 days after the purchase. As the entrepreneur knew the distributor personally, he didn't ask for any security deposit.

During September, Nishka Toys found another distributor to cater to another market in the outskirts of the town. The distributor was called FNO Traders. On 1st October, a small batch of 500 units were invoiced and supplied to them, against their purchase commitment. The business with this distributor was not a smooth ride. The rate at which it agreed to sell to FNO Traders was INR 250 per unit with 30 days as the payment term. FNO Traders paid for 400 units. However, it returned 50 units and for 50 units it didn't pay in 2017 following a dispute. Nishka Toys was not expecting to receive any money from it. The 50 units returned by FNO Traders didn't have any resale value. It could be sold on scrap, but no value could be assessed for the same.

Since, FNO failed to pay the security deposit of INR 75k that it had agreed to pay on 30th September, the contract with them was rescinded by mutual consent by both parties on 10th October. FNO paid the amount for 400 units on 31st October.

As the sales transactions with RMO Enterprises started quite late, resulting in a delay in cash generating activities, Nishka Toys had to rely on the bank overdraft facility to fund the temporary fund requirements in March and May. The bank charged interest and fees of INR 750 for the borrowed period. This was settled on 14th April and 30th June. The first set of interest paid was INR 500 and the balance was paid in the second set of overdraft taken in May. With money flowing consistently from the second half and having produced enough stock, the business didn't have to seek the overdraft facility in the second half of the year.

As it was mentioned earlier, Nishka Toys manufactured 10000 toys during the year. However, it is important to note here that around 1000 toys were pending to be invoiced as RMO Enterprises had not provided a purchase order before 31st December 2017. The purchase order came only on 5th January, when the books of accounts were already closed. The shipment and invoicing took place on 6th January 2018.

One more relevant point to be considered is that all the expenses incurred on machinery, people's salaries, or the facility was for manufacturing the goods. Without these, the goods wouldn't had been manufactured. So these costs are associated with manufacturing inventory, which is then available to be sold in the market.

The transactions stated in this part of the case study relates to sales. This is the most important section as it relates to **revenue generation activity**. A business can earn revenues either by selling goods or selling services. It's very important to understand when to record a sales transaction. A sale transaction is complete only when significant transfer of ownership in goods and services is transferred from the seller to the buyer. Revenue recognition is in itself a separate topic and there's an accounting standard dedicated to it. Let's understand the nuances of revenue recognition using this case study.

All transactions done to RMO Enterprises and FNO Traders from Feb to Dec would be recognised when the goods were shipped and invoiced. Here, the transfer of ownership in goods is considered to have taken place when the distributors had provided their willingness and acceptance to buy goods in the form of purchase orders or other documents expressing their commitment to the purchase for a certain amount of money. Goods are then invoiced and delivered. So there is clearly a contract of sales where the buyer has agreed to buy goods and the seller has accordingly provided the requisite goods. So these can be recognised in accounting at the time when they were invoiced and delivered. But there are certain peculiar transactions that need special consideration. Let's take them one by one.

- There's one transaction where RMO had expressed its desire to buy the products before 31st Dec. However, it gave a purchase order only in the next accounting period. So, the transaction should be recognised in the next year. The goods already manufactured against this specific transaction should be considered as an inventory which is ready and available for sale. The treatment of this inventory in the records is provided in this part of the case study below.

— There's one transaction with FNO Traders where it didn't pay for 50 units. However, there was nothing to indicate, in the beginning, that FNO wouldn't be paying that amount. So, in this case, a provision should be made for a potential loss, even if FNO Traders might change its mind and pay in the future. This would have been different if fraud happened. If the distributor turned out to be a fraud, then in that case, there was no intention from the distributor to pay money since the beginning. The distributor in that case would have intended to buy the goods to deceive the seller. It would had been a one-sided contract where only the seller was willing to provide goods, but the buyer was not willing to pay money for it. In that case, revenues, if at all recognised, should be reversed. But the cost of the goods should still be recognised. This will reduce the earnings of the business, suggesting the impact of loss due to goods moving out but money not coming in. However, in our case, no such intention prevailed at the time of the transaction. But we still have a potential loss. So, the loss is to be separately provided, but the sales transaction can't be reversed. A fraud can be identified when the customer suddenly disappears or couldn't be contacted or is able to forge records which put business in a difficult situation to recover money or goods. There can be more examples to how this fraud can occur. But the intention of not paying and not getting into a relationship with the business is a feature of a fraud transaction. It's always advisable to conduct a credit check beforehand to avoid getting into such a crisis. There are multiple vendors available who can provide such credit check facilities.

As mentioned earlier, one of the journals maintained by a business is the sales book. The quantum of credit sales are typically higher for any business; it's relevant to have this journal in place.

In case of any sales or revenue generation activities, goods or services are going out of the business. So the sales account or income generating account always gets credited. Normally, in most businesses, the customer buying goods will seek some credit period to pay for the goods or services. Cash comes at a later stage. So while the goods or services are going out of the business, business creates debtors or people who owe money to the business. They are the ones receiving goods or services. So they are debited. A typical credit sales transaction will have the following entry:

Customer Account Dr.
To Sales Account

The transactions recorded in the sales book are normally the ones related to crediting the books with income generated from sales. It provides the details of customers who bought goods or services on credit. This is how the sales book will look.

Sales Book				
Date	Particulars	L.F.	Details	Amount
27-Feb-17	RMO Enterprises			125,000
	500 units @ INR 250/unit			
15-Mar-17	RMO Enterprises			375,000
	1500 units @ INR 250/unit			
25-May-17	RMO Enterprises			275,000
	1100 units @ INR 250/unit			
1-Jul-17	RMO Enterprises			375,000
	1500 units @ INR 250/unit			
1-Aug-17	RMO Enterprises			250,000
	1000 units @ INR 250/unit			
1-Sep-17	RMO Enterprises			500,000
	2000 units @ INR 250/unit			
1-Oct-17	FNO Traders			125,000
	500 units @ INR 250/unit			
1-Dec-17	RMO Enterprises			225,000
	900 units @ INR 250/unit			

Please note that the transactions with RMO Enterprises are recorded at INR 250 per unit and not INR 360 per unit. Even though Nishka Toys has decided to keep the retail price at INR 360 per unit, it cannot record the transactions at INR 360 per unit as the difference is paid towards distributor margins, retail margins, and indirect taxes (VAT/GST). The first set of transactions happens with the distributor and only that gets recorded as the ownership in goods gets transferred from Nishka Toys to the distributor. When the distributor sells to the retailer, the distributor will record at the price at which it will sell to the retailer. Again, this will not be at retail price as the distributor has to give allowance for retailer's margins. VAT/GST will be paid at different levels, but that is out of the scope of this case study. The business must record sales value excluding these taxes. The taxes are collected by the business on behalf of the government and they have to be deposited to them through the regular filing of returns to tax authorities.

There was one transaction of returning the goods. Normally, a business also maintains purchase returns and sales returns journals, especially when the volume of returns is high. Here, I'll try to explain the sales return through a record maintained in the sales return book. A typical sales return entry will be:

Sales Return Account Dr.
To Customer Account

Goods are coming back, so sales return is debited. The customer is the one giving back the goods; so his account gets credited.

Sales Return Book				
Date	Particulars	L.F.	Details	Amount
27-Feb-17	FNO Traders			12,500
	50 units @ INR 250/unit			

Normally, returns coming back from the customer are considered inventory as it might be possible to sell them again. But in this case, no money is expected to be coming from the goods returned. So, the inventory value of the goods returned back is zero. So we shouldn't be carrying any value as an asset for these goods.

While returning goods is one aspect, the other one relates to a provision that needs to be made for a potential loss expected due to non-receipt of money.

In this case, there is no money expected to be received for 50 units. So, a provision for bad debts needs to be made, which will be a journal entry and it will be as follows:

				Amt in INR
Date	Account Title or Description	Ref	Debit	Credit
31-Dec-17	Profit and Loss Account Dr		12,500	
	To Provision for Bad Debts Account			12,500
	Provison for Bad Debts Expected to Arise from FNO Traders			

This indicates that there is a loss which is represented by a debit and it comes from provision which will go to reduce the amount recoverable from debtors.

The last set of transactions that occurred for which no entry was yet made relates to **bank overdraft** transactions. Overdraft is a facility granted by banks to its current account holders, where they can withdraw more than the amount they have deposited in the bank. For this, the bank charges interest and fees.

These set of transactions will be shown when a consolidated cash book for the whole year is made, which is covered later.

Here, we have not assumed that the bank charges fees for maintaining a current account with a bank. Normally, a bank would charge fees for maintaining a current account with itself. These are expenses related to the normal running of the business and should be debited. The bank balance will get reduced because of this and so bank accounts will get credited towards payment of fees.

Having recorded all sales and sales return transactions, we now move towards making certain adjustments to assess the financial performance during calendar year 2017. These adjustments are related to **depreciation** on machinery bought during the year and **inventory** left at the end of year.

Let's start with **depreciation**. As explained earlier, capital expenditure is incurred for long term. This is more than one year. It is expected that once the expenditure is incurred, it will last for a longer duration. In this case, machinery is expected to last for 5 years and the computer is expected to last for 4 years.

The depreciation amount on the same will be INR 1 Mn/ 5 years = INR 200k.
Similarly, the depreciation on computer will be INR 20k/4 years = INR 5k.

It is irrelevant whether the expenditure is of higher value or of a lower value. If it's expected to last for a longer duration, the value of the capital expenditure must be split over the useful life of the asset and depreciation needs to be provided to ensure that its cost is properly allocated over the life of the asset. These are considered as miscellaneous transactions and are covered in journal proper. So, the journal entry will be as follows:

| | | | | Amt in INR |
Date	Account Title or Description	Ref	Debit	Credit
31-Dec-17	Profit and Loss Account (Depreciation) Dr.		205,000	
	To Provision for Depreciation (Machinery) Account			200,000
	To Provision for Depreciation (Computer) Account			5,000
	Depreciation Provided for Machinery and Computer			

The above is an adjustment entry and is used to recalculate the value of the asset after providing for the wear and tear that the asset might have gone through due to the usage. Depreciation records this value. It is considered an expense for the normal running of the business and is revenue expenditure.

The balance, which is INR 1.02 M minus INR 205k, represents the revised value of the assets based on the remaining useful life, which will be 4 years in case of machinery and 3 years in case of the computer.

Depreciation allows us to record only the value related to utilisation of the asset. This will help us not to charge the full value of the asset in the year when the asset was purchased. The balance value of the asset will be carried forward in the balance sheet and will represent the value of assets owned by the business.

Like depreciation, we need to assess the value of the **inventory** as well. The inventory is the stock which remains with the business at the end of the accounting period. The inventory can be related to raw materials not yet consumed or finished goods not sold or work in progress which is not turned into finished goods yet during the period.

The value at which the inventory will get recorded is important. It must be at cost price or it has to be at the market price, whichever is lower. Selling price, in typically all or most of the cases, is higher than cost price. But if these are not sold by the business, inventory cannot be recorded at selling price. However, if due to some competitive pressure, all of a sudden the selling price falls down dramatically and the business is not able to cover even the costs associated in manufacturing the product or creating a service, then the inventory should factor in such loss and its value should be recorded at the expected selling price to make a provision for loss. Similarly, sometimes there are returns done by customers. The revised selling price of the goods, after returns, normally tends to go down. If this is the case, then such inventory has to be recorded at its expected revised selling price. If nothing is expected to be realised, then the inventory value will be zero, as we have seen above in case of sales return.

As called out earlier in one of the paragraphs, the business must take a conservative approach at the time of recording. It has to provide for all possible and anticipated losses, but realise gains only when the activity takes place.

Now, let's assess the value of the inventory first before recording the value of purchases, which will be utilised in subsequent reporting period. In the earlier part of our case study, we had identified INR 60k of cotton and INR 10k of cloth that was not utilised. This must be carried as inventory.

There remains another 1000 units of finished goods, which also should be carried forward to the next period. This is available for sale in subsequent period, as called out in the earlier paragraph. The value of these finished goods is critical. This must be based on the total cost incurred to manufacture these finished products. This includes the raw material cost, the cost of processing and the labour involved in manufacturing the product. Let's try to assess the value of the finished product through developing a cost sheet.

All materials procured before July were already consumed. The business is controlling its stock on FIFO basis. It means that the stocks manufactured first are sold out first. The business had manufactured 5000 units before July and total units sold during the year were 9000 units. So, the 5000 units produced before July were already sold out. Their valuation therefore has no impact on inventory valuation. So let's concentrate on the transactions occurring after July to value the inventory. The same has been calculated with the cost sheet, which gives the details of costs for the period 1st July to 31st Dec for 5000 units manufactured during this period.

Cost Sheet				
Total Units Manufactured from July to Dec 2017			**5000 units**	
Consumption of Raw Materials for Manufacturing 5000 Units				
	Units	**Rate**	**Cost value**	**Comments**
Consumption of Raw Materials from Jul to Dec 2017				
Consumption of Cotton	2250 kgs	80	180,000	
Consumption of Cloth			110,000	INR 10 k is carried in stock. It's not been used.
Consumption of Dyes			30,000	
Consumption of Other Materials			55,000	INR 5k of other material was returned and refunded by local agency.
Value of Raw Materials Consumed			**375,000**	
Depreciation for the Period			102,500	INR 205k is depreciation for full year, so for half a year it's INR 102k. These assets are used for normal operations and manufacturing the product. So their cost forms part of the finished goods.
Salaries Paid to Workers from Jul to Dec 2017			90,000	These are salaries of individuals who were directly involved in manufacturing. If this was related to salaries of sales or administration departments, then those salaries will not be considered.
Electricity Cost			16,500	Electricity bill for the second half

Maintenance Cost			25,000	Maintenance costs equally spread between both the half
Total Cost Incurred to Produce 5000 Units			**609,000**	
Value of One Unit			**121.80**	
Value of Inventory - 1000 units			**121,800**	

From the above, you'll notice that I've not considered all finance costs related to manufacturing. Bank interest and interest on overdraft are not considered here. Finance costs are completely different. They are like fees charged for a temporary arrangement to meet funding requirements. If the manufacturer had the requisite means, she might not have borrowed funds from outside. But electricity costs include interest to the landlord as it's considered a service by the landlord and an integral part of getting electricity even if interest is shown separately in P&L. If there are costs associated with selling and administration, which in this case study is not present, then these will also be not considered at the time of valuing the inventory. So marketing and advertising costs, administration costs, or sales facilities costs will be charged directly to the profit and loss statement and will not be considered at the time of inventory valuation.

This value of the inventory will be adjusted from the profit and loss statement. The value of the inventory will reside as an asset in the balance sheet and the expenses forming part of the inventory like labour cost or maintenance cost will get reduced in the profit and loss statement when the value of inventory is recorded. This will be carried forward into the next period or year and will be considered an expense when they are sold. We will see this at the time of preparing the profit and loss statement and the balance sheet. An entry for the inventory will appear as follows:

Inventory Account Dr.
To Profit and Loss Account

The inventory being an asset is coming to the business from normal operations. Profit and loss is a representative of normal operations.

The journals are now translated into ledgers. Businesses maintain general ledgers, considering the volume of transactions they work with.

All the transactions from Part 1 to Part 4 of the case study are considered in order of their occurrence while preparing the ledgers. There will be a balance available at the end of the year, which will get either transferred to the profit and loss account or those balances will be carried forward to the next year. Again reiterating, balances related to accounts which are related to normal running of business like salaries or rent are transferred to the profit and loss statement. In the case of capital expenditure or assets, individual or business accounts, cash or bank accounts, their values are carried forward directly into the balance sheet. The balance in the profit and loss statement, which can be a profit or a loss, will either increase the capital of the entrepreneur or reduce it, and will also appear in the balance sheet.

All records related to ledgers will be consolidated, as it does not make any sense to repeat the transactions for each date. So a consolidated entry will be made at end of the period for all transactions occurring on different dates, which are similar in nature.

The purpose of creating these ledgers is to understand the balances at the end of accounting period against each set of accounts, which is either carried to the profit and loss account or the balance sheet.

Before moving to the consolidation, let's summarise all the major frequently occurring transactions, which are related to purchases and sales.

An analysis of purchases will help in understanding how much of raw material is required to produce saleable goods and how rate changes impact the overall cost value.

Given below is an analysis on purchases.

Analysis of Purchases, Returns and Raw Materials Consumed During the Year					
Purchases from 1st Feb to 30th June					
Vendor Name	Raw Material Procured	Units	Rate	Cost Value	
ABC Traders	Cotton	2500	120	300,000	
XYZ Company	Cloth			235,000	
PQR Limited	Dyes			40,000	
Local Agency	Miscellaneous			50,000	
Total Value of Purchases from 1st Feb to 30th June				625,000	(A)
Purchases from 1st Jul to 31st Dec					

ABC Traders	Cotton	3000	80	240,000	
MNO Company	Cloth			120,000	
PQR Limited	Dyes			30,000	
Local Agency	Miscellaneous			60,000	
Total Value of Purchases from 1ˢᵗ Jul to 31ˢᵗ Dec				**450,000**	**(B)**
Total Value of Purchases During the Year				**1,075,000**	**(D)**
Returns During the Year				5000	(E)
Net Purchases During the Year				**1,070,000**	**(F) = (D)-(E)**
Material Not Utilised for Production During the Year					
ABC Traders	Cotton	750	80	60,000	
MNO Compnay	Cloth			10,000	
Material Unutilised During the Year				**70,000**	**(G)**
Total Value of Materials Consumed During the Year				**1,000,000**	**(H) = (F)-(G)**

Like purchases, it's also advisable to have such a basic analysis for sales. This analysis is important for both manufacturing, trading and services business. It helps in understanding how revenue is coming and from which quarters. It can further augment in making decisions related to more market penetration and pricing. which we'll cover in the planning section of this book.

Analysis of Sales and Returns During the Year

Sales for the entire year				
Customer Name	**Products Sold**	**Units**	**Price**	**Revenues**
RMO Enterprises	Toy	8,500	250	2,125,000
FNO Traders	Toy	500	250	125,000
Total Value of Sales During the Year		**9,000**	**250**	**2,250,000**
Less: Returns During the Period				
FNO Traders	Toy	50	250	12,500
Net Sales During the Period				**2,237,500**

The cash book is unique. It acts like a journal and a ledger. We will not have separate ledgers maintained for the cash or bank account. However, a month-on-month consolidated cash book will be presented after presenting all the other ledgers. This will also help you understand the cash position, which is critical for any business. Also, it will help you understand how the bank overdraft facility works.

Now let's take the **ledgers** one by one.

The first set of ledgers that I'll be considering will be the ones related to capital brought by the entrepreneur and the capital expenses incurred or assets created in the form of machinery and computer, which are partly funded by the owner and the third party.

Dr				Capital Account			Cr
Date	Particulars	JF	Amount	Date	Particulars	JF	Amount
31-Dec-17	To Balance c/f		520,000	1-Jan-17	By Cash Account		500,000
				1-Jan-17	By Computer Account		20,000
Total			520,000				520,000

Dr				Computer Account			Cr
Date	Particulars	JF	Amount	Date	Particulars	JF	Amount
1-Jan-17	To Capital Account		20,000	31-Dec-17	By Balance c/f		20,000
Total			20,000				20,000

Dr				Machinery Account			Cr
Date	Particulars	JF	Amount	Date	Particulars	JF	Amount
20-Jan-17	To Bank Loan Account		800,000	31-Dec-17	By Balance c/f		1,000,000
	To Bank Account		200,000				
Total			1,000,000				1,000,000

Dr				Bank Loan Account			Cr
Date	Particulars	JF	Amount	Date	Particulars	JF	Amount
31-Dec-17	To Bank Account (Sundries)		171,186	20-Jan-17	By Machinery Account		800,000
31-Dec-17	To Bal c/f		628,814				
Total			800,000				800,000

Below is the story coming out from these ledgers. The business was started with some cash and assets (computer) brought in by the entrepreneur. While incurring the expenditure on machinery, the business relied on a bank loan. In total, INR 1.320 M worth of assets was created by the business in the form of machinery, computer, and bank balance. Of this,

INR 520k came from the entrepreneur and INR 800k from the bank in the form of a loan. Of the INR 520k, INR 220k (INR 200k for machinery and INR 20k for computer) was utilised towards creating assets for normal operations and a balance INR 300k was kept as the bank balance for the operational needs of the business.

Now, let's turn to the operational elements of the business. There are activities done to generate revenues during the period. They relate to purchasing raw materials to manufacture products, renting a facility, incurring expenditure on electricity and maintenance, employing people to manufacture products, and the normal wear and tear of the asset during the year. The balances in these accounts will directly get transferred to the profit and loss statement.

Dr			Purchases Account					Cr
Date	Particulars	JF	Amount	Date	Particulars	JF	Amount
31-Dec-17	To Sundry Vendors		965,000	31-Dec-17	By Profit and Loss Account		1,075,000
31-Dec-17	To Bank Account		110,000				
Total			1,075,000				1,075,000

Dr			Purchase Returns Account					Cr
Date	Particulars	JF	Amount	Date	Particulars	JF	Amount
31-Dec-17	To Profit and Loss Account		5,000	31-Dec-17	By Bank Account		5,000
Total			5,000				5,000

Dr			Salaries Account					Cr
Date	Particulars	JF	Amount	Date	Particulars	JF	Amount
31-Dec-17	To Bank Account (Sundries)		165,000	31-Dec-17	By Profit and Loss Account		165,000
Total			165,000				165,000

Dr			Rent Account					Cr
Date	Particulars	JF	Amount	Date	Particulars	JF	Amount
31-Dec-17	To Bank Account (Sundries)		120,000	31-Dec-17	By Profit and Loss Account		120,000
Total			120,000				120,000

Dr	Electricity Account						Cr
Date	Particulars	JF	Amount	Date	Particulars	JF	Amount
31-Dec-17	To Landlord Account		28,000	31-Dec-17	By Profit and Loss Account		28,000
Total			28,000				28,000

Dr	Maintenance Account						Cr
Date	Particulars	JF	Amount	Date	Particulars	JF	Amount
31-Dec-17	To Bank Account		50,000	31-Dec-17	By Profit and Loss Account		50,000
Total			50,000				50,000

Please note that two provisions have been made. One relates to the wear and tear of an asset and the other for a potential loss. They are part of the operating costs and should be recorded in the ledger, as follows, as revenue expenses.

Dr	Provision for Bad Debts						Cr
Date	Particulars	JF	Amount	Date	Particulars	JF	Amount
31-Dec-17	To Bal c/f		12,500	31-Dec-17	By Profit and Loss Account		12,500
Total			12,500				12,500

Dr	Provision for Depreciation Account						Cr
Date	Particulars	JF	Amount	Date	Particulars	JF	Amount
31-Dec-17	To Bal c/f		205,000	31-Dec-17	By Profit and Loss Account (Depreciation)		205,000
Total			205,000				205,000

Inventory adjustment ledgers are critical as they point out the value of the inventory that will remain in stock and helps in identifying costs related to manufacturing these inventories which will be carried forward to the subsequent accounting period. They will have a debit balance coming from the profit and loss account which, as mentioned earlier, is a representation of the normal operations of the business.

Dr	Inventory (Raw Material) Account						Cr
Date	Particulars	JF	Amount	Date	Particulars	JF	Amount
31-Dec-17	To Profit and Loss Account		70,000	31-Dec-17	By Bal c/f		70,000
	(Refer to analysis on raw material purchased and raw material consumed)						
Total			70,000				70,000

Dr	Inventory (Finished Goods) Account						Cr
Date	Particulars	JF	Amount	Date	Particulars	JF	Amount
31-Dec-17	To Profit and Loss Account		121,800	31-Dec-17	By Bal c/f		121,800
Total			121,800				121,800

If we take the balances in all these accounts, which are transferred to the profit and loss statement, we get a summary of all operational expenses incurred during the period. This will be appearing in the profit and loss statement. The value of these expenses is **net debit balance**, also reflected as transfers to profit and loss statement, and are derived from the above ledgers.

Operating Expenses Incurred During the Period

	Amt (INR)
Net Purchases of Raw Material Less Returns	1,070,000
Less: Inventory of Raw Materials	70,000
Consumption of Raw Materials During the Year	1,000,000
Rent	120,000
Salaries	165,000
Maintenance	50,000
Electricity	28,000
Depreciation	205,000
Total Manufacturing Related Costs	1,568,000

Less: Inventory Not Utilised During the Period	121,800
Total Cost of Goods Sold	**1,446,200**
Provision for Bad Debts	12,500
Total Operating Costs for the Year	**1,458,700**

Now, let's turn to the sales ledger.

Dr			Sales Account				Cr	
Date	**Particulars**	**JF**	**Amount**	**Date**	**Particulars**	**JF**	**Amount**
31-Dec-17	To Profit and Loss Account		2,250,000	31-Dec-17	By Sundry Customers		2,250,000
Total			**2,250,000**				**2,250,000**

Dr			Sales Returns Account				Cr	
Date	**Particulars**	**JF**	**Amount**	**Date**	**Particulars**	**JF**	**Amount**
31-Dec-17	To Sundry Customers		12,500	31-Dec-17	By Profit and Loss Account		12,500
Total			**12,500**				**12,500**

The net balance in the sales and the sales returns account or ledgers represent the total income generated by the business during the year. Some of it will be realised in the form of cash and some will still have to be recovered from the respective individuals or businesses.

In the above case, the income generated by the business is INR 2,237,500, which is the net balance of INR 2.25 M in the sales ledger reduced by the sales return which is INR 12.5k.

Now, let's turn to the most important book, which is the lifeline of any business i.e **cash book**. The cash book helps in understanding how cash or bank balance is utilised. It also helps you to plan activities and maybe avoid indulging in a lot of overdraft activities. It also would facilitate taking decisions related to credit. More on this will be covered in the subsequent part of the book.

There are financing costs related to borrowing funds for the running the operations and creating assets. These are referred to as interest and fees costs. This will be considered now. Below is a month-on-month view of the cash book.

Dr											**Cr**
		Receipts						Payment			
Date	Particulars	Ledger folio	Discount	Cash	Bank	Date	Particulars	Ledger folio	Discount	Cash	Bank
Jan Cash Book											
1-Jan-17	To Capital Account			500,000		1-Jan-17	By Cash Account	C		490,000	
1-Jan-17	To Bank Account	C			490,000	1-Jan-17	Security Deposit				120,000
						20-Jan-17	By Machinery Account				200,000
						31-Jan-17	By Rent Account				10,000
						31-Jan-17	By Bank Loan Account				13,623
						31-Jan-17	By Bank Interest Account				6,667
						31-Jan-17	By Bal c/f			10,000	139,710
	TOTAL			**500,000**	**490,000**		**TOTAL**			**500,000**	**490,000**
Feb Cash Book											
1-Feb-17	To Bal b/f			10,000	139,710	1-Feb-17	By Local Agency				10,000
						16-Feb-17	By PQR Limited				20,000
						28-Feb-17	By Salaries Account				15,000
						28-Feb-17	By Bank Loan Account				13,737
						28-Feb-17	By Bank Interest Account				6,553
						28-Feb-17	By Rent Account				10,000
						28-Feb-17	By Bal c/f			10,000	64,420
	TOTAL			**10,000**	**139,710**		**TOTAL**			**10,000**	**139,710**
Mar Cash Book											
1-Mar-17	To Bal b/f			10,000	64,420	1-Mar-17	By Local Agency				10,000
3/3/2017	To Bank Overdraft				91,000	3-Mar-17	By ABC Traders				60,000
29-Mar-17	To RMO Enterprises				125,000	3-Mar-17	By XYZ Company				85,000

Date	Particulars					Date	Particulars				
31-Mar-17	To Bank Overdraft				65,000	31-Mar-17	By Salaries Account				15,000
						31-Mar-17	By ABC Traders				60,000
						31-Mar-17	By XYZ Company				75,000
						31-Mar-17	By Bank Loan Account				13,851
						31-Mar-17	By Bank Interest Account				6,439
						31-Mar-17	By Rent Account				10,000
						31-Mar-17	By Bal c/f			10,000	10,130
	TOTAL			**10,000**	**345,420**		**TOTAL**			**10,000**	**345,420**
			Apr Cash Book								
1-Apr-17	To Bal b/f			10,000	10,130	1-Apr-17	By Local Agency				10,000
14-Apr-17	To RMO Enterprises				375,000	14-Apr-17	By Bank Overdraft				156,000
						14-Apr-17	Bank Overdraft interest				500
						16-Apr-17	By PQR Limited				20,000
						30-Apr-17	By Salaries Account				15,000
						30-Apr-17	By Bank Loan Account				13,967
						30-Apr-17	By Bank Interest Account				6,323
						30-Apr-17	By Rent Account				10,000
						30-Apr-17	By Bal c/f			10,000	153,340
	TOTAL			**10,000**	**385,130**		**TOTAL**			**10,000**	**385,130**
			May Cash Book								
1-May-17	To Bal b/f			10,000	153,340	1-May-17	By Local Agency				10,000
						1-May-17	By ABC Traders				60,000
						31-May-17	By Salaries Account				15,000
31-May-17	To Bank Overdraft				107,000	31-May-17	By ABC Traders				60,000
						31-May-17	By XYZ Company				75,000
						31-May-17	By Bank Loan Account				14,083

					31-May-17	By Bank Interest Account			6,207
					31-May-17	By Rent Account			10,000
					31-May-17	By Bal c/f		10,000	10,050
	TOTAL			**10,000**	**260,340**		**TOTAL**		**10,000**	**260,340**

Jun Cash Book

1-Jun-17	To Bal c/f			10,000	10,050	1-Jun-17	By Local Agency			10,000
25-Jun-17	To RMO Enterprises				275,000	25-Jun-17	By Bank Overdraft			107,000
						25-Jun-17	By Bank Overdraft Interest			250
						30-Jun-17	By Salaries Account			15,000
						30-Jun-17	By Bank Loan Account			14,201
						30-Jun-17	By Bank Interest Account			6,089
						30-Jun-17	By Rent Account			10,000
						30-Jun-17	By Bal c/f		10,000	122,510
	TOTAL			**10,000**	**285,050**		**TOTAL**		**10,000**	**285,050**

Jul Cash Book

1-Jul-17	To Bal c/f			10,000	122,510	1-Jul-17	By ABC Traders			60,000
						1-Jul-17	By Local Agency			10,000
						16-Jul-17	By PQR Limited			15,000
31-Jul-17	To RMO Enterprises				375,000	31-Jul-17	By Salaries Account			15,000
						31-Jul-17	By ABC Traders			40,000
						31-Jul-17	By Bank Loan Account			14,319
						31-Jul-17	By Bank Interest Account			5,971
						31-Jul-17	By Rent Account			10,000
						31-Jul-17	By Bal c/f		10,000	327,220
	TOTAL			**10,000**	**497,510**		**TOTAL**		**10,000**	**497,510**

Aug Cash Book

1-Aug-17	To Bal c/f			10,000	327,220	1-Aug-17	By Local Agency			10,000
31-Aug-17	To RMO Enterprises				250,000	31-Aug-17	By Salaries Account			15,000

					31-Aug-17	By Bank Loan Account				14,438
					31-Aug-17	By Bank Interest Account				5,852
					31-Aug-17	By Rent Account				10,000
					31-Aug-17	By Bal c/f			10,000	521,930
	TOTAL			**10,000**	**577,220**		**TOTAL**			**10,000**	**577,220**

Sep Cash Book

1-Sep-17	To Bal c/f			10,000	521,930	1-Sep-17	By Local Agency				10,000
						1-Sep-17	By ABC Traders				40,000
						1-Sep-17	By MNO Company				40,000
						30-Sep-17	By Salaries Account				15,000
						30-Sep-17	By Bank Loan Account				14,559
						30-Sep-17	By Bank Interest Account				5,731
						30-Sep-17	By Rent Account				10,000
						30-Sep-17	By Bal c/f			10,000	386,640
	TOTAL			**10,000**	**521,930**		**TOTAL**			**10,000**	**521,930**

Oct Cash Book

1-Oct-17	To Bal c/f			10,000	386,640	1-Oct-17	By Local Agency				10,000
1-Oct-17	To RMO Enterprises				500,000	1-Oct-17	By ABC Traders				40,000
31-Oct-17	To FNO Traders				100,000	1-Oct-17	By MNO Company				40,000
						17-Oct-17	By PQR Limited				15,000
						31-Oct-17	By Salaries Account				15,000
						31-Oct-17	By ABC Traders				40,000
						31-Oct-17	By Bank Loan Account				14,680
						31-Oct-17	By Bank Interest Account				5,610
						31-Oct-17	By Rent Account				10,000
						31-Oct-17	By Bal c/f			10,000	796,350
	TOTAL			**10,000**	**986,640**		**TOTAL**			**10,000**	**986,640**

		Nov Cash Book							
1-Nov-17	To Bal c/f	10,000	796,350	1-Nov-17	By Local Agency				10,000
				30-Nov-17	By Salaries Account				15,000
				30-Nov-17	By Bank Loan Account				14,802
				30-Nov-17	By Bank Interest Account				5,488
				30-Nov-17	By Rent Account				10,000
				30-Nov-17	By Bal c/f			10,000	741,060
	TOTAL	**10,000**	**796,350**		**TOTAL**			**10,000**	**796,350**
		Dec Cash Book							
1-Dec-17	To Bal c/f	10,000	741,060	1-Dec-17	By Local Agency				10,000
				1-Dec-17	By ABC Traders				40,000
				1-Dec-17	By MNO Company				40,000
				26-Dec-17	By Maintenance Account				50,000
31-Dec-17	To RMO Enterprises		225,000	31-Dec-17	By Salaries Account				15,000
31-Dec-17	To Local Agency	5,000		31-Dec-17	By Bank Loan Account				14,926
				31-Dec-17	By Bank Interest Account				5,364
				31-Dec-17	By Rent Account				10,000
				31-Dec-17	By Landlord Account				30,000
				31-Dec-17	By Bal c/f			15,000	750,770
	TOTAL	**15,000**	**966,060**		**TOTAL**			**15,000**	**966,060**

As you would have noticed above, there are overdraft facilities taken from the bank and temporary funds coming to the business in the form of a loan. The financing activities that the business entered during the period can be classified as three major activities for which business needs to maintain separate accounts or ledgers. We have already covered two activities earlier. These pertain to bank loans for machinery and the advance given by the landlord for electricity charges. Now, we need to record the ledgers related to the interest element. Also, we need to cover the overdraft transactions, where we need to have two ledgers, viz. one related to the overdraft and the other covering the interest component of it.

Dr	Bank Interest (Loan Account)							Cr
Date	Particulars	JF	Amount	Date	Particulars	JF		Amount
31-Dec-17	To Bank Account (Sundries)		72,294	31-Dec-17	By Profit and Loss Account			72,294
Total			**72,294**					**72,294**

Dr	Interest on Advance (Landlord) Account							Cr
Date	Particulars	JF	Amount	Date	Particulars	JF		Amount
31-Dec-17	To Landlord Account		2,000	31-Dec-17	By Profit and Loss Account			2,000
Total			**2,000**					**2,000**

Dr	Bank Overdraft							Cr
Date	Particulars	JF	Amount	Date	Particulars	JF		Amount
14-Apr-17	To Bank Account		156,000	3-Mar-17	By Bank Account			91,000
25-Jun-17	To Bank Account		97,000	31-Mar-17	By Bank Account			65,000
				31-May-17	By Bank Account			97,000
Total			**253,000**					**253,000**

Dr	Bank Overdraft Interest							Cr
Date	Particulars	JF	Amount	Date	Particulars	JF		Amount
14-Apr-17	To Bank Account		500	30-Jun-17	By Profit and Loss Account			750
25-Jun-17	To Bank Account		250					
Total			**750**					**750**

Having covered the transactions related to expenditure (capital expenses and revenue expenses), income (sales), capital and financing, it's now time to understand who owes the business how much and how much the business owes to the creditors. The amount owed or owned by the business from creditors or debtors is respectively reflected in the balance sheet.

To understand that, we need to have ledgers of all the vendors and customers. This will be covered below.

Let's start with the vendor's ledgers.

Dr				ABC Traders			Cr
Date	Particulars	JF	Amount	Date	Particulars	JF	Amount
31-Dec-17	To Bank Account		500,000	31-Dec-17	By Purchases (Sundries)		540,000
31-Dec-17	To Bal c/f		40,000				
Total			540,000				540,000

Here, the balance of INR 40k represents the amount which the business owes to ABC Traders during the year. Once it gets settled, there will be no balance left with ABC Traders.

Dr				XYZ Company			Cr
Date	Particulars	JF	Amount	Date	Particulars	JF	Amount
31-Dec-17	To Bank Account		235,000	31-Dec-17	By Purchases (Sundries)		235,000
Total			235,000				235,000

In this account, business has settled for all transactions done with XYZ Company. Nothing is pending. Nothing will flow into the balance sheet.

Dr				PQR Limited			Cr
Date	Particulars	JF	Amount	Date	Particulars	JF	Amount
31-Dec-17	To Bank Account		70,000	31-Dec-17	By Purchases (Sundries)		70,000
Total			70,000				70,000

Again, in this account, there's nothing that the business owes to PQR Limited. Nothing flows into the balance sheet.

Dr				MNO Company			Cr
Date	Particulars	JF	Amount	Date	Particulars	JF	Amount
31-Dec-17	To Bank Account		120,000	31-Dec-17	By Purchases (Sundries)		120,000
Total			120,000				120,000

Like above, nothing is owed to MNO Company and nothing will flow into the balance sheet.

Dr	Local Agency						Cr
Date	Particulars	JF	Amount	Date	Particulars	JF	Amount
31-Dec-17	To Bank Account		110,000	31-Dec-17	By Purchases (Sundries)		110,000
31-Dec-17	To Purchase Returns		5,000	31-Dec-17	By Cash		5,000
Total			115,000				115,000

In the case of the local agency, there's going to be no balance as everything was settled in cash immediately. There's one entry related to returns, which was settled in cash immediately. The same is reflected separately for your understanding. It helps you to know how returns will reflect on the vendor's ledger.

Now, let's move on to the customer's ledger.

Dr	RMO Enterprises						Cr
Date	Particulars	JF	Amount	Date	Particulars	JF	Amount
31-Dec-17	To Sales (Sundries)		2,125,000	31-Dec-17	By Bank Account		2,125,000
Total			2,125,000				2,125,000

In this case, everything is paid by RMO Enterprises on time. As there's nothing owed to the business, no debtors are created. If, for example, the last transaction settled on 31st Dec of INR 225k wasn't paid, then RMO Enterprises would have owed business INR 225k and would become a debtor. Thus, instead of increasing the bank balance, we would have seen an increase in the debtor's position, in that case.

Dr	FNO Traders						Cr
Date	Particulars	JF	Amount	Date	Particulars	JF	Amount
31-Dec-17	To Sales (Sundries)		125,000	31-Dec-17	By Bank Account		100,000
				31-Dec-17	By Sales Returns		12,500
				31-Dec-17	By Bal c/f		12,500
Total			125,000				125,000

Here, FNO Traders has still not settled INR 12.5k of dues, for which provision for bad debts is created. We're not expecting this money to come in at any time, but as long as there's an attempt made to recover the dues, we have to show it as debtors. The provision will help in reflecting the true view. In case the money comes back from FNO Traders, then the provision is taken off and income is realised to the extent for which the provision was created. If nothing is received after a considerable point in time, then the amount is written off. The FNO Traders account is closed by the balance amount. The provision too is taken out and actual loss is recorded. But as provision has taken care of the loss earlier, there is no profit and loss impact in the subsequent period. **Thus, prudent accounting ensures we take the impact of a potential loss in the period in which it occurred, rather than taking it at a later stage**.

Apart from these vendors and customers ledgers, there is one ledger left related to the landlord. The transactions that appear out here are related to security deposits, rent, advance on electricity, and interest paid on electricity charges. Let's see the ledger below.

Dr				Landlord Account				Cr
Date	Particulars	JF	Amount	Date	Particulars	JF	Amount
1-Jan-17	To Security Deposit (Bank)		120,000	31-Dec-17	By Rent		120,000
31-Dec-17	To Bank Account		120,000	31-Dec-17	By Electricity		28,000
31-Dec-17	To Bank Account		30,000	31-Dec-17	By Interest on Electricity		2,000
				31-Dec-17	By Bal c/f		120,000
Total			**270,000**				**270,000**

In the first transaction, the security deposit was paid to the landlord. The landlord owes that, which is INR 120k. Then, in the second set of transactions, the rent is to be paid, which is also settled. So nothing is due related to rent. In the third set of transactions, electricity was paid by the landlord on behalf of the business for which it charged INR 2k of interest. This was also settled by the business promptly on the last day of the year for INR 30k (INR 28k electricity charges + INR 2k interest on advances taken) This means that the amount which the landlord owes to the business and which is as good as a debtor for the business is INR 120k.

The last ledger is related to provision of income tax. The entry for this will be known only when we prepare the profit and loss statement. The provision will be carried forward in the balance sheet and will reflect as a liability that the business needs to pay to the government.

Having completed all the ledgers, it's now time to assess the impact of this on the profit and loss account and balance sheet. We know the transactions which were carried to the profit and loss account. These are all related to purchases, sales, revenue expenses (operating and finance expenses), and provisions. Below is a P&L for the period in a **T** format. The **T** format puts credit entries on the right side and debit on the left, similar to a ledger.

Profit and Loss Account for the period 1st Jan to 31st Dec 2017				
Dr				**Cr**
Particulars	**Amount**	**Particulars**		**Amount**
Purchases	1,075,000	Sales		2,250,000
Sales Returns	12,500	Purchase Returns		5,000
Rent	120,000	**Inventory**		
Salaries	165,000	Raw Materials		70,000
Maintenance	50,000	Finished Goods		121,800
Electricity	28,000			
Provision for Depreciation	205,000			
Provision for Bad Debts	12,500			
Interest				
Bank Loan	72,294			
Overdraft	750			
Landlord	2,000			
Provison for Tax	**140,751**			
Profit for the Period	563,005			
Total	**2,446,800**	**Total**		**2,446,800**

The total of all debits before provision for tax and profits is INR 1,743,044. The provision that needs to be made for tax is INR 140.8k. This is calculated assuming a rate of 20% on the total profits made. The total profits are worked out by deducting INR 1,743,044 from INR 2,446,800. The provision created for tax will be reflected in the journal as follows:

Account Title or Description	Ref	Amt in INR	
		Debit	Credit
Profit and Loss Account Dr		140,751	
To Provision for Tax Account			140,751

The provision for the tax account will appear as follows in the ledgers:

Dr			Provision for Tax Account				Cr
Date	Particulars	JF	Amount	Date	Particulars	JF	Amount
31-Dec-17	To Bal c/f		140,751	31-Dec-17	By Profit and Loss Account		140,751
Total			140,751				140,751

The provision for tax represents the liability that the business owes to the government.

Regarding P&L presentation, I personally do not like the above form of presentation of P&L. I would do the presentation in the following manner, which is simple to comprehend and gives a proper classification of income and expenses for further analysis to business person, investors and analysts.

Profit and Loss Statement for 2017	
Income Generated During the Period	
Gross Sales	2,250,000
Less: Returns	12,500
Net Sales	2,237,500
Less:	
Purchases	1,075,000
Less: Returns	5,000
Net Purchases	1,070,000
Less: Inventory of Raw Material	70,000
Raw Material Consumption During the Year	1,000,000
Less: Adjustment of Finished Goods Inventory	121,800
Other Operating Expenses	
Rent	120,000
Salaries	165,000
Maintenance	50,000
Electricity	28,000
Depreciation	205,000

Bad Debts Provision	12,500
Total Operating Expenses	**580,500**
Finance Costs	
Interest on Bank Loan	72,294
Interest on Overdraft	750
Interest to Landlord	2,000
Total Financing Costs	**75,044**
Total Expenses During the Period	**1,533,744**
Net Income/Profit During the Period Before Tax	**703,756**
Less: Provision for Income Tax	140,751
Net Income/Profit For the Period	**563,005**

Now, let's assess the balances that other businesses owe to the business or for which Nishka Toys has to pay. Also, let's cover the balances related to cash and bank accounts and assets (capital expenditure). Please note that the balance in the profit and loss statement is a credit balance of INR 563k, which is the **value addition** done by the entrepreneur during the period and will increase the total capital of the entrepreneur. Let's try and put all the balances in a small table and then go ahead with the preparation of the balance sheet.

Particulars	Debit	Credit
Capital		520,000
Computer	20,000	
Security Deposit (Landlord)	120,000	
Machinery	1,000,000	
Bank Loan		628,814
Inventory (Raw Material)	70,000	
Inventory (Finished Goods)	121,800	
Provision for Depreciation		205,000
Provision for Bad Debts		12,500
ABC Traders (Creditors)		40,000
FNO Traders (Debtors)	12,500	
P&L Account (**Amount by Which Capital Will Increase or Decrease**)		563,005
Provision for Taxation		140,751

Cash	15,000	
Bank Account	750,770	
Total	**2,110,070**	**2,110,070**

You will notice that the balance of the debits and the credits are the same. As called out earlier, this is due to the fact that accounts record both the give and take side of any transaction. **In short, the business created INR 2.11 M of assets in the form of capital expenditure, cash, and bank balances which were provided through the entrepreneur's capital and acumen and the rest through borrowings from banks and the creditor. This is the essence of a balance sheet.**

The above balances were carried forward (c/f) from individual ledgers.

As mentioned while explaining ledgers, if something has a debit balance, its debit side will be higher. The amount by which the debit side is higher than the credit side will be considered the debit balance that will be carried in the balance sheet. Similarly, if the credit side is higher than the debit side, the same will be considered the credit balance. **This represents the value of the respective asset or liability at the time of preparing the balance sheet.**

Debits are receipts by the business and are therefore the assets employed by the business. They represent either the value of capital expenditure or the debtors created or the cash/bank balances available with the business.

On the other side, credits represent the amount coming from the entrepreneur or borrowed sources or creditors. They represent the source of funds that were used to build assets or it represents how capital was employed either through the entrepreneur's funds or borrowed funds. **The profit earned by the business is something that the business owes to the entrepreneur for providing value addition by employing her/his acumen and will go on to increase the entrepreneur's capital. We call these reserves and they add to the capital. If a loss occurs, the amount of capital will get reduced by the loss or the reserves will fall by the loss amount.**

Reading a balance sheet is very important just like the profit and loss statement. There's a lot that a balance sheet describes. It describes how the business is funded, it describes where the funds are being deployed, and it helps in understanding what profits are derived and accumulated over a period of time.

Balance Sheet as on 31st December 2017	
Source of Funds (Liability)	
Owner's Funds	520,000
Capital Introduced	
Add/Less: Additions/Deletions (Drawings)	-
Add: Reserves	563,005
Total Owner's Funds	**1,083,005**
Borrowed Funds	
Bank Loan	**628,814**
Short-Term Borrowings	
Creditors	40,000
Provision Towards Taxation	140,751
Total Short-Term Borrowings	**180,751**
Source of Funds Total	**1,892,570**
Capital Employed (Assets)/Utilisation of Funds	
Fixed Assets	
Machinery	1,000,000
Computer	20,000
Less: Provision for Depreciation	205,000
Net Value of Fixed Assets	**815,000**
Short-Term Assets	
Debtors	12,500
Less: Provision for Bad Debts	12,500
Net Debtors	-
Cash	15,000
Bank	750,770
Security Deposit (Landlord)	120,000
Inventory	
Raw Materials	70,000
Finished Goods	121,800
Total Short-Term Assets	**1,077,570**
Capital Employed/Utilisation of Funds Total	**1,892,570**

In the above balance sheet, asset values for fixed assets and debtors were reduced by the provision amount. By deducting them from the debit balance, it is as good as recording it on the liability side.

Reading the Balance Sheet

The above balance sheet tells you that from a capital of INR 500k, the entrepreneur was able to earn more than 100% in terms of returns or profits during the year. It didn't have much of a burden from debt or borrowed funds and it has generated enough bank balance to pay off the loan in one shot, if it desires. Apart from machinery, there was no major capital expenditure incurred and so many of the assets that were generated were in the form of the bank balance.

Can this performance be replicated next year? The answer might be different. It also depends on how the entrepreneur wants to invest the surplus bank balance. Does she want to penetrate further markets with that bank balance or add more assets in form of additional machinery or other assets? It can be anything. But that is to be considered at the time of planning and controlling. I'm just setting the scene out here. **Also, answers to the above questions can help potential investors to take a decision on buying the shares of any specific company.**

IX.   Tool to Manage Personal Finance

The principles, as outlined above, for accounting for businesses can be of great help to individuals as well for maintaining their personal monetary records. However, the numbers of transactions will be limited and it's not important to maintain a journal or a ledger. But it's worthwhile to track and record all expenses, whether you have paid for it or not, which means it's due to be paid. It's critical to understand the difference between them. Many individuals tend to have a sudden shortage of funds as they do not make a provision for expenses which are due to be paid in the subsequent months, and so would overspend and will have to borrow from some other source to make a payment or seek more time for payment. This can result in a temporary cash crunch or, in extreme cases, create a debt trap.

Maintaining tools that can facilitate spending wisely, based on the above accounting principles, is therefore highly advisable. Speaking very lightly, such wise spends could have avoided the 2008 sub – prime mortgage crisis, where people borrowed more than their income without realising that eventually they would have to pay it back.

Even individuals have complex personal transactions. They can be related to loan or capital expenditure incurred like buying a house, car, home appliances or kitchen appliances.

Though it might sound trivial, maintaining depreciation on such transactions can help in making a provision for their replacement in future. Also, it forces an individual to think about the timeframe for replacement and thereby creates discipline in spending on big ticket expenses.

Let's say you buy a smart HD television with all the great features. You buy that television keeping a 4-year horizon into consideration. Suddenly something new appears after a year and you replace your television with a new one. The amount realised from selling the old television is very less and does not even cover a quarter of your earlier spends as the technology has changed. This will suddenly strain you a bit or heavily depending on your income levels. If there are not many features to offer than your existing television, the expense can be considered to be going down the drain.

Maintaining a depreciation or deducting a fixed sum of money each year will ensure that you provide money for a replacement. This will also help you in assessing the loss or financial impact you would be incurring by a sudden change of your mind to switch to a new television after one year and might force you to reconsider your decision. The expenditure that you would have incurred on a new television could be channelised into getting something better which might add more value or convenience to your life.

The above principle applies to a great extent to smartphone purchases which have become more like revenue expenditure than capital expenditure these days.

My advice would be to always maintain a month-on-month record of all expenses. Expenses should be properly classified, and separate records should be maintained for each expense type as it might help to reconcile things whenever required. Below is a format of income and expenditure and total assets created, which I can prescribe, but one can develop their own templates. Remember to apply the principles of accounting while maintaining the records. The format tries to explain the same with an example of an individual who's getting a fixed salary. Transactions are classified as either cash or credit transaction. Monthly provisions are created for some expenses which will be due in future. This will help in avoiding any cash crunch at the time of making such an expenditure. This should be considered in while preparing cash flow projection which we will see in the next section viz. funds management section. This will help in spending cash judiciously and ensuring enough cash balance. Also, provision for depreciation is maintained and separate funds are provided for the same for future replacement.

Depreciation will apply only to capital expenditures which have a finite life and will have a reduction in value every year. Houses do not come under this bucket as houses will normally have an appreciation in value. But we shouldn't be measuring that appreciation. If we wish to track this appreciation, we can do it separately. Some capital expenditures are funded by a loan. In such cases, one can opt to create a depreciation fund if they wish to replace those assets in future without any borrowings. Sometimes, it's not possible to create such a fund given the kind of income and expenditure and future obligations which an individual might have.

Expenses are classified into two broad areas viz. basic costs and lifestyle expenses. The format can be further modified as per one's convenience and can be increased or decreased. It's completely up to an individual to maintain this. This is just a blueprint that provides a view of how your records should appear. If one does it diligently, it might take a one-time investment to build this and then regular maintenance can be done by spending 5–10 minutes of the day recording all monetary transaction you entered into. It might take another half an hour every week on your weekly offs to evaluate it. One can do it on monthly or quarterly basis as well. This might also help you to plan for your next big capital expenditure, a holiday abroad, investments for future, your kid's education, your wedding or even a trip to space, who knows!

Personal Income and Expenditure Statement for June 2018

	Cash/ Bank	Credit Cards	Provisions	Depreciation	Jun-18	Comments
Income Excl. Taxes						
Salary	125,000				125,000	
Business					–	
Rental Income					–	
Investment Income	10,000				10,000	
Others					–	
Total Income	**135,000**	**–**	**–**	**–**	**135,000**	
Less:						
Basic Costs						
Groceries	5,000	5,000			10,000	(half paid through cash and half by credit card)
Rent/Interest on House Loan	15,000				15,000	**(Interest on EMI, if any, is a recurring expense. Principal amount should be covered from the surplus. It's a repayment. If surplus is not becoming sufficient, it should ring alarm bells.)**
Clothes			2,000		2,000	(provision made for future purchases)
School/ College Fees			10,000		10,000	(provision made for future payout)
Telephone/ Internet/Cable Costs	2,000				2,000	
Gas/Fuel	4,000				4,000	
Medical Expenses			1,500		1,500	(provision made for any contingencies)
Total Basic Costs	**26,000**	**5,000**	**13,500**	**–**	**44,500**	
Lifestyle Expenses						

Club Fees/ Future Trip Provision		3,000		3,000	(Provision made every month for yearly payment)
Restaurant	2,000			2,000	
Movies/Play	1,000			1,000	
Outing	1,500			1,500	
Luxury Shopping (Perfumes, Paintaings etc)	5,000			5,000	
Total Lifestyle Expenses	**9,500**	**–**	**3,000**	**–**	**12,500**	
Depreciation on Assets					
Furniture			2,000	2,000	
Home Appliances			1,250	1,250	
Car			7,500	7,500	
Gadgets/Smart phones & Televisions			5,000	5,000	
Total Depreciation	**–**	**–**	**–**	**15,750**	**15,750**	
Total Recurring Expenses	**35,500**	**5,000**	**16,500**	**15,750**	**72,750**	
Surplus/ Deficit					**62,250**	
Transferred to					
Investments/ Loan Principal Amount				30,000	(INR 10k on Fixed deposits, INR 10k on shares and INR 10k on mutual funds.)
Cash/Bank Balance	99,500		(15,750)	83,750	Amount provided for Depreciation already transferred to Fixed Deposit

Statement of Net Assets Created		
Assets/Capital Expenditure		
Cash/Bank Balance	333,750	(assuming INR 250k of previous balance and adding surplus plus all provisions from this month)
Home		
Furniture	96,000	(expected to last 4 years)
Home Appliances	60,000	
Car	630,000	(expected to last 7 years)
Gadgets/Smart Phones/Computers & Televisions	180,000	(expected to last 3 years)
Gross Value of Assets	**1,299,750**	
Less: Accumulated Depreciation	189,000	assuming everything was purchased last year
Net Value of Assets	**1,110,750**	
Investments		
Bank Fixed Deposits	1,000,000	
Shares/Mutual Funds	2,000,000	
Business		
Additional Home/Land		
Total Investments	**3,000,000**	
Provision for Fixed Assets	**189,000**	Creating a fixed deposit to cover cost of assets in future
Lendings to Friends/Relatives/Others	**10,000**	
Total Value of All Assets	**4,309,750**	
Less: Long Term Liabilities		
Pending Loan Amount to Be Repaid	0	
Net Value of Assets Created*	**4,309,750**	

*Net assets = Total value of assets minus long-term liabilities to obtain these assets

In the above, the most important element to understand is cash/bank balance. The total balance was INR 250k before June 2018. However, there were some expenses which were just provided for and some were done using a credit card. The expenses which were just provided and the ones which were done using credit card would be paid on the due date. Cash balance will be impacted then. But by making a provision for the same, one can prevent unnecessary expenditure. This can avoid any strain in the future. In this example, we didn't assume any payout due to the credit card for the last month. If it was there, it should be deducted and shown as an outflow of cash from the exercise. **Please refer to the funds management section for more understanding on determining personal cash flow projection. All provisions and credit card payment to be done in future should be considered in these cash flow projections in the period when cash will flow out.**

The amount kept for depreciation can help in further replenishing the asset in the future, through a fixed deposit specifically created for the same. There's no instance of EMI (equated monthly installment) on loans that are covered in the example above. Principal and interest are paid in installments in the form of EMI against a loan taken to buy an asset. Every month it will lead to a cash outflow till the period of the loan ends. The same must be considered in the personal cash flow projection. Interest is the charge by the bank for advancing money and is a recurring cost. So, this should be considered an expense as this is the cost you bear every month for the loan taken. By doing this, we can maintain a proper discipline on our expenses. The principal is the amount that you pay for the value of the asset in installments. Principal represents the value of the asset. This further helps you in tax planning and taking advantage of interest and the principal amount in your direct tax.

Your bank, which provides a loan, also provides a schedule of principal and interest payment.

The above type of exercise can help you assess the value of the asset properly and facilitate decision making in certain situations. For example, if for some unforeseen reasons, the income suddenly drops, this can help in raising the alarm bells and can help you in taking a decision swiftly with respect to the asset. It can help you to sell out the asset at appropriate prices quickly. Similarly, if income increases suddenly, it can help you understand the surplus available and help you in repaying your loan quickly and save some money on interest costs.

X. Conclusion

As the heading says, accounting is the backbone of finance and business in general. The principles of accounting can be a great tool for individuals as well. If you do not have a strong recording mechanism, you will not be able to understand all transactions that you entered into and that might impact your decision-making ability as well. It will limit you to assess and get a complete picture about your business. The books that we created in the case study were maintained by the entrepreneur. Similarly, the vendors and customers or the financing agency will also be maintaining their own set of books. Whenever there are transactions done with such parties, there is a likelihood of some discrepancy at some stage and this requires to be sorted out through a **reconciliation** process. The transactions that were presented to you were limited. But in reality the volume of these transactions are huge and it's also important that there is a reconciliation mechanism in place when variances occur in two sets of records. Such a process will help in settling dues quickly and ensure the smooth running of the business. This can be done by checking your records with the records provided by the third party and then discrepancies from the same can be evaluated.

Another point that needs consideration is related to revenue recognition. This is one of the most important principles that any business needs to know as this will help them understand how it impacts their overall profitability for a given period. The case that I had presented to you was a simple manufacturing case study. However, the principles apply to services and trading businesses as well. The only difference in service business is that instead of goods, there are services involved. In the case of services, if services are agreed to be delivered, for a specific period is not complete or executed, the transaction cannot be recorded as revenue. There must be acceptance from the buyer acknowledging to have received such services. All important elements of the contract need to be agreed beforehand. If those elements as agreed are not fulfilled, the contract wouldn't be complete, and revenues cannot be recognised. Example: A firm provides accounting services on a monthly basis. Revenue should be recognised only after the month is over. There could be a provision in the contract that if the seller decides to rescind in between the month, they will not be paid for the services offered in the interim and the contract will be considered null and void. In that case, unless the month doesn't expire, no revenues should be recognised. Maintaining prudence in such cases is the key.

Similarly, there could be another provision where the contract would have been considered fulfilled only when certain work-related documents or statements are provided at the end of the month. Unless they are provided to the satisfaction of the buyer and agreed with her/him, revenues shouldn't be recognised.

While the above considers transactional elements of revenue recognition, sometimes huge projects have complex arrangements. They last for more than a year. Mostly in such cases, the stages of completion are decided at the time of framing the contract. After finishing important milestones, performance is reviewed and agreed by both the parties. Only then proportional revenues and expenses associated with it will get recognised. Remember the principle of inventory valuation for finished goods in the above case study. The balance portion of the inventory which remains to be recognised in P&L is recognised in the balance sheet. The statement of work which gives a detailed description of the work is very relevant in such kind of businesses.

Accounting can be of interest to individuals, business person, investors, students from finance and non-finance backgrounds. When more people plan to do something of their own, such an understanding of accounting can be very vital for making decisions and recording and assessing their financial performance properly. In case someone is not able to hire the services of accountants, then the above can help in maintaining at least the basic records by themselves.

One can refer to more accounting books for more details in case one has an interest to know more about accounting. There are numerous books available on accounting from different publications.

However, I feel whatever I have covered so far is sufficient to give a conceptual understanding of accounting in general and one can take it forward from here to understand the other aspects of finance.

Section 3

Funds Management

I. Introduction and Cash Conversion Cycle

Cash is king. Without cash or bank balance (hereinafter referred to as cash), nothing moves for individuals and businesses. Let me try to prove this point.

An individual or a business gets into numerous commercial activities or transactions at any given point in time. All these entail money or funds. Most of the time, they tend to get credit in the form of a credit card or in case of businesses, credit from vendors. They also need to give credit to customers. Suppose, suddenly due to some issues or lack of control, the economy starts to feel distress. Funds starts disappearing from the system and the economy. The customers to whom businesses had given credit find it difficult to make payments. This further leads to businesses curtailing their buying activities or they in turn stop paying money. Individuals start feeling the heat and they too don't have anything to spend on. All the economic activities of a society or a nation slow down or come to a grinding halt. This is how recession occurs. A business that typically has spare cash, in the form of hard cash and bank balance, will sail through such a tide and survive. Businesses in over significant debt find it difficult during such a period. Even individuals who take excessive loans to fulfill their dream house at times face difficulty in repaying their debt and could sell their assets at distress values, especially when they don't have jobs. So, having adequate amount of cash is quintessential for businesses and individuals. The one with cash or even gold is the one who survives on a rainy day.

This in no way indicates that debt is a sin. Just like an individual's or businesses own cash, debt also acts like catalyst and mitigates shortage of funds temporarily but borrowing or lending in excess creates problems.

As mentioned in the introductory note, cash is the catalytic force that brings all elements of business together. Cash ensures the smooth running of business operations and thereby helps in generating more income. In normal business operations, cash gets converted to purchases of goods or services, from purchases of goods to inventory, from inventory to debtors, from debtors to cash. The same applies for services business as well except that there might not be an inventory, but services when sold get converted to debtors and debtors to cash. Similarly if a big expenditure is made, cash converts to assets and those assets help to convert to cash, over a period of time through normal business operations.

The above is referred to as a **cash conversion cycle**. Let's try to summarise it in a simple chart as given below:

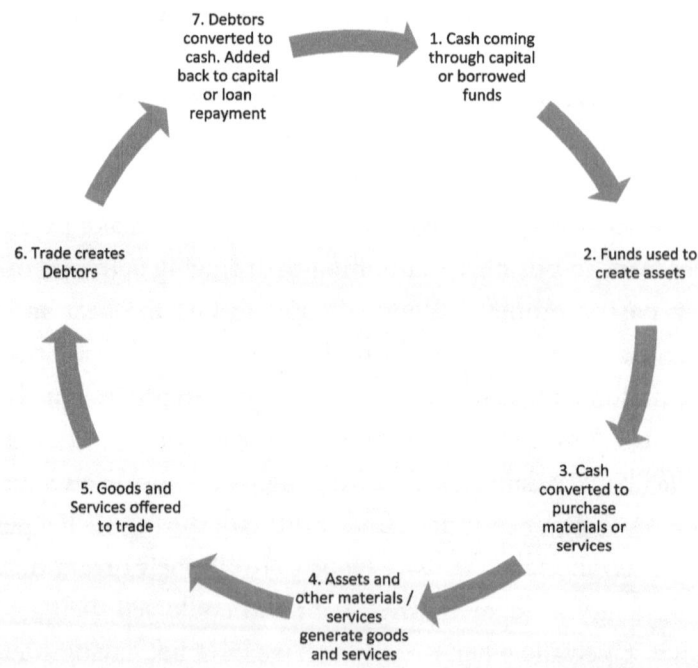

As seen in the above chart, cash can come directly from the entrepreneur or from their associates or it can be borrowed. Running a successful business would normally depend on how much value you generate in the whole conversion process in the form of **profits**. Most of the profits are transferred back to capital in the form of cash (there are always some outstanding debtors for the business). The cash is further utilised to create more assets or expand the markets. This, in turn, facilitates the business to grow and scale further. Thus, cash attracts more cash if invested wisely and so, cash is the king.

A good fund management depends on proper planning and controlling of funds, which also includes having proper accounting in place. This is a part of the business and financial planning and controlling exercise. Much of it will be covered when we cover planning and controlling in the second part of this book.

The principles, as given above, related to cash conversion apply to individuals in personal capacity as well. The cash earnings and utilisation chart for an individual is as follows:

The above can't be represented in a cash conversion cycle as for an individual and her/his family, the money earned is normally spent. Investments provide returns, but normally it takes time to give regular inflows. But this helps in understanding how individuals channelise funds to improve their wellbeing.

II. Currency

The first thing to know in funds management is the currency in which you'll receive your income or in case of a business, the currency in which you'll be operating your business. It's simple to understand and often taken for granted. Every country operates with its own currency. In India, it's the Indian Rupee (INR). One has to maintain a sufficient balance of local currency at any point in time. Ideally it should be available in the bank, rather than keeping cash, as most of the transactions happen through banking channels. Most of the transactions happen in the local currency in which the business is established.

In today's world, most of the businesses have some sort of global presence. Either they buy their stuff or get services from different countries or they sell their wares and services in more than one country. With more money at their disposal, many individuals also travel abroad for holidays where international currency is required. In that context, having a basic understanding of the currency market is critical.

The currency market is the market in which all the major currencies of the world operate. In most of the countries, USD (United States Dollar) is the most recognised currency for international transactions. In that context, understanding how your currency is moving against the USD is important. One can go online and track the movement of currencies through different online portals. One specific portal that I use to track currency movement is www.xe.com. There are also other portals that provide such services and one can use them as well to track currencies.

In the case of high volume of international transactions, appropriate hedging should be used to protect yourself against the volatile movement in currencies, which could impact your profitability.

III. Hedging

Hedging is a mechanism through which one can protect themselves in international trade. It is a process through which you buy or sell a specific pair of currencies at a future date at a particular agreed rate or locked rate. These agreed or locked rates give you visibility on the amount that you can expect from selling or buying in your home currency and facilitates taking proper business calls with respect to pricing and costs in international markets. Many major banks or financial institutions provide hedging facility. There are different hedging methods and products available but I'll cover only futures and options in this book.

A Currency Future or Futures contract is where one agrees to buy and sell a pair of currencies at a specific rate in future. The rate is locked for a future date. So, one has visibility of how much they can expect from selling their stuff in international markets or they know how much they need to pay for their international purchases and business operations during a given period. Any change in exchange rates will not impact your earnings or purchases.

Example: You agree to buy 10k USD at the rate of INR 70 for every USD, after one month. After one month, if the rate falls and USD is less in demand and the value of one USD goes below INR 65, then you tend to lose the benefit of INR 5 for every dollar that you had hedged. Alternatively, after one month, if the cost of buying a USD is say INR 72, then you save INR 2 for every USD that you had hedged. However, as mentioned above, because of this hedging, you can be rest assured on the amount that you will get and thereby can take appropriate business calls with respect to pricing and costs in advance. The loss or gain that you make during the process goes to increase or reduce your hedging expenses.

However, in **Options**, you get an option to exercise your contract at a particular rate in future by paying a premium money, unlike Futures where you're bound by the contract. You may or may not decide to exercise the option depending on where the currency is moving. If rates are lesser, like in the above example, you may decide not to exercise the option. However, you will not get the premium money back if you do not exercise the option. The payment done towards the premium is the cost that you're incurring to protect against the risk of unfavourable movements. It's like a short-term service or something like an insurance premium, which is undertaken by the seller in this case, to protect you from the risks of the foreign exchange market.

Example on Buying an Option: Suppose you expect USD to be at INR 70 after one month. So you buy a USD contract available in the Option market at INR 70, by paying a premium of say INR 0.50 for every USD, that can be exercised after one month. Here, the seller has to sell this option to you at INR 70 after one month even if the rate goes to INR 72 or INR 75 or any higher rate. This way, you're protected from adverse movements. But there will be a premium charged by the seller which will be dependent on interest rates and volatility. Higher the volatility, higher the interest rates, higher the premium. If the rates after one month is say INR 65 or INR 68, you can decide not to exercise the option. In such an event you have to forego the premium amount that you paid to the seller which is INR 0.50 for every USD hedged by you.

Let's try to understand the difference between Options and Futures. In the above case, you pay INR 0.50 as the premium to obtain the above option contract. If exchange rates go below INR 69.50 for every USD, in this case, your maximum loss will be INR 0.50 for every USD that you had hedged. But in futures, it can be much more than INR 0.50. In case of options, your maximum loss is defined. Options therefore appears more lucrative, but it's not simple like that.

These expenses on premium or any other fees associated with hedging are hedging expenses. The premium money that needs to be paid can become expensive if the markets are highly volatile. Similarly, if the probability of rate going up is higher, the option premium could be higher and futures might be more attractive at that point in time.

Therefore, it is always advisable to use a mix of different hedging products that are available and that can work out at an optimal cost to save on hedging expenses. At times, you may decide not to hedge your complete exposure, depending on market conditions. Here, I mean that you might hedge only a part of your expected foreign income or expenses.

In case of big businesses, having high global presence, they would have a policy towards hedging different currencies, especially for big multinational companies.

IV. Working Capital

Broadly speaking, a business requires funds for two reasons. This can be for running the day-to-day operations and one for a long-term purpose.

The amount that is required for running the day-to-day operations of the business is also referred to as working capital. On the other hand, the amount that is required for creating or buying assets that typically lasts for longer duration is called capital expenditure. Now, let's go back to the different expenses which we covered at the time of accounting that can help us in connecting with this topic. There are basically two types of expenses viz. revenue expenditure and capital expenditure.

Revenue expenditure is required on a regular and daily basis. This is representative of the working capital.

For example, a business needs money for procuring raw material for running its operations on a regular basis. Similarly, if you have bought a facility on rent, rent must be paid every month. The same goes if you hire someone for assisting you, in the form of salaries, who needs to be paid on a monthly basis. Also, you would need money to advertise your product or conduct different marketing activities. The list can be endless. For some of these expenses, you tend to get a credit facility but for some of them, you must pay money immediately. Cash moves in a cycle as seen in the above chart. Every business converts its inputs into final products or services over a period of time. This can be a few days or months. In some cases, it can be as good as a year. The amount of money required to sustain during this period is the working capital required by the business.

Most of the business is done on credit. When the vendors are giving you goods or services on credit, it forms a short-term liability for the business in the form of creditors. These are also called current liabilities. They are supposed to be settled in a few days or months. Similarly, when you sell goods or services on credit, you're creating debtors. They are not converted into cash immediately but might take a few days or months to get converted. They are part of the short-term assets, also referred to as current assets.

Similarly, the inventory purchased from the vendors is stored, processed, and then converted into finished goods. It takes time to get this thing done. The amount is locked during the process. The material that is unused or in the process of manufacturing or stored as finished goods, which are not yet sold, is also the current assets of the business.

Thus, current liabilities are short-term liabilities that need to be paid in a short period of time, which is typically less than a year, and similarly current assets are short-term assets that are paid by customers or debtors or converted into sales within a short period of time, which again is less than a year.

The difference in the value between these current assets and current liabilities represents the working capital required by the business.

For example, let us say you have to collect INR 1 Mn from debtors and pay INR 500k to creditors and other suppliers and employees. If you have a stock of goods, which costs INR 500k, and is available for selling, then the working capital required by you to sustain in the short-term is as follows:

Current Assets

Debtors	INR 1 Mn
Stock/Inventory	INR 500k
Total Current Assets	**INR 1.5 Mn**
less: **Current Liabilities**	
Creditors & others	INR 500k
Working Capital	**INR 1 Mn**

V. Sources for Getting Working Capital

The above kind of exercise helps a business in determining the money required at any point in time for normal business operations. To run the business smoothly, sufficient funds need to be there to cover these working capital requirements. Sometimes there can be a situation where everything can't be funded by own sources. A business might have to rely on borrowed funds for a short time. One of this can be a **Bank Overdraft**. We saw in our case study that the business was short of funds in March and May-June period, which was funded by a bank overdraft. There are many products offered by vendors dealing in financial products that cater to this short-term requirement of finance. While bank overdraft is one of them, there are factoring, credit cards or letters of credit in international transactions and many more. However, I'll touch upon factoring, credit cards, and letters of credit. A letter of credit is not a funding source but is an important instrument in case of international transactions.

Factoring

Normally when sales transactions are huge in number and happen via credit, one can resort to factoring for temporary arrangement of funds. In this facility, the business would sell its debtors or invoices, also referred to as accounts receivable to a third party providing these services. This third party is referred to as factor. A factor provides the money to the business at a discount. So if the business is selling say INR 1 Mn of its account receivables to the factor, it will receive less than INR 1 Mn, say for example INR 995k. The right to receive money from the debtors now resides with the factor. This can be a great source to fund a temporary cash crunch. It is also used in international trade where exporters would sell their receivables to a forfeiter. Forfeiting is a factoring arrangement used in international trade, where the forfeiter will collect the money from the debtors. This removes the hassle of collecting money.

Credit Cards

A credit card can be a great source to fund transactions if utilised properly. Normally a credit card issuer gives 45 days credit term. If payments are done using credit card at the start of the credit cycle, a business can enjoy close to full period of credit term. But at the same time, the business too must give this facility to its customers. In that case, the bank or the credit card issuing company will charge fees to the business. When business provides credit card facility to pay money to its customers, then it becomes a merchant in credit card terminology.

There are risks associated with credit cards, especially related to frauds. In case of fraud, there are chances of chargebacks by the original card holder, where the amount is held by the bank. Chargeback would mean that the credit card holder might contest that the amount charged to him for purchases are not genuine purchases. So the bank providing the credit card to the card holder will hold the money to the merchant. Normally, in such cases, the merchant must contest the case if he has to get the money and this could take away a good amount of time. Normally such kind of chargebacks should be properly provided in the books of accounts and should be created as a provision. This provision should reduce the sales or revenues of the business. This will ensure prudence in accounting.

Credit cards can be a great source of funding for individuals if proper records are maintained and if spends are tracked properly. They also allow individual to earn interest on their bank accounts for a short period, if they use this facility.

Overall, credit card can be a great source of funding for businesses that are transactional in nature or the ones that deal with multiple consumers in a day. For example, retail stores, online stores, doctors, professionals etc.

Letter of Credit

A letter of credit is not a funding arrangement but it's an important instrument in international trade where buyers and sellers are governed by their respective country laws and assessing credit is difficult. The banking system can come to the rescue. Here there is a written commitment from the bank on behalf of the buyer that money will be paid to the seller on submission of all the documents in relation to the transaction. The seller must provide all requisite documents as agreed upon to get the money from the bank. It's quite administrative but one of the best tools while dealing with international transactions.

The different financial instruments or products as described above are not exhaustive but a representation of the different products available in the market. The products can be many, but it's important to assess if it suits your need and comes at the least possible interest costs. Proper cost benefit analysis needs to be done while evaluating all alternatives. Also, it's important to maintain proper credit rating. Many of the financial institutions could charge a higher interest rate if they perceive high risk from the person or business availing credit and has less credit rating score. It's important to assess the credit rating on a regular basis. There are many vendors that provide such services.

VI. Determining Working Capital Requirement

Having understood the concept of working capital requirement and the different sources to fund it, let's turn to assess the quantum of working capital requirement. Let me try to give a small example around this.

Let's take our example of Nishka Toys with some changes. Let's assume that Nishka Toys does INR 3 Mn of revenues in any given month, on an average. 50% of its revenues goes towards buying raw materials. 10% of its revenues goes towards converting raw materials into finished goods. This does not include any depreciation. It holds raw materials after it has come to its warehouse for 5 days. Then it takes another 10 days to process them into finished goods and it holds the finished goods for 5 days before they are dispatched to its customers. It pays its vendors in 30 days and it gives a credit of 30 days to its customers.

To determine the quantum of funds required as working capital, let's create a replica of a monthly P&L. We learnt about P&L in the last section. We'll now use the principles out here.

For the convenience of readers, **conversion costs** is the cost of labour, fuel or electricity or any other expenses required to convert raw materials into finished goods. This is part of the cost of manufacturing.

	% of Rev	Monthly Amt	Amt per day
Average Sales During the Month	100%	3,000,000	100,000
Raw Material Cost	50%	1,500,000	50,000
Conversion Costs	10%	300,000	10,000
Total Cost of Goods Sold		1,800,000	60,000
Gross Profit		1,200,000	40,000

So, now we have details of average sales happening during the day. We also have details of average raw material consumption and average conversion costs incurred during the day. However, this is not complete. There are other elements to it.

Let's turn to the inventory first.

- Raw material is held for 5 days. So, at any point in time, there is 5 days of raw material which is in inventory. Raw material consumed per day is INR 50k. So inventory of raw material available at any point in time will be worth **INR 250k** (INR 50k * 5 days).
- Raw material gets processed into finished goods in 10 days. This means the value of goods which are work in progress will be INR 600k. The calculation is given below.

Raw Material Consumed per Day	50,000	
Raw Material Consumed for 10 Days (INR 50k * 10 Days)	**500,000**	**A**
Conversion Cost per Day	10,000	
Conversion Costs for 10 Days (INR 10k * 10 days)	**100,000**	**B**
Work in Progress Inventory for the Period	**600,000**	**A+B**

Finally the goods are stored for 5 days before they are sold. This means the value of the goods in the finished goods inventory will be as follows. The calculation is given below.

Raw Material Consumed per Day	50,000
Conversion Cost per Day	10,000
Value of Finished Goods Inventory per Day	**60,000**
Finished Goods Inventory for the Period (Inr 60K * 5 Days)	**300,000**

Thus, the value of the inventory required at any point in time for the business is approx. INR 1.15 Mn. The breakup of it is INR 250k (Raw materials) + INR 600k Work in progress + INR 300k (Finished goods).

Now, let's turn to determine the value of the debtors and the creditors which will be available at any point in time.

- The average daily sales of Nishka Toys is INR 100k. So, if it gives a credit of 30 days, then the debtors at any point in time will be on an average INR 3 Mn (INR 100k * 30 days).
- The average raw materials consumed during the month is INR 1.5 Mn (INR 3 Mn * 50%). Thus, INR 1.5 Mn is purchased through vendors during a month, which is paid after 30 days. Thus, in a nutshell, INR 1.5 Mn of the creditors will always be reflected in the balance sheet.

Now, let's sum all of these together to assess the working capital requirement.

Working capital required at any point in time	
Inventory	1,150,000
Debtors	3,000,000
Current Assets at Any Point in Time	**4,150,000**
Less: Creditors	1,500,000
Working Capital Required	**2,650,000**

Thus, at any point in time, the working capital required is INR 2.65 Mn. Ideally, it's always advisable that the business maintains this kind of cash, plus some buffer, in case the realisation into cash is delayed at times.

The above can also be represented differently. It can be said that the business requires 26.5 days of its average daily revenues in the form of working capital. Please note that the amount of working capital required must be assessed on a regular basis as business would grow and attain a scale or at times it can shrink.

Working capital requirement forms the basis for determining the policies with which a business can operate with creditors and debtors after mutual agreement with them.

It is inevitable for most of the business to offer credit in some form or the other to its customers. Similarly, a business receives credit from its vendors, where you are their customers. In such a scenario, the quantum of period for which credit needs to be given must be determined very carefully. It can be 30 days or 45 days or 60 days or 15 days. While lower credit terms for customers and higher credit terms from suppliers is always favourable and is on one end of the extreme, but things do not work on these extremes. The market might be offering a different set of credit terms to its customers or suppliers. So, apart from assessing which terms works best for you, it is equally important to consider what is offered by the market to different vendors and customers. At times, to reduce the credit period to customers or getting additional credit facility from suppliers, a business might have to entail a higher cost. It can be in the form of higher discounts to customers or increased prices from suppliers. Factoring services offered by some financial institutions to cater to the working capital need can also form a critical piece of puzzle while fixing the credit terms. We already went through factoring earlier. Such things should be evaluated properly and proper prudence has to prevail while determining these terms.

Working capital represents just one aspect of funds requirement. The above is a very simplistic view of working capital needs. For a business which is in the services sector, the dynamics could be different. The current assets and current liabilities in this case could be different. For example, if a company is providing online accounting services for which it charges a subscription fee every month, then its cash from the debtors is locked for a month. It needs to pay for administration and other overheads during the period. It must assess its working capital accordingly. But the basic principles outlined above remain valid, to determine working capital, and this is applicable whether it's a manufacturing, trading or services business.

An individual can determine her/his working capital requirement by preparing a cash projection, which we'll see later in this book.

VII.   CAPEX (Capital Expenditure)

Apart from the revenue expenditure, a business would need funds to make investments for big-ticket items. This can be a factory or machinery in case of a manufacturing concern. It can be a giant warehouse in case of a trading concern. This can be a facility to run services business. It can also be an acquisition of another business to improve revenue generation and profitability. Now let me go back to the car and fuel analogy. The expenditure incurred on car is an example of the above kind of expenses. The car is an asset out here. It's a CAPEX (capital expenditure) or a big ticket expense.

VIII.   Payback Period

We often read in business dailies that a company incurred some INR 1 Bn in setting up a plant or factory or it is investing INR 2 Bn in putting its software centre facility somewhere in the country. These are all CAPEX. The revenue and profits generated from these facilities or assets take some years to recover the asset cost. But the expenditure is incurred before these revenues start coming. The period it takes to recover the asset cost is called the **payback** period.

Let's take an example here. If a business is incurring INR 10 Mn in building a factory and is expecting to generate INR 50 Mn of revenues in a year from that factory, its cash profit is expected to be INR 5 Mn in a year, after factoring the interest component on borrowed capital. In this case, it will take 2 years to recover the cost (INR 10 Mn factory cost divided by cash profit of INR 5 Mn). As reiterated above, these expenses are funded by either the entrepreneur's capital or borrowed funds.

In case these expenses are funded from the entrepreneur's capital, an entrepreneur can even think of diluting his share from the business and offering the partnership to someone else who brings capital. In case of public limited or private limited companies, the company might do a public issue or invite some more shareholders to invest in their venture.

In the above case, if the entrepreneur is an individual running the operations directly, then she/he can decide to bring in another partner who can provide finance and share the profits with her/him. As profits will get diluted, proper care should be taken to ensure how much dilution you can afford. This requires extensive calculation and all factors should be considered. This further helps in determining the share of profits that you can afford to part with.

These expenses always pose some kind of risk. If assessed properly, this paves the path for growth for the business. If something gets miscalculated or caution is not taken, it can lead to a disaster. It can put the business into a debt trap if incessant borrowings are done and earnings are not in line to recover all the costs. Sometimes, even after caution is taken, some external factors put the business to risk and create troubles for the business. These factors can be political and international factors or change in market conditions (disruption brought by an alternative demand fulfilling source or some better offering by a competitor). At times it can be natural calamities as well. Political and international factors and market conditions can work both ways.

A proactive government, which follows a reforms path, can provide immense benefits to the business. Post liberalisation in India, you can see the balance sheets and profit and loss statements of the companies improving significantly. This was noticed for most of the public traded companies. Any CAPEX done during the time of liberalisation had significantly benefitted most of those companies at a later stage.

The risk taken by the business depends on the risk appetite of the entrepreneur/s or management in the case of companies. There are some businesses that have a moderate risk-taking appetite. They will wait for having sufficient internal accruals or cash reserves in place and only thereafter they will incur expenses on creating assets. Similarly, a risk-taking business might want to utilise funds from a third party to fund its expansion programmes. There is no right or wrong approach. But it requires a lot of prudence at the time of decision making. I don't wish to influence readers with my approach. I'm saying there's no right or wrong approach. But if you ask me, my perspective would be to fund these expenses from borrowed capital, only if you're short of funds and there is good visibility on earnings expected from certain assets or projects.

Let me take the analogy of a house purchase done by an individual with a particular fixed income. Let's assume there is an individual who earns INR 150k per month. There is a good visibility that the job will continue in the same place and there's no major risk to the job. Rentals are shooting up every year. Land value too is appreciating. In such a scenario, it's always advisable to own a house and pay the value of the house through EMIs (equated monthly installments).

The same principle should be applied when borrowing funds. If there is lack of visibility, it can work against you. Also banks too need to take this into consideration while granting loans. A bad loan is worse than no loan. However, there are instances of successful ventures where a risk was taken and it helped those organisations grow multifold, even when there was no good visibility to earnings. The entrepreneurs were able to envision the future much better or had to offer a much superior product or service. Here, the lender also needs to have that vision to understand the concept before granting the credit.

These days, a lot of high net worth investors, venture capitalists and angel funding are also available to fund such big expenditures. They are interested in getting a stake against the capital poured into your business and would expect strong returns on it through appreciation in value brought about by revenue and profit growth. These investors take a big risk out here as their funds can wipe out completely if the business does not survive. Many of today's online platforms are funded this way.

Now, the question is what financial considerations need to be considered while making a decision on CAPEX.

The entrepreneur or management needs to assess the viability of these spends through a rigorous study of the market conditions that will be prevailing in future. They also need to assess the incremental costs in the form of extra manpower and materials or other business development costs required to run business operations. A lot of planning goes in such an exercise. I'll attempt to give a comprehensive view of this part when I'm covering planning. There is a separate case study dedicated to this.

There are different tools available to facilitate the decision making process. Apart from the payback period, which I had covered earlier, there are two other tools that are used for the decision-making process. These are **discounted cash flow (DCF)** and **internal rate of return (IRR)**.

IX. Time Value of Money and the Tools That Facilitate Its Calculation

DCF and IRR consider the **time value of money**. I personally believe that the time value of money is one of the best methods of doing cost benefit analysis.

The value of money is not the same year over year. If you keep your cash in bank as fixed deposit or government or corporate bonds, they tend to earn some interest. After one year, their value is higher than the amount initially invested in. So, if you invest INR 100k for 1 year at 10% interest, its value is INR 110k at end of one year. If this is reinvested for one more year, it will be INR 121k [INR 110k + (INR 110k * 10%)] and so on. This is the beauty of compound interest. The money if invested for a specific number of years, say 5 years, will get compounded by the value of principal and interest and every year will earn interest income on principal and interest of previous years. This can be represented by the formula **principal * (1+interest rate) ^no. of years**.

In the above case, say INR 100k is invested for 5 years at 10% interest rate, then the value of money at end of five years can be represented as INR 100k (Principal value) * (1+10%)^5 years in a spreadsheet. The value will be INR 161.05k.

Thus, the value of INR 100k in five years will be INR 161.05k or, alternatively, it can be said that the projected 5th year income of INR 161.05k, if discounted by 10% for five years, will have a present value of INR 100k.

Thus, the **time value of money** gives an assessment of the **present value of expected future cash flows.** It represents what futuristic revenues are worth today, by discounting them at a prevailing interest rate or what is also called the cost of money.

If the value of the cash flows after discounting is lower than the investment value, then it makes more sense for the business to put money in safe places like banks, treasury bills or bonds rather than investing and taking risk, if it's funding the investment from its own money. If it's a case of a borrowed investment, it makes more sense to avoid any borrowings and avoid any financial strains.

Now let's turn to **DCF**. DCF tries to evaluate the present value of future cash flows from the investment made. The present value of future cash flows is determined by discounting the future cash flow for each year with the cost of money. If the present value of future cash flows is more than the cash outflow on account of investments, then the investment is considered feasible.

Let's take an example. XYZ and Company plans to invest INR 50 Mn in a facility. This is a software development centre. They estimate the cash flow in terms of cash profits to come in the following manner throughout the year.

	Year 1	Year 2	Year 3	Year 4	Year 5
Rev (in INR Mn)	50	60	70	90	100
Cash Profit (in INR Mn)	20	22	25	30	35

In this case, the present value of cash flow for the above earnings will be:

	Year 1	Year 2	Year 3	Year 4	Year 5
Rev	50	60	70	90	100
Cash Profit	20	22	25	30	35
Cost of Money	10%	10%	10%	10%	10%
Present Value of Cash Flow from Earnings/Profits	18.18	18.18	18.78	20.49	21.73
Cumulative Present Value of Cash Flow from Earnings	**18.18**	**36.36**	**55.15**	**75.64**	**97.37**

The cash profit is discounted by 10%, which is the cost of money or interest rate every year to calculate the present value of cash flows. The formula for arriving at the present value is cash profit * $(1/(1+r)^n)$. Here, r stands for interest rate or cost of money and n for number of completed years. Thus, in the 2nd year, the calculation of the present value will be INR 22 * $(1/(1.1)^2)$ which is equal to INR 18.18 Mn. The cumulative value of cash flow from earnings for 2 years will be INR 18.18 Mn for 1st year and INR 18.18 Mn for the 2nd year, which equals INR 36.36 Mn.

In the above example, you'll see that the cumulative value of DCF was covering the investment cost or CAPEX in the third year itself. If a 5-year horizon is comfortable enough for assessing revenues and profitability, then this investment really looks lucrative. It will generate a positive discounted cash flow of INR 47 Mn at the end of 5 years as can be seen below in the calculation.

	Year 0	Year 1	Year 2	Year 3	Year 4	Year 5	Total	
Present Value of Cash Flow from Earnings		18.18	18.18	18.78	20.49	21.73	97.37	A
Cumulative Present Value of Cash Flow from Earnings		18.18	36.36	55.15	75.64	97.37		
Investment Made	50						50.00	B
Net Present Value of Cash Flow from Investment							47.37	C=A-B

This is a more robust way of assessing investments or CAPEX. This is because it factors in the time value of money.

Another method of assessing investment rationale is **IRR** or **internal rate of return.** Here, an attempt is made to assess the percentage of returns from an investment after factoring in the time value. An investment is more feasible if its IRR is significantly higher than the cost of obtaining funds.

The aim is to arrive at the rate at which the present value of future cash flows will be equal to the investment made. An attempt is made to see at what rate the net present value of cash flow is the same as the investment made. If the rate of return is higher than the cost of obtaining funds or cost of money, the investment is considered feasible. For the interest of readers, the following is the technical formula of IRR:

$$0 = CF_0 + \frac{CF_1}{(1+IRR)} + \frac{CF_2}{(1+IRR)^2} + \frac{CF_3}{(1+IRR)^3} + ... + \frac{CF_n}{(1+IRR)^n}$$

or

$$0 = NPV = \sum_{n=0}^{N} \frac{CF_n}{(1+IRR)^n}$$

Where:
CF_0 = Initial Investment/Outlay
CF_1, CF_2, CF_3,...CF_n = Cash flow
n = Each Period
N = Holding Period
NPV = Net Present Value
IRR = Internet Rate of Return

However, this is made more easy by the present-day Excel spreadsheet. The screenshot below provides a wizard that can guide you to calculate IRR in Excel.

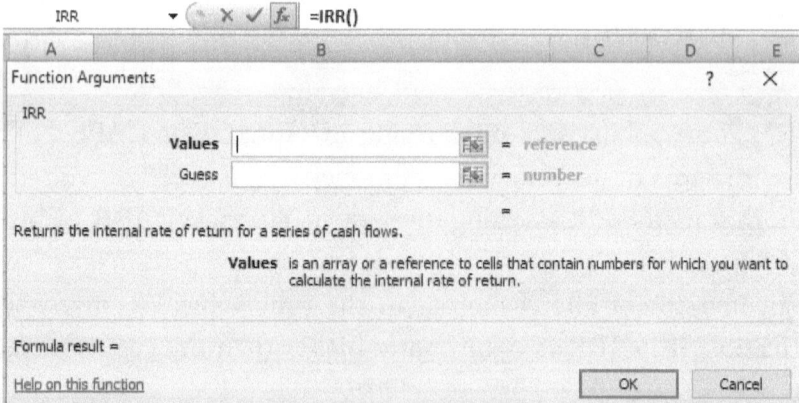

In the spreadsheet, you must show investments at a negative value and the year-on-year cash profits in one single row or column. While calculating the IRR, select those rows or columns where you had incorporated the cash outflow and cash inflows. This range needs to be incorporated in the 'values' section. The guess no. can be kept as 10%. You can keep 5% as well, but as a standard, it's better to keep it as 10%. It represents the interest rate against which you're comparing. It's up to you what rate you wish to guess.

Let me show you how it should look like in Excel. In columns 'C' to 'H' of the Excel spreadsheet, I have incorporated cash flows. Column 'C' has a cash outflow of INR 50 Mn represented in negative value. Column 'D' to Column 'H' has cash inflows expected in the next 5 years. Column 'I' calculates IRR. As you'll notice in the wizard shown below, I have taken values from cells **C15:H15**. I have considered rate or cost of money as 10%. However, it's up to you to consider which rate should be incorporated. The IRR will work out to 38.86% represented in decimal values, as shown below.

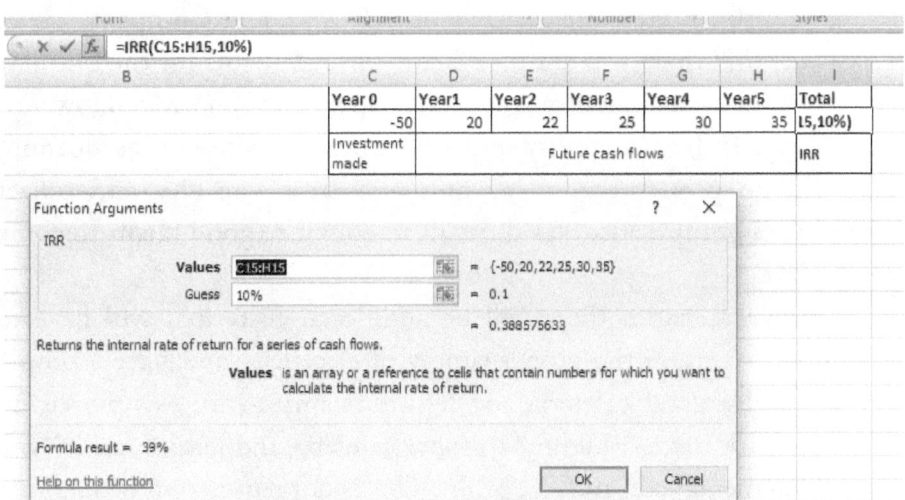

Below is the IRR result from the above exercise.

Year 0	Year 1	Year 2	Year 3	Year 4	Year 5	Total
-50	20	22	25	30	35	**39%**
Investment Made	Future Cash Flows					IRR

It means that the return on investment is 39%, which is way above the interest rate or cost of money of 10%. This makes the investment more favourable.

Evaluating Alternative options while assessing CAPEX:

If a business wants to incur a CAPEX and buy an asset, it will be faced with multiple choices of vendors. Some might be able to provide the asset at least possible cost but might not have enough capacity to meet the requirements of business. Some might be a bit expensive but would bring much more incremental benefits in terms of revenues and would require less running costs. Sometimes, even though the capacity of the asset is superior, the market is not big enough to absorb everything that gets produced. The extra capacity might be of no relevance. There are many alternatives available to a business. Each option must be carefully evaluated and assessed before taking a final call on picking any specific option. Let's understand it with an example.

Let's continue with our example of M/s XYZ and Company. Here, let's assume that there was another facility also available for the business to evaluate. The other facility is much cheaper at INR 45 Mn. However, the challenge is the availability of proper infrastructure in that location. There are no proper roads. It's quite far from the city and power availability is abrupt. Also, it's difficult to convince good talent to come to that place.

In such a scenario, there will be additional costs that will have to be incurred to ensure the proper supply of electricity and have a proper transport and a good cafeteria and leisure facility to woo employees to come and work there. Building a proper cafeteria and leisure facility will cost an incremental cost of INR 3 Mn. This is not required to be incurred when purchasing the facility for INR 50 Mn. It's inbuilt into it. The cost of transport and uninterrupted power supply will cost an additional INR 1.5 Mn every year. Cash profits will decrease by INR 1.5 Mn versus the above estimate. The revised cash flow scenario will be as follows.

	Year 1	Year 2	Year 3	Year 4	Year 5
Rev	50	60	70	90	100
Cash Profit	18.5	20.5	23.5	28.5	33.5

Using the DCF method of assessing the investment, the present value of cash flows will be as follows, after discounting the earnings at 10%.

	Year 0	Year 1	Year 2	Year 3	Year 4	Year 5	Total	
Present Value of Cash Flow from Earnings		16.82	16.94	17.66	19.47	20.80	91.68	A
Cumulative Present Value of Cash Flow from Earnings		**16.82**	**33.76**	**51.42**	**70.88**	**91.68**		
Investment Made	-48						(48.00)	B
Net Cash Flow from Investment							**43.68**	**C=A-B**

The original investment cost is not just the cost of facility of INR 45 Mn, but you need to consider the additional cost for the cafeteria and leisure which is INR 3 Mn. That makes the total investment value **INR 48 Mn**.

Now, you'll notice that the net cash flow from this investment proposal works out to INR 43.68 Mn v/s 47.37 Mn in the first option. That means you tend to earn INR 3.7 Mn of higher profits in the first option even if your investment in the first case was on the higher side.

However, if the entrepreneur can negotiate and bring the selling price down to INR 40 Mn, then the equation changes. In that case, the DCF will be as follows.

	Year 0	Year 1	Year 2	Year 3	Year 4	Year 5	Total
Present Value of Cash Flow from Earnings		16.82	16.94	17.66	19.47	20.80	91.68
Cumulative Present Value of Cash Flow from Earnings after Discounting Earnings at 10%		**16.82**	**33.76**	**51.42**	**70.88**	**91.68**	
Investment Made	-43						(43.00)
Net Cash Flow from Investment							**48.68**

The amount of net cash flow in this case will be INR 1.3 Mn higher than the first option. This makes this option more lucrative and it can be considered for buying the facility.

However, if I have to make such a decision, I would have still preferred the first option if I did not see any potential of the remote land developing any time in future. Such a remote location normally tends to keep you on the edge. Many times, to attract better talent, you have to incur more expenses than competition. Many times, you tend to pay a premium to your employee to come and work in these locations. This still does not guarantee any reduction in attrition rates. The amount of visibility available to determine cash flow is limited. However, it also depends on the kind of business. Maybe if I had a manufacturing plant, I would have still considered negotiating the price and going after option 3. Similarly, if there was a proactive government and infrastructure development that was running smoothly, it would make more sense to go after negotiating the prices or to reevaluate option 2 with a revised cost estimate.

While DCF and IRR can help you assess the financial feasibility, it should not be the decisive factor. Other factors must also be taken into consideration. The above kind of scenario can hold true for manufacturing facilities as well. Sometimes, a particular plant or machinery can be available at distress value. For a small or medium business, this amount can still be material enough or significant enough and you would need to borrow money or raise additional capital through shareholders or partners. If the earning potential from the plant and the machinery is not great due to the quality of machines or labour disputes existing at such facilities, then even if the purchase price is lucrative, it wouldn't make sense to invest in such facilities. It might only make you incur more expenses in the future. Your interest costs will keep mounting if you're unable to generate enough income to cover your operating and financial costs and finally you end up in a debt trap and you might have to be bailed out by someone. This is like buying an old obsolete car at nearly no cost and every year you have to incur money on its repairs, maintenance, and additional fuel as it might not give enough mileage.

In modern times, with the service industry becoming more mature and with the concept of asset light business, there are many more alternatives available rather than just evaluating buying an asset. These days, there are companies that provide office spaces for rent. Sometimes, machinery may be available on lease. Here, much of the risk lies with the supplier of the services. These services can, at times, provide much better returns even if the fees paid for subscribing to these services might be a bit higher.

Let's assume in the above example, that instead of buying a facility, the firm decides to rent a facility that is already providing all required services. The total cost of rent, inclusive of the services offered by the service provider, is INR 10 Mn per year, which will be deducted from the cash profits. Some INR 5 Mn goes through renovating the premises as per the requirement of the business. The revised present value of cash flow from earnings will appear as follows:

	Year 0	Year 1	Year 2	Year 3	Year 4	Year 5	Total	
Present Value of Cash Flow from Earnings		9.09	9.92	11.27	13.66	15.52	59.46	A
Cumulative Present Value of Cash Flow from Earnings after Discounting Earnings at 10%		**9.09**	**19.01**	**30.28**	**43.94**	**59.46**		
Investment Made	− 5						(5.00)	B
Net Cash Flow from Investment							**54.46**	**C=A-B**

As you'll notice, the only investment is related to renovation which is INR 5 Mn. The net cash flow from the investment is the maximum versus any other option that we have considered so far. The payback is quick and renovation costs can be recovered in the first year itself. This makes this option the most lucrative of all the options.

But even here, try to assess if such kind of arrangements will have more demand in the future. Will this continue for a much longer duration? What would be the capital appreciation available if you own the facility? The choice must be made after considering all of these elements. Sometimes, the above kind of benefit as seen from the rent option might not last long and is in the form of arbitrage. As demand increases, this alternative starts to lose its shine.

Arbitrage is a temporary benefit available from a particular option which provides similar benefits like other options but at reduced costs.

DCF and IRR can be of great help for individuals who buy properties for investment purposes or invest in shares, mutual funds or any other asset. They can do such a kind of analysis to evaluate their investments.

If I have INR 7Mn of money saved from my earnings and investments from my salary over 20 years and I plan to buy a house for investment purposes, considering that the land value will appreciate and double after similar projects come up in that location in 5 years. In such a case, it's worthwhile to check what returns I can generate by investing in the house. There is a possibility of earning a rent of INR 30k per month. I assume that the house might remain vacant on an average of 1 month per year.

Expenses incurred every month on maintenance will be INR 30k. If I keep INR 7Mn in some corporate deposit or other fixed return assets, I would get 10% interest on the same. In such a scenario, my investment will look something like this:

							Amt in INR k
	Year 0	Year 1	Year 2	Year 3	Year 4	Year 5	Total
Rev from Rentals		330	330	330	330	14,330	
Expenses		30	30	30	30	30	
Cash Profit		300	300	300	300	14,300	
Interest Rate		10%	10%	10%	10%	10%	
Present Value of Cash Flow from Earnings		273	248	225	205	8,879	9,830
Cumulative Present Value of Cash Flow from Earnings		273	521	746	951	9,830	
Investment Made	-7000						(7,000)
Net Cash Flow from Investment							2,830
Rental Income	INR 30k * 11 months	INR330k					
Year 5 Income	INR 7 M invested is expected to be INR 14 Mn by end of 5 years.						
	INR 14 Mn is added on top of rental income						
Tax Assumptions	Here tax is not assumed on rental income.						
	Similarly capital gains tax while selling is not considered						
	One has to consider this as well before making a decision						

The results will not vary significantly even after taking tax into consideration. The bottom line is that this is more lucrative than putting it in bonds. The risk that you would be taking will give incremental INR 2.8 Mn of additional returns. The IRR works out to 18%.

Year 0	Year 1	Year 2	Year 3	Year 4	Year 5	IRR
-7000	300	300	300	300	14,300	18%

Being a finance professional, I'll also evaluate other alternatives. As I understand business to a fair extent, I will also evaluate if I can invest in fairly valued small or midsized or even undervalued large companies. Let's assume I find some companies that can possibly appreciate two and half times in five years in value. However, since they are small and mid-size companies, I'm not expecting any major returns in the form of dividends. My alternative option will possibly give me the following returns.

							Amt in INR k
	Year 0	Year 1	Year 2	Year 3	Year 4	Year 5	Total
Cash Profit		–	–	–	–	17,500	
Interest Rate		10%	10%	10%	10%	10%	
Present Value of Cash Flow from Earnings		–	–	–	–	10,866	10,866
Cumulative Present Value of Cash Flow from Earnings		–	–	–	–	**10,866**	
Investment Made	–7000						(7,000)
Net Cash Flow from Investment							**3,866**

Year 0	Year1	Year2	Year3	Year4	Year5	IRR
–7000	–	–	–	–	17,500	20%

This is better than investing in property and it gives me nearly INR 1.05 Mn higher returns. But investing in shares carries a lot of risk. Proper care should be taken to see if the likelihood of getting the above kind of returns is high. If I assume that the likelihood of getting the above returns is 90%, then I should reduce my cash profit by 10% to factor such risk and then evaluate. However, I'm very sure of the property investment doubling in 5 years and I don't wish to factor any risk out there. My revised calculation on share investments will be as follows.

							Amt in INR k
	Year 0	Year 1	Year 2	Year 3	Year 4	Year 5	Total
Cash Profit		–	–	–	–	15,750	
Interest Rate		10%	10%	10%	10%	10%	
Present Value of Cash Flow from Earnings		–	–	–	–	9,780	9,780
Cumulative Present Value of Cash Flow from Earnings		–	–	–	–	**9,780**	
Investment Made	-7000						(7,000)
Net Cash Flow from Investment							**2,780**

Year 0	Year1	Year2	Year3	Year4	Year5	IRR
-7000	–	–	–	–	15,750	18%

When I factor such a risk, the investment on the house looks more lucrative. If I was expecting 3 times the returns and the risk was still 10%, then I would have gone with the option of investing in small companies. These are not straightforward decisions. A lot of qualitative factors also need to be considered. Market factors viz. demand and supply factors are also important. Diversifying investments if you have more money is also an option in itself.

X. So now the big question is how much funding does a business require at any point in time?

While doing the DCF analysis, we realised that it's important to understand the level of operating cash that will be available at the end of each period. This is then discounted by the interest rate or the rate at which funds are procured, which is also referred to as the cost of money. However, the most tricky and exhaustive exercise is related to assessing cash flows. We will determine this by undertaking an exercise on cash projection. Cash projection will help in determining when receipts from sales will come and when payouts on the account of purchase for goods and services have to be done. Cash projection will also show how much money is received from borrowed sources and what interest is paid on them. However, when doing a DCF exercise, one must be cautious and consider only operational cash flows, which is nothing but receipts coming from operating income and payouts happening on the account of operating expenses as financial expenses are part of discounting.

The first step in cash projection is to determine the expenses required to produce goods or services that can be sold. Unless you don't have the inventory or services to sell, you can't make any money. All expenses related to producing the initial set of goods or services is a part of the capital required. Most of the time, the CAPEX is also required to kick-start the business.

The second step is determining the projected sales. One must carefully evaluate how much time it will take to produce goods and services and how much time it will take to sell them eventually to someone. After goods are sold, how much time will it take to finally recover money on such sales? The time projected will determine the funds required. The cycle continues as we saw in the cash conversion cycle. However, this exercise helps in determining the funds that one needs to keep running the business smoothly.

A well-planned approach will result in getting the funds at the best possible rates, which will reduce the cost of procuring these funds.

For an existing business, it is always advisable to understand historical cash movement. This helps in determining the future cash projection in a much better way. Let's use our example of cash book from the accounting section related to Nishka Toys to develop a historical monthly cash flow statement. The principles used below will also help you develop short-term cash projection which is normally done on a monthly basis. The same can be applied to build long-term cash projection which we'll see soon after this exercise. In short, the cash flow projection that we will build for long term will be a projected cash book.

												Amt (INRk)
	Jan	Feb	Mar	Apr	May	Jun	Jul	Aug	Sep	Oct	Nov	Dec
Cash and Bank Balance at the Beginning of the Period	–	150	74	20	163	10	133	337	532	397	806	751
Add: Receipts												
Capital Introduced	500											
Income			125	375		275	375	250		600		225
Other Receipts												5
Borrowings	800		156		97							
Total Receipts	**1,300**	–	**281**	**375**	**97**	**275**	**375**	**250**	–	**600**	–	**230**
Less: Payouts												
Rent	10	10	10	10	10	10	10	10	10	10	10	10
Purchases		30	290	30	205	10	125	10	90	145	10	90
Salaries		15	15	15	15	15	15	15	15	15	15	15
Electricity												28
Maintenance												50

Borrowings Repaid	14	14	14	170	14	111	14	14	15	15	15	15
Interest on Borrowings	7	7	6	7	6	6	6	6	6	6	5	7
Security Deposit	120											
CAPEX	1,000											
Total Payouts	**1,150**	**75**	**335**	**232**	**250**	**153**	**170**	**55**	**135**	**190**	**55**	**215**
Cash and Bank Balance at the End of the Period	**150**	**74**	**20**	**163**	**10**	**133**	**337**	**532**	**397**	**806**	**751**	**766**

For a new business, it's difficult to assess things beyond six months, as there is lot of uncertainty. But if risk is assessed properly by doing appropriate ground work in relation to projecting the revenue generation activities and expenses, and proper actions are taken to achieve those goals, it helps to avoid any major hiccups. However, still there are times when things might not go your way inspite of proper assessment due to some internal or external factors. This is the risk that business must take. But the risk is not an abrupt risk, it would be considered a **calculated risk**. A calculated risk has to be taken by every business person. Without this, a business can't even see the light of the day.

The principles outlined above in preparing the short-term cash projection applies to long-term cash projection as well. The only difference is that instead of doing it on a monthly basis, we do it on a yearly basis. This is an important exercise that should be undertaken by the entrepreneur while undertaking the capital expenditure exercise. Not only that, this exercise can also help in understanding the working capital requirement. This long-term cash projection can be done for 3 years, 5 years, or 10 years. It depends on what time horizon you wish to take and how much visibility you have about the business you're in. Given later is a view of a 3-year- plan.

The above exercise helps in determining **capital structure**. Before I go through an example, let me briefly mention capital structure. Capital structure describes how you will fund your business. As mentioned earlier, the funds of the business can come from either the promoters, entrepreneurs or shareholders, who are also referred to as owned sources. Or it can come from third party sources which can be bank loans and loans from financial institutions. The proportion of borrowed funds to owned funds that the entrepreneur or management wishes to keep determines capital structure. It is assessed by a ratio called debt equity ratio, which is calculated by dividing debts or borrowed funds with the entrepreneur's capital. It can be represented as below:

Debt – Equity ratio: Total Borrowed funds / Capital.

If borrowed funds are higher than capital, the equation will be higher than 1 and vice versa. If it's significantly higher than 1, it should raise alarm bells, unless there is a good visibility on earnings and profits. As mentioned earlier, debt is a catalyst but its overdependence is worrisome. One has to tread cautiously while relying too much on debt. Debt can be leveraged successfully for projects having a good visibility on potential future earnings. It can even allow a much better control and swift decision making as stakeholders or owners influencing decision would be less. However, a proper and balanced approach can help you in protecting capital and also the interest of the vendors providing you with borrowed funds.

Now, let's move to our example. Nishka Toys did a study of its existing market and potential other markets and has built a projection of the following revenues and expenses for the next three years.

				Amt (INRk)
	2017 Actuals	**2018 Estimates**	**2019 Estimates**	**2020 Estimates**
Units	8950	20000	22000	34200
Rev per Unit	250	250	275	275
Revenues	**2,237.5**	**5000**	**6050**	**9405**
Material Consumption	1,000.0	1,575.0	1,846.4	2,872.8
Rent	120.0	130	150	150
Salaries	165.0	365	420	630
Maintenance	50.0	100	100	150
Electricity	28.0	45	50	70
Depreciation	205.0	410	410	615
Inventory Adjustment	(133.8)	(125.0)	(141.8)	(213.7)
Marketing Costs		200	200	300
Selling Costs		300	330	363

Bad Debts Provision	12.5	10	10	10
Interest Costs	75.0	99.6	68.5	34.3
Profit before Tax	**715.8**	**1,890.4**	**2,606.9**	**4,423.6**
Tax	143.2	378.1	521.4	884.7
Profit after Tax	**572.6**	**1,512.4**	**2,085.5**	**3,538.9**

There are two CAPEX of INR 1 Mn, each are considered for 2018 and 2020 at the start of the year. Let us assess the funding requirement in this example.

The entrepreneur decides to maintain a specific inventory in place at all times. She decides to have 5 days of sales in the form of raw material stock, 10 days of sales as Work in progress stock and 5 days of sales as finished goods stock. She does an input output analysis and understands how much raw material is required to make a finished product and determines the cost of materials required to produce a unit of finished product. Using this, the following inventory as given below is planned to be kept at all times for the next three years.

Work in progress and finished goods inventory includes conversion costs. The conversion costs include the cost of rent, the salaries of workers, maintenance, electricity, and depreciation which are incurred to produce the goods. These costs are directly associated with manufacturing the product and are therefore conversion costs. These are calculated on a per unit basis. These are calculated by adding all the costs and dividing it by the sum of the finished goods sold and the inventory of work in progress and finished goods created.

Inventory – Raw Material Equivalent to Finished Goods									
	2018			2019			2020		
	Units	Rate	Cost Value	Units	Rate	Cost Value	Units	Rate	Cost Value
Raw Material	330	75.0	24,750	370	80.0	29,600	570	80.0	45,600
Work in Progress Stock	670	125.0	83,750	730	128.9	94,110	1140	125.0	142,470
Finished Goods	330	125.0	41,250	370	128.9	47,700	570	125.0	71,235

The following is the projected purchases for the next 3 years. This considers the above inventory, and the inventory which was available at the start of the year in 2018. It provides the purchases that need to be made to maintain a particular inventory and expected sales of finished products.

Purchases of Raw Material (RM) – Equivalent to Finished Goods									
	2018			2019			2020		
	Units	Rate	Cost Value	Units	Rate	Cost Value	Units	Rate	Cost Value
Sales & Finished Goods/WIP Inventory	21000	75.0	1,575,000	23100	79.9	1,846,350	35910	80.0	2,872,800
Closing Stock	330	75.0	24,750	370	80.0	29,600	570	80.0	45,600
Less: Opening Stock	933	75.0	69,975	330	75.0	24,750	370	80.0	29,600
Purchases	20397	75.0	1,529,775	23140	80.0	1,851,200	36110	80.0	2,888,800

The credit policy for customers is kept at 30 days and for vendors it is kept at 30 days. For vendors, the last month's purchases will remain as a due and paid in the subsequent year. This means for the year 2018, INR 1.53 Mn of purchases will happen, but the amount that will be paid will be INR 1.442 Mn only as last month's purchases of 2018, worth INR 127k, will be paid in the year 2019. Also creditors of 2017 will get paid in 2018. In 2019, the outstanding of INR 127k will be added to the purchases of 2019 and last month's purchase of INR 154k will be paid in year 2020. Thus, the purchase payout for 2019 will be INR 127k of 2018 + INR 1.851 Mn of 2019 purchases minus INR 154k of last month's purchases of 2019 which will be paid in year 2020.

The same principle will apply for the amount received from sales or income. Thus, for the year 2019, INR 417k of outstanding debtors related to year 2018 will be received + sales income will be INR 6.05 Mn minus debtors of INR 504k will come in 2020. It is expected that some amount will never get paid, which is assumed at INR 10k, and is bad debts provision. This will also get reduced from the above. So the calculation of income for 2019 to be received will be INR 417k+INR 6.05Mn minus INR 504k minus 10k.

Now, let's build a cash projection or projected cash book for CY 2018 to CY 2020. The calculation behind the amount to be paid or received from purchases and sales is also provided below for reference.

	2017	2018	2019	2020	2018	2019	2020	2018	2019	2020	Comments
		Amt (INRk)			Purchases/Sales			Dues to Be Received/Paid			Comments
Cash and Bank Balance at the Beginning of the Period	–	766	1,113	2,383							
Add: Receipts											
Capital Introduced	500										
Income (Net of Bad Debts Provision)	2,225	4,573	5,953	9,115	5,000	6,050	9,405	417	504	784	Total sales minus debtors and bad debts provision
Other Receipts	5										
Borrowings	1,053	500									Bank Loan taken including overdraft
Total Receipts	3,783	5,073	5,953	9,115							
Less: Payouts											
Purchases	1,035	1,442	1,824	2,802	1,530	1,851	2,889	127	154	241	Refer to Purchases of Raw Material table
Rent	120	130	150	150							
Salaries	165	365	420	630							
Electricity	28	45	50	70							
Maintenance	50	100	100	150							
Borrowings Repaid	424	296	327	361							
Interest on Borrowings	75	100	69	34							
Security Deposit	120										
Capital Expenditure	1,000	1,000		1,000							
Marketing Expenses		200	200	300							
Selling Expenses		300	330	363							

Drawings		605	834	1,416
Taxes Paid		143	378	521
Total Payouts	**3,017**	**4,726**	**4,682**	**7,798**
Cash and Bank Balance at the End of the Period	**766**	**1,113**	**2,383**	**3,701**

Cash Profits from Operations	**832**	**1,991**	**2,878**	**4,650**

The above analysis shows how INR 500k can get converted into INR 3.7 Mn in 4 years. Initially, for the first two years, the business is expected to be reliant on getting funds from borrowed sources. The scale of the business is expected to be such that cash profit from operations can take care of funding requirements in the subsequent years. However, this will not be the case if the business wants higher scalability and requires more funding which exceeds the cash generated from operations. In that case, it might have to rely on borrowed funds or seek funds by developing more partners, associates or shareholders.

In the above case, the capital structure will be tilted towards entrepreneur's capital and not towards borrowed funds. There is no need to seek more funds from outside.

The above case can be considered a simple case. However, businesses, especially the new ones, face a lot of challenges. The quantum of cash requirements is very high initially. Sales take a long time to come by or the gestation period is very high. For such kind of businesses, cash flow projection can be a great tool to understand how long they need to pump in capital before it starts generating cash inflows. This can be a great monitoring and controlling tool to ensure things happen on timelines in order to get the cash inflows at the earliest. Potential investors can assess this before making the requisite decisions.

Also, there are times when business is coming in smoothly, but it requires scalability at every stage. So whatever is earned has to be continuously invested. This is particularly true for modern internet businesses, which face high competition. Sometimes, it also entails further investment in the form of marketing or additional distribution costs or it can be the continuous development of the product or service range that the business has to offer. Cash flow projection helps in understanding the time till which business will continue to scale and will require investment. Again, this facilitates potential investors with decision making. It can also help the business in finding potential investors or lenders.

XI.   Sources for Funding CAPEX (Assets)

Businesses can either take loans from banks or financial institutions for which EMI needs to be paid on a monthly basis or companies can raise debentures or bonds. They are generally backed by the general credit worthiness of the company issuing them. There are many other sources of borrowed funds, but the important point to note is some debts are secured against the property or assets of the business and some are not.

A business can also obtain money from its own internal sources. It can also ask some more partners to join in or it can seek more share capital in case of the company. It can even ask angel investors or venture capitalists to fund their requirements. These are those people who take the risk of investing in business. Their returns are in the form of profits. This arrangement works when a business does not want to get into a financial risk and a debt trap if something goes wrong. Determining their share of profits can be a daunting task and a subject of negotiations. Proper care should be taken to ensure that you get a fair share of profits in the whole exercise as ultimately you provide the value addition from operations.

Inspite of having its own funds, a business can go through borrowings at times if it does not want to reduce its holding in the company. When you invite others to invest in your business, you're reducing your own holding or stake in the business. The business might plan to temporarily engage other vendors to provide funds and then create a good surplus during operations to take care of its funding requirements internally. This helps in avoiding diluting the stake. Only an interest element has to be paid for the borrowing period. That can be considered as one of the costs to retain the stake. This normally works when there is a good visibility on earnings for the future.

XII.   Personal Cash Flow Projection

The above principles of cash flow projection can be applied to individuals as well. We already saw in the accounting section how records can be maintained. It had a split between cash and credit transactions. There were separate sections covering provisions and depreciation. It can be argued that it's a simple tool and covers everything and why we need to have a separate cash flow projection.

The idea is to make a projection on how much funds are required to cover for credit transactions and other provisions and within what timeframe one can obtain those funds. Also, it facilitates in identifying adjustments that need to be taken in order to achieve a specific goal. The records that an individual prepares can help in creating such cash flow projection.

An individual can have any goal and there is nothing right or wrong about it. An individual can plan to go on holiday around the world or the goal can be to start a venture or business, make savings for future, buy house or car, or it can be anything. Cash flow projection can act as a guiding tool to make plans; it can help in estimating the timeframe and this can be further compared with the regular records, as seen in the accounting section, to identify variances.

Let me present to you an example of personal cash flow projection. This is a plan of a person who wishes to start a business and currently has INR 2Mn in cash for her personal needs. She wants to understand if this INR 2Mn makes sense and if it will cover all her expenses on personal needs during the period when the business is not earning her any money. She is confident that her venture will start giving her returns from the month of November onwards.

The cash flow projection will help in assessing if the fund kept by the potential entrepreneur is sufficient enough to cover her personal needs, while she is building her business. The template below should help her with the same.

												Amt (IINRk)
	Jan	Feb	Mar	Apr	May	Jun	Jul	Aug	Sep	Oct	Nov	Dec
Opening Balance	2000	1905	1810	1715	1620	1525	1430	1335	1240	1145	1050	985
Income											30	50
Less												
Cash Expenses	15	15	15	15	15	15	15	15	15	15	15	15
Credit Card	20	20	20	20	20	20	20	20	20	20	20	20
Rent/EMI	20	20	20	20	20	20	20	20	20	20	20	20
Insurance Premium Paid Monthly	10	10	10	10	10	10	10	10	10	10	10	10
Adhoc	10	10	10	10	10	10	10	10	10	10	10	10
School Fees Paid Monthly	10	10	10	10	10	10	10	10	10	10	10	10
Contingency Savings (Fixed Deposit)	10	10	10	10	10	10	10	10	10	10	10	10
Closing Balance	1905	1810	1715	1620	1525	1430	1335	1240	1145	1050	985	940

The above one is kept very simple, but one should provide for cash flow in the month when funds are moving out, especially for provisions made. Here school fees is assumed to be paid on a monthly basis, but typically the fees is paid either once a year or in two or three installments. In such case, the month in which you're expected to pay has to be provided in cash flow. The rest of the months will remain at zero value. This should be tied with the monthly provision created in the record keeping section when making the actual payout. This way, you'll never feel stressed on account of a high payout in any particular month. **Provisions** as seen in the record keeping section restrict you from making excessive spending and creates discipline. Above all, it helps you to meet your personal objectives.

One should also make room for contingencies, as in the above case, in case the plan doesn't work. Maintaining a contingency fund is highly advisable when venturing into a business having inherent risks.

Insurance

The last topic on funds management is insurance. An individual or business must always take adequate insurance to cover for any risk in case of contingencies. Insurance can be health insurance, life insurance, asset insurance, theft insurance, and many more products. Insurance always facilitates recovering the losses occurring due to health issues, theft or natural calamities or any other circumstances for which cover is taken. It provides money to start things again. In the case of life insurance, it provides money to the loved ones in the case of unforeseen circumstances. One must take their personal lifestyle and future goals into consideration while determining the value of insurance to be taken. An insurance premium must be paid mostly every year to maintain the insurance coverage. The higher the value of insurance taken, the higher the premium will be.

Also, one must assess her/his personal needs or that of their business and thereafter take adequate insurance coverage. Proper diligence must be applied at the time of selecting the insurance that matches your needs. Also, an insurance premium is revenue expenditure or normal recurring expenditure incurred every year. Proper care must be taken to evaluate the premium amount while taking the insurance coverage. It needs to be compared with the premium and services provided by different insurance providers or insurance companies. Care must be taken to ensure that the premium amount is reasonable and not exorbitant. Once a premium is paid in pure insurance policies, it's not possible to recover them if the incident doesn't occur.

PART B

Section 4

Planning

I. Types of Plan

Accounting is the backbone of finance. Without proper records, it's difficult to assess the financial performance and it's not possible to assess the value creation done by the business. Managing money is a critical aspect of any business. Cash must be managed properly to generate more cash through value-added processes that are typically offered by business. To carry out those actions that create value addition and bring incremental money in the form of profits to the business, proper planning is required.

Any business activity must be properly planned to obtain the requisite resources to fulfill the objectives. Without proper planning, much of the value addition is not possible. Without planning, it's not possible to determine when resources will be required, or one may end up obtaining these resources at the wrong time.

Also, it's also important to keep a track of plans. It's important to measure whether activities are going as per plans and understand the variances. There are always inherent risks associated in the business but planning and subsequently proper controlling can help you negate much of these risks. In other words, planning and controlling help in measuring risk. We'll cover planning in this section and controlling will be covered in the next section. We'll start with things that impact businesses. I'll touch upon personal branding, which is quite interesting for individuals when they plan their own career. This will be covered at the end in the planning section. This can act as an interesting guideline for individuals to foresee and shape their career, and it includes an assessment of the monetary part as well.

We often hear about businesses attaining scale over a period and generating significant assets. We hear how their utilisation of funds helped them in earning more profits. But have you ever wondered if this was abrupt or was a result of a well-thought out and properly executed business plan? One's destiny must be super strong to achieve things as they wish on an abrupt basis without a proper plan. For the rest of the pack, proper planning is required. One needs to think in advance how they'll get business in the future and they need to determine what will be required to achieve it.

The next thing that I wish to be very clear with is regarding strategy. Many times, this term is used loosely for planning. But one needs to understand that strategy is a part of the planning exercise. Planning is a much wider term and encapsulates strategy in it. Broadly speaking, there are three **types of plans** viz. strategic plan, tactical plan, and operational plan. Let's understand these in detail.

Strategic Plans

Let me take our example of Nishka Toys. The entrepreneur of Nishka Toys was highly successful and decided to diversify into the business of theme parks or adventure parks. In this case, the entrepreneur is striving to get into an activity which provides an opportunity to local residents of the city to relax and engage in some fun and adventurous activities outside the perimeter of the city in a much more peaceful place. This objective with which the entrepreneur is planning to start the commercial venture describes the **MISSION** of her new business. Every organisation or business is established to accomplish a specific task. The specific task for which the business is established is nothing but the mission of the company. It defines the business which the entrepreneur wants to be in. It defines the objectives for which the business was established and lays down an approach to reach its objectives.

The mission might have been undertaken when the entrepreneur sensed the need to have an enterprise which provides a much better value-added entertainment avenue to local residents. The idea would have made a lot of commercial sense as there would be many takers of this idea. The expectation to get a strong return on investment (ROI) would have been sensed. This would have laid the framework to define the future state of a potential business idea. All this tells us about a likely future state of a potential business idea. It describes the **VISION** with which business is started. A vision describes the desired future position of the business.

A strategic plan starts with an organisation vision. The objectives are laid down in the mission. Given the fact that a mission defines the long-term objective of the business, the planning horizon is also for a higher duration. These plans are normally set for more than a year. Depending on the visibility that a business can obtain from the scope of their activities, these plans can be for say 3 years, 5 years, 10 years or more. Let's assume in the above case, the entrepreneur is quite sure that for 4 to 5 years she can expect a growth which could be anywhere between 40% to 50% every year. In such a case, it's worthwhile to check the commercial feasibility of the idea for a period of 4 to 5 years by factoring what earnings it can make and what resources it might require.

In a consumer-centric market, there is the possibility to get visibility for a higher time frame. There the plans can be for a much longer duration. However, if the business is into a technology industry where things change very fast, it might be difficult to get visibility for more than 2 or 3 years. However, irrespective of this, one must have a strategic plan in place. This is also needed to commit the resources required to achieve the objectives.

A strategic plan must be made by the entrepreneur, promoter or management in large corporations. In large corporations, everyone in the top management should be involved in the strategic planning exercise. During the course of this exercise, they set the direction of the organisation. A strategic plan becomes the framework for building tactical plans or lower level operational plans. Normally, a business would plan strategically for 3, 5, 10 or more no. of years.

Strategic planning is covered in more depth in the case study.

Tactical Plans

In our above example, once the commercial feasibility of the strategic plan related to theme park or adventure park is confirmed, the entrepreneur should engage in getting the activities done to attain the long-term objective. It's worthwhile to split the plan into a quarterly or monthly basis every year. It's also important to understand the different products or services offered by the business to its customers. Let's assume in the above exercise that the business wants to provide a picnic spot and an adventure park to the local residents as part of its strategy. In this case, there must be a yearly plan for both these businesses. This should describe in detail how resources will be procured and utilised by a picnic spot and an adventure park during the year and how earnings or revenue will flow during different months or quarters of the year for each of these businesses. This breakdown of the long-term plan into a monthly or quarterly plan for each business separately is the **tactical plan** of the business.

Tactical plans are the means to achieve the strategic plans. Tactics follow a strategy to obtain the requisite objectives. An organisation can be made of different divisions. A tactical plan is concerned with achieving these divisional goals. The person in charge of those divisions is responsible for executing these plans. In the case of small businesses, the entrepreneurs are running the show. So they are responsible for achieving these plans. These plans are for a shorter duration and are normally a year. While defining the strategic plans, certain milestones are defined to achieve those objectives. A tactical plan is concerned with achieving these milestones. One of the best tools available to assess these tactical plans is budgeting or yearly financial projections. These are typically broken into months or quarters.

Operational Plans

Once the yearly budget is created for the above business, all activities that are required to attain the commercial goal should be spelt in depth. One such activity could be related to marketing. To create visibility, there could be a need to get a certain minimum number of spots in the local radio and the newspaper during prime and non-prime time over the course of the year. There might be a need to pay search engines that can facilitate creating visibility on the internet. A plan might have to be made with advertising or media agencies which suggest how different campaigns will be executed during different months. Thus, the plan is broken down at execution level. Such a breakdown of a plan into individual planned activities help in realising the ultimate goal, which is defined in the tactical and strategic plan. These plans are related to the operations required to run the business and are at very granular level and are called **operational plans**.

Operational plans are concerned with the activities that the business needs to accomplish to achieve its tactical plans. For the sales function, this can be processing a certain level of transactions in a day, meeting a certain set of retailers or customers during a day. For the manufacturing function, this can be producing a certain quantity of goods during a day. One should develop an operational process map to define operational plans.

While tactical plans and operational plans are not covered in the case study, they can be built in a similar way as a strategic plan except that they will have more details about the year. Operational plans will have more details regarding the activities that need to be carried out during the year in different months. One thing I would like to call out is that planning is a continuous activity. Certain activities which are planned earlier might be difficult to pursue due to some changing circumstances. So there might be a revision required. So plans have to be continuously monitored and where required, they should be changed.

II.   Inception Stage of Any Business

This is referred to as a period when business is not even established. Entrepreneurs have to incur expenses from the time they come up with an idea to start the venture. The first thing any potential entrepreneur needs to do is assess if their idea can be converted into a product or service that can be accepted and recognised by a particular set of buyers, which is also called a market. Sometimes, the products are themselves revolutionary and they create a market for themselves. Once entrepreneurs get a sense that it's likely that the product or service will be accepted and it could have a market for itself, they should then proceed further. This must be evaluated critically because after this step, funds have to be committed to start the venture. The journey after this is filled with some struggles. It's only after you surpass this stage that you tend to start getting success.

At the operational level, money is spent on building an inventory or putting an infrastructure in place to deliver a service. These days a lot of mobile applications that act as a platform to connect the service provider and consumer are in vogue. Expenses are incurred on building such applications (apps) as they act as the essence of such a business. Many new service providers can't function without having the relevant apps in place. Apart from that, expenses are incurred in getting approvals from local authorities and the tax department and developing contracts with vendors, customers, investors etc. Many times, the ideas are brilliant, but funding is not properly estimated and such ideas would go down the drain before they see the light of the day. It's therefore important to critically evaluate the estimates you have made, revisit them again and again, and find the sources of your funds. Above all, for individuals it's also important to have a personal cash flow in place, which was discussed in the previous section, to ensure that they have sufficient funds to look after themselves and their family before they start making revenues and profits.

While it's manageable to assess the administrative costs of a startup as much of them have a predictable cost, certain things are difficult to assess, especially when you're planning to build a new product or a platform for delivering your services or creating some asset which will be a revenue generator. A critical assessment is required at every stage. It's always better to keep some buffer in case you run over your estimate. A lot of things are hard to predict and it is always useful to maintain contingency funds. The most handy tool that can be used by any entrepreneur is a cost sheet/ estimate. The format and contents may vary but more or less it should be something like the one below to track your spending. One can modify it as per their requirements.

	Units reqd	Rate	Cost value	Inventory available	Usable	Inventory value
Material Consumption						
Material A						
Material B						
Material C						
Total Material Consumption			–			
Service Costs						
Outsourcing						
Inhouse						
Development Costs						
Product Development						
Application Development						
Employee Costs Working on Product/Service						
Utility Costs						
Fuel and Electricity						
Spares						
Maintenance						
Rent of the Facility, If Any						
Total Estimate for Bringing the Product/Service to Usable Form			–			
of which	Ratio					
Incurred in Trial Runs	80%		–			
Incurred in Building Product/Service in Usable Form	20%		–			
Incidental Costs						
Administrative Costs						
Legal Costs						
Patent Costs						
Registration Costs						
Other Administrative Costs						
Selling or Marketing Expenses, at Inception, If Any						
Advertisement						
Other marketing costs						

Sales Person's Salary/Fees/Commission			
Other Selling Overheads			
Total costs estimate			–

The above is not exhaustive but can throw some ideas on how to evaluate costs. Secondly, some of these costs might require further analysis. For example, product development costs may have the following elements:

Product Development Costs
Product Design Costs
Advisory Expenses
Processing/Conversion Costs

Every expense can be dissected further. But one needs to draw a line out here and consider what needs to be deep dived into and what should not be. Sometimes you can do away without getting into the depth of things, which is not material or which is known that it has to be incurred. But certain costs are critical and here a proper deep dive is required. An example could be product development cost.

The above exercise gives an indication of the likely costs that need to be incurred to develop an asset. There will be certain costs that will be written off especially the ones incurred on trial runs. A lot of expenses incurred only give the requisite experience to forge ahead or not. If you decide to kickstart your venture, there could be some inventory which gets built up in the process which can be further used when the operations kick in. It's important to keep them separate in order to have a proper control over these startup expenses. Also, keep a stock of things built as assets during the process, which helps you in running your operations.

Before the business starts and before you start committing funds to it, it is always advisable to make an estimate of the preliminary revenues and costs for running the operation. The visibility is not that great. But nevertheless one should have some plan in place. Even after the product or service is developed, the same exercise should be repeated. The assumptions made by you should be continuously monitored. Certain actions are needed on the part of the entrepreneur like proper networking with intermediaries or customers to assess the revenue potential. As I mentioned above, costs are critical during the early phases; so hiring has to be done with utmost care. Don't spend too much on recruiting many people as this can significantly backfire if things don't turn your way. However, care should be taken to hire the right number of people of proper caliber because without the people element, the business can't operate.

It's always advisable to have the following assessment done for revenues and it should be quantified, as given below in the chart, before and after you commit funds for doing your venture. This will also help in optimal resource deployment be it in the form of assets, people or services.

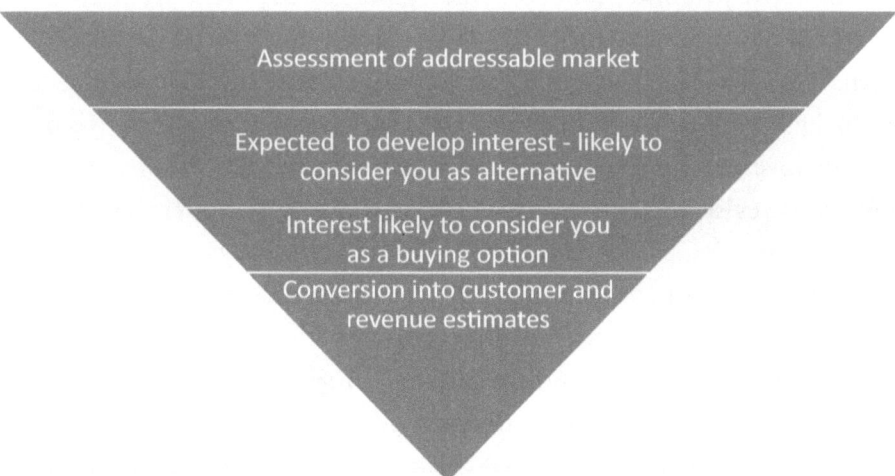

Any entrepreneur must have a good understanding of the market in which they are operating. Normally, an entrepreneur starts operating in a local market and then expands, but it's important to know the market size. It's not necessary to express it firmly in terms of money, but one has to have a fair understanding of the size. Within this market, there will be a section in which your products or services will fit and where you can have a presence. It's a place where you might be considered an option. It's important to know the estimated size of this market.

It's worthwhile to check if there's some space or opportunity outside this section. There could possibly be a section that is not catered to or poorly organised so far. Such a space gives you a leading edge over others. I personally consider online food logistics firms like Swiggy and Zomato as smart enterprises catering to a market space which never existed before but had the potential of getting accepted with a proliferating internet and urban class. Personally, I'm a big fan of these enterprises. They are classic examples of businesses that find a space or create a presence for themselves outside the conventional markets. In the overall market, there will be always some section of potential customers who're willing to try something new. They are in most probability likely to consider you as a buying option.

The above pyramid should provide a guideline to potential entrepreneur to examine the market properly and critically analyse potential buying alternatives available with the customer, understand how its products can make a presence out there and evaluate potential customers who can generate revenues for the business. It's a painstaking task and could involve long hours revisiting the exercise multiple times and frequent visits to the market to understand the dynamics of it in a better way.

Once an assessment is made, requisite arrangements are to be made to procure materials and services. Please don't go for economies of scale and get into a trap where you end up buying a huge stock, which you might have to write off at some point in time. So purchase wisely. It's similar to hiring, which I mentioned above. Also, try to keep capital expenses or assets to minimal levels if there is not much of visibility on earnings. Where possible, outsource things. Care has to be taken to ensure that the costs are within your reach and you don't end up in a debt trap. If needed, try to find a like-minded individual or firm who can invest in your venture. But don't sell your stake in a distress manner, which basically gives all the benefits to the investor and leaves you with no major motivation to continue your business.

The following will be a preliminary projected P&L and balance sheet for first year that a business needs to develop in advance.

	Amt (INR)
Revenues Estimated	
Less	
Material Consumption	
Salaries	
Rent	
Electricity	
Administrative Costs	
Selling and Marketing Costs	
Operational Profit or Loss	0
Financial Expenses	
Interest	
Bank Fees and Charges	
Net Profit or Loss before Tax	0

Balance Sheet

	Amt (INR)
Sources of Funds	
Capital	
of Which	
From Entrepreneur	
From Other Investors	
Total Capital	
Borrowed Funds	
Source of Funds	0
Utilisation of Funds	
Fixed Assets, If Any	
Inventory	
Debtors	
Cash/Bank Balance	
Utilisation of funds	0

III. Factors Impacting Planning Exercise

At times, it's possible to make an assessment for a longer duration, especially when the market is not surrounded by too many sellers. Also the technology or process is such that not many sellers will be able to enter that particular business. It means the barriers of entry, in marketing terminology, is high. But sometimes the market is surrounded by too many sellers and here many factors have to be considered while making an assessment for long and short-term.

Sometimes, a business has to borrow funds from banks or other financial institutions and in those cases multi-period profit and loss and balance sheet projections are required for banks or financial institutions to fund these ventures. Banks have their money at stake, so expect more grilling from their side. So your assessment has to be very exhaustive in order to convince yourself and the bank before putting money in your venture. All factors impacting your business have to be incorporated properly in the plan.

In order to undertake such exercise, one needs to have a very strong understanding of the different factors that play an important role in the planning exercise. We will cover these factors one by one below.

Market Reach

A business operates in different markets and each business needs to know the size of those markets. A market is made of different vendors. They offer different products and services which are comparable to what you have to offer. Some might be directly related to yours and would act as direct competition. Some are similar to yours but are relatively very different. One can consider that a potential market. A business can even address these markets with their unique selling proposition (USP).

These markets are facilitated by different intermediaries or at times you need to sell directly. In case you are an intermediary, you need to know your customers. Today there are multiple channels offering products and services. It's not just the retail or resell format that is predominant as in the past. Today businesses want to tap customers using technology. There are many websites that act as intermediaries. Vendors selling their stuff are using more of traditional retailers or resellers and online retailers or resellers to make their presence felt and to capture a sizeable portion of the market. Tapping this multi-channel model is omni channel. In fact, many traditional brick and mortar intermediaries are adapting and are willing to sell using different channels. They too are becoming more omni channel.

The above pyramid is applicable to established businesses as well. An assessment of this can help you understand where to tap the market for growth while remaining profitable. More importantly, any business needs to know where its revenues are coming from.

Below, I'm suggesting a tool that can be used to determine the potential market opportunity for different types of products (at a broader level, not at individual brands) in different types of markets. A business can go through intermediaries or it can go directly to its customers. But it's important to evaluate the opportunity available in different route to markets. This way a business can really evaluate its full potential by considering all available avenues.

Route to Market							
		Intermediaries		Direct Model			
		Distributor Model	Direct to Retailer/ Reseller/Online Intermediaries	Direct Stores/ Sales Force	Direct Online Store	Agents	Total
No. of Partners Available	A						0
% That Can Be Tapped	B						0
No. of Total Partners at Your Disposal	C=A*B						0
Likely Units to Be Bought by Each Partner	D						0
Sales Realisation Expected	E						0
Estimated Revenues	F=D*E*C						0
TOTAL		0	0	0	0	0	0

Margins to intermediaries – The sales realisation is not the price at which the products or services are offered to the final customers/consumers. This is the price at which the business transfers products or services to either the end customer or the consumer or most of the times to **intermediaries.** Intermediaries are interested in selling your products for getting some margins or commissions. The difference between the final price at which the consumer receives the product or services and the price at which the business sells the product or services to intermediaries, after deducting all taxes, is the margin that the intermediary receives. The margins can be paid to a single or multiple intermediary and this depends on how further you wish to reach a particular geography and how the value chain operates in specific areas.

Products or Services Offered

A business can offer different products or services in the market. While understanding the market is critical, it is equally important to assess the relative position of your products or services in the market. The number of products or services offered may vary. Sometimes, a business has to offer just one product, but some variation might be required to suit the customer's expectations. At times, in order to cater to a wider audience, more products might have to be offered. Similarly, for services, different offerings will be available depending on customers' needs.

Some products or services carry a premium value compared to others. They have better quality, are costly, and command a better price. They tend to cater to specific groups or at times a niche market. In most of the cases, they tend to be more profitable than others. In order to drive better profitability, a business needs to understand how the mix of these products in total sales is trending and what actions can be taken to drive more profits from such a mix. A higher mix tilted towards a premium product may offer more profits. Better management of the product mix can drive operating leverage.

But before that, one needs to know the cost of manufacturing each unit of these products or service lines. In order to do that, any business needs to separate the production costs from the selling and marketing costs. Production costs can be related to the manufacturing of a product or cost incurred on delivering services. These costs can be either variable or fixed costs. Variable costs change with every unit of goods manufactured or service delivered; fixed expenses are same irrespective of the quantity that is manufactured or service lines created. Examples of variable costs will include raw material costs. With more quantities being produced, more raw material costs are required. On the contrary, fixed costs can be expenses like rent, electricity, maintenance, depreciation, and others which are more or less the same irrespective of the units manufactured or service lines created.

Again, these costs can be directly associated to the manufacturing of the product or service or indirectly related to overall production. Expenses like raw materials can be directly identified to a product or a service. However, some expenses like a common facility or supervisory costs incurred to manage the entire production line are not directly related to production but are essential to manufacture specific product or services. They should be allocated to the cost of the manufacturing of products using some criteria. For example, rent can be allocated on the basis of space utilised by the respective product or service line for production. Supervisory costs can be allocated on the basis of the number of employees managed for each product/service line.

All these costs are incurred to bring the goods in a tradable form to generate revenues. The costs incurred in the overall process are called cost of operations to bring the goods or services in saleable form. These costs are assimilated at the end of the period to work out the total cost of manufacturing a product or service. Some of these goods that are manufactured are utilised for generating revenues during the period and some of it goes in the inventory for trading in the future. The actual costs should be compared to the estimates in order to understand variances and check leakages, if any, which we'll see in the controlling section. However, for planning, it is important to make an assessment of these costs in advance in the form of estimates, which needs to be rigourously carried out. Let's take an example of this.

A business manufactures two products. Product A and product B. Product A requires certain raw materials which will cost INR 1Mn during the quarter, based on the assessment of units expected to be manufactured. Similarly, Product B requires certain raw materials which will cost INR 800k during the quarter. The business expects to manufacture 10k units of both of them.

There are 5 workers employed to manufacture Product A and 4 workers are employed to manufacture Product B. The cost of each worker is INR 10k per month. A supervisor manages all the workers and earns a salary of INR 20k per month.

Both products are manufactured on different machines, which cost INR 2Mn each and are expected to last for 10 years. Electricity consumption on a machine employed to manufacture product A is higher by 10%. Expected electricity units to be consumed are 3300 units during the quarter and would cost INR 42k at the current rate. Rent is paid for the manufacturing facility of INR 40k per month. Maintenance on both machines is INR 30k per quarter.

Now, let's try to find an estimate of the cost of production of these goods and assess how much it costs to bring the goods in a saleable form.

	Expense Type	Total Costs	Product A	Product B	Comments
Units Manufactured			10000	10000	
Raw Materials Consumption	Variable	1,800,000	1,000,000	800,000	
Worker/Labour Cost	Fixed				
No. of Workers			5	4	
Cost per Employee per Quarter			45000	45000	(INR 15k * 3 months)
Total Cost of Workers		405,000	225000	180000	
Depreciation	Fixed				
Machine Value			2,000,000	2,000,000	
Useful Life (In Years)			10	10	
Depreciation for the Year			200,000	200,000	based on value of machinery used and useful life of asset
Depreciation for the Quarter		100,000	50000	50000	
Maintenance Costs	Fixed	40,000	20000	20000	
Electricity Costs	Variable	42,000	22,000	20000	based on units consumed
Total Direct Costs		2,387,000	1,317,000	1,070,000	
Direct Cost per Unit			131.7	107	
Indirect Costs					

Rent	Fixed	120000	60000	60000	allocated equally assuming that the facility is equally shared with both machines
Supervisor	Fixed	90000	50000	40000	allocated on the basis of no. of employees managed
Total Indirect Costs		**210000**	**110000**	**100000**	
Cost of Production or to Bring Goods to Saleable Form		**2,597,000**	**1,427,000**	**1,170,000**	
Cost of production per unit			**142.7**	**117**	

The above estimates play a critical role in fixing the price of the product or service. We'll see this below. These are normally controlled against actual costs at the end of the period and the variance is either something that helps business get more profits or bear some extra costs.

Pricing

Every product or service produced is offered at a certain price. The net price of the product or service helps in determining the revenues of the business. Certain products or services are generic in nature and are not able to command better prices. However, certain products are at a premium and cater to a niche market. The value of the product is reflected in its price. Determining the price is a key to success for any business. Proper pricing covers all the costs and helps to generate more profits. Poorly devised pricing creates troubles for the business. That's why it's important to plan pricing properly. In order to plan pricing, one needs to understand costs, apart from understanding the market dynamics in which the business is operating. Here, costs contain two elements. One is the cost of producing each unit of product or service, which we saw above, and the other is fixed costs related to administration, selling and marketing, which I call **trading investments**. Even discounting pricing at certain times is a kind of trading investment as it has a direct impact on demand, most of the times and is especially true in the online space. These investments are made to drive sales and generate revenues. In this highly competitive market, the market dynamics have to be considered and appropriate investments have to be made to drive revenues.

If one takes a view that capital expenditure (CAPEX) is the only investment, then they are taking a myopic view of business. Investments can be capital expenditure or revenue expenditure. Accounting only tries to segregate them as long-term or short-term investments. Sometimes, even the short-term investments have an impact for a longer duration, especially advertising campaigns. Trading investments are strategic in nature and have to be incurred quarter after quarter or year after year. They form the basis for future CAPEX or long-term investments.

There are two factors to be considered while pricing a product or service.

i.   The price of similar products or services needs to be taken into consideration. Also, the market penetration that you intend to capture. It's important to note what premium customers are willing to give to your products.

ii. The other crucial factor is the assessment of product profitability. This helps in making better pricing decisions and optimises a brand's profitability.

In order to understand profitability at product level, one needs to know the concept of gross margins or gross contribution. Irrespective of the term you might want to use, they represent gross profits of the business. They are the costs associated directly with selling the products or services. These profits help firms to cover trading investments and financial expenses. The entrepreneur needs to continuously evaluate the quantum of gross margins or contribution per unit of a product or service. If this is done in conjunction with assessing the opportunities available in the market, it can help in driving a better product mix and of course more profits.

In the above example, if a business is selling Product A at say INR 300 per unit and Product B at INR 220 per unit, then the gross profits are as follows:

	Product A	Product B
Selling Price per Unit	300	220
Cost of Production per Unit	142.7	117
Gross Profits per Unit	157.3	103
Gross Profits %	52.43%	46.82%

If the business is able to identify more opportunities for Product A vis-à-vis Product B, it can help it generate more gross profits.

Let's assume the business is currently selling 8k units of Product A and 10k of Product B. In this case, it generates INR 2.1Mn of gross profits. However, the business is able to identify some other route to market for Product A and generate 2k additional units. Here, the profits will increase by 14%, which is higher than the revenue growth of 13%. The overall gross profit per unit increases from INR 117 to INR 120 per unit or in other words overall gross profit margins will be higher by 38 bps (basis points). This is the building block for driving operating leverage, which deals with generating more profitable growth versus revenue growth.

	Scenario 1 (Current Scenario)			Scenario 2 (Exploring Opportunity for Product a with Different Route to Market)			Variation
	Product A	Product B	Total	Product A	Product B	Total	
Selling Price per Unit	300.0	220.0	255.6	300.0	220.0	260.0	
Units Sold	8,000	10,000	18,000	10,000	10,000	20,000	
Revenues	2,400,000	2,200,000	4,600,000	3,000,000	2,200,000	5,200,000	13.0%
Cost of Production per Unit	142.7	117.0	128.4	142.7	117.0	129.9	
Cost of Production	1,141,600	1,170,000	2,311,600	1,427,000	1,170,000	2,597,000	
Freight Costs per Unit	10.0	10.0	10.0	10.0	10.0	10.0	
Freight Costs	80,000	100,000	180,000	100,000	100,000	200,000	
Cost of Goods Sold	1,221,600	1,270,000	2,491,600	1,527,000	1,270,000	2,797,000	
Cost of Goods Sold per Unit	152.7	127.0	138.4	152.7	127.0	139.9	
Gross Profits per Unit	147.3	93.0	117.1	147.3	93.0	120.2	
Gross Profits %	49.10%	42.27%	45.83%	49.10%	42.27%	46.21%	38 bps
Gross Profits	1,178,400	930,000	2,108,400	1,473,000	930,000	2,403,000	14.0%

A projection of the above basically helps you in assessing how much investments you can make in selling or marketing or other activities to drive business. In Scenario 1, the maximum a business can invest in order to remain at no profits or no loss is INR 2.1Mn. But if it's able working towards driving more of Product A, the available investment opportunity increases to INR 2.4 Mn. If the business goes more aggressive and wants to identify more opportunities for Product A, then in that case, the investment kitty increases further. The maximum investment opportunity is a point of breaking even and is directly related to operating leverage. Let me briefly touch upon both the points before venturing further. We might need them going forward and they are important tools.

Break-Even Point

It is that point at which the firm makes no profit or loss. Understanding this point is important to understand the number of units or services that should be sold to keep a business floating without any additional burden or loss. It is the point at which the revenue of the business is equal to all the costs. Businesses do not earn any profits or loss at this point. Any revenue earned after the break-even point results in profits. The break-even point also helps in determining the number of units to be sold, the price point feasible for the business, and the trading investment that a firm can make without stretching it much. To understand how a break-even point impacts your profitability, let's take an example.

In the above case, if the business decides to spend INR 2.1 Mn on trading investments, then the revenue of INR 4.6 Mn at 45.8% gross profits represents the break-even point. In order to achieve this, the business has to sell 8k units of Product A and 10k units of Product B.

However, when it changes to 10k units of Product A and Product B and if its trading investments is still INR 2.1 Mn with other cost parameters more or less staying the same, then the profit will be INR 2.4 Mn minus INR 2.1 Mn or approx. INR 300k. Since all costs do not vary in the same proportion as the increase or decrease in the revenues, the break-even point helps in defining the minimum sales volume.

Mathematically, the break-even point can be expressed as the following:

Break-even point = Gross Profits/Gross Profit %
In the above case, the formula can be expressed as:
Break-even point = INR 2.1 Mn/45.83% = INR 4.6 Mn
(which is equal to revenues).

If one has an understanding of gross profits, one can easily understand the potential money available with them to invest to flourish in the trade or survive in the trade.

Operating Leverage

Equally important as the break-even point is the operating leverage and both are very much related to each other. This is also one of the best tools to assess pricing and trading investments. Every increase in revenues is normally accompanied by growth in profits. But a higher growth in profits than revenue growth can be achieved by improving the product mix and getting more synergies through fixed costs. So the degree by which a business gets more operating profits by increasing revenues is operating leverage.

Below is example of operating leverage.

Please refer to the below P&L which provides the current scenario in which business is operating and its strategy to increase the sales of Product B through more discounts and some marketing investments, which is presented in the proposed scenario.

| | Current scenario | | | Proposed Scenario (Pushing Product B) | | | | |
| | Products | | | Products | | | Variance | |
	A	B	Total	A	B	Total	Difference	% Difference
Units	1,000	500	1,500	1,000	700	1,700	200	13.3%
Selling Price	100	200	133	100	190	137		
Revenues	**100,000**	**100,000**	**200,000**	**100,000**	**133,000**	**233,000**	**33,000**	**16.5%**
Cost of Goods Sold	70,000	50,000	120,000	70,000	70,000	140,000	20,000	16.7%
Gross Contribution	**30,000**	**50,000**	**80,000**	**30,000**	**63,000**	**93,000**	**13,000**	**16.3%**
Gross Contribution %	**30.0%**	**50.0%**	**40.0%**	**30.0%**	**47.4%**	**39.9%**		
Direct Marketing /Sales Costs	10,000	10,000	20,000	10,000	12,000	22,000	2,000	10.0%
Net Contribution	**20,000**	**40,000**	**60,000**	**20,000**	**51,000**	**71,000**	**11,000**	**18.3%**
Net Contribution %	**20.0%**	**40.0%**	**30.0%**	**20.0%**	**38.3%**	**30.5%**		
General Marketing/ Sales Costs			20,000			20,000	–	0.0%

General Administration Overheads			20,000			20,000	–	0.0%
Operating Profit			**20,000**			**31,000**	**11,000**	**55.0%**
Operating Profit %			10.0%			13.3%		

In the above example, a business is operating with two product lines. The proposal is to push more of Product B by reducing the price by INR 10 per unit. This will bring the gross contribution down for Product B and the overall gross contribution will also grow lower than revenue growth by a small proportion. In our example, revenues are growing 16.5%, but gross contribution is growing 16.3%. However, the costs are fixed. Product B has a higher selling price and gross contribution than Product A. So any sales of Product B will result in a higher absolute value of gross contribution than Product A. Most of the costs are more or less fixed except direct marketing and sales costs which increased by INR 2k to support additional volumes of Product B. But inspite of this, the net contribution is expected to grow 18.3%, higher than the revenue growth of 16.5%. Now coming to some general marketing and sales and administration expenses, they are expected to remain the same. As operating profit in absolute terms has increased, it will have a multiplying effect in the growth of operating profits as you notice above. This brings a net increase in operating profit by 55% versus sales growth of 16.5%. Thus operating profits will grow by 3.3 times the revenue growth just by pushing more volumes of the highly profitable Product B. This is the essence of operating leverage.

It tries to gauge factors that can drive more profitable growth than revenue growth.

Trading Investments

A good product with proper pricing has to be supported by marketing and sales investments, along with a proper support ecosystem in the form of human resources or talent acquisition folks, business finance and finance folks, and sales operations folks. A good product can be penetrated deeply into the market with better pricing and trading investments. One has to apply her/his discretion to determine pricing and trading investments. They have to go hand in hand. Also this has to be monitored rigorously to ensure you're getting optimal returns on your investments. Care has to be taken to see that you don't over or under invest.

But first, let's first understand marketing and sales investments. Marketing investments are those which are incurred to identify the customers and create the demand for the product or service. People buy a product or service to satisfy their needs or wants. With a plethora of options available to them, the business needs to facilitate them in making the right choices. They should be able to connect their benefits with the customer's needs. A business has different vehicles available to create visibility about its products. It can be advertising or different types of promotions. Once the business attains scale, they need to hire marketing managers to run the show. All costs associated with these are marketing investments.

For some businesses, there is something called product development costs. These are businesses that continuously try to provide a unique innovative offer to its customers at all times. I would like to classify them under the broader classification of marketing investments.

Sales investments are the costs associated in building a network of partners or sales force to drive business. The investments in this space are in the form of remuneration that you provide to your intermediaries or sales force. So, salaries of sales staff and their travel costs are included in these investments. Incentives given to intermediaries in the form of rebates or concessions are also included. However, one can argue that rebates directly impact gross margins and so it should not be included out there, which is completely fair. But while assessing return on investments, it's important to consider the amount paid on these incentives and take a holistic view of all sales investments. Investment in this space is critical to drive relationships with customers, who help in driving business.

Special discounts on pricing can be argued as a sales or marketing investment, but I wish to keep it separate. This is a trading investment to drive more demand by leveraging the discounts.

In order to understand how much to price and invest, one needs to know the life cycle of the product and this has to be evaluated properly.

Broadly speaking, a product goes through four cycles. It is first introduced in the market. Once it survives, gets accepted and moves ahead, it will enter a growth phase and penetrate the market more. After some time, it matures and finally it starts declining with some other alternative offering. The period of this life cycle is different for different products. Some products are still in the matured phase for so many years now. This helps in understanding the kind of pricing and investments that need to be incurred to either retain the current position, grow or react to a declining phase.

When a product is initially introduced, capital has to be brought in. A good amount of money goes in developing the product. Marketing and sales investments required to create visibility are very high. Pricing has to be lucrative to attract attention and create demand in the market. So during this period, there should ideally be no expectation for any profits. Everything is invested to create a presence.

Once the product starts to grow, continuous marketing and sales investments are required to get the tempo going. Pricing again has to be lucrative in order to penetrate more in the market. Profits are likely to be low or even if there are some profits, they get invested back into the business.

During this phase, the products can start getting a higher market share and higher growth. Investments might still be required to maintain the momentum, but profits are likely to be low. There is a possibility of having a low share, even though the growth might be high due to a low baseline. Money will be pumped in continuously to get more shares. In this phase, a business either creates star products or their products become a question mark. It means a decision needs to be made to either continue with them or come out.

Once the business matures, the market share stabilises. Either a product attains a significant market share or it has a low market share. However, growth is likely to be very low in this phase. Normally, high value profits are seen in this phase. Typically, a business succeeds in creating either cash cows or creates laggards. One needs to come out if a laggard is spotted. Cash cows generate significant profits and are cash generating engines but more growth is not expected.

Not much investment is required in this phase. Investments are required just to sustain things. Pricing has to be aligned to the market or at times it should help in beating the market.

After the business declines, it has a high share but negative growth. However, profits are still very decent. No big investments should be planned. As the product loses interest from customers, prices should reduce. There is a possibility that a low market share and growth might turn the operations unprofitable as well.

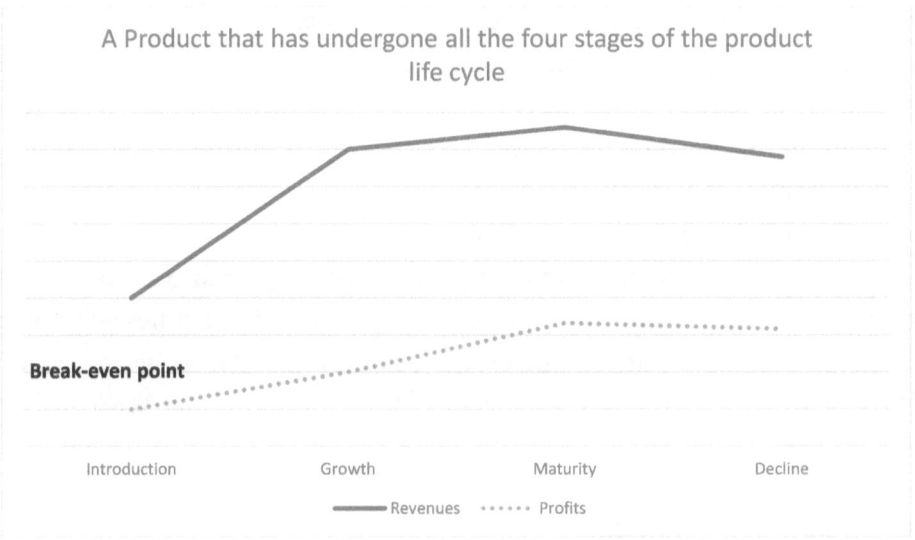

A Product that has undergone all the four stages of the product life cycle

It's not necessary that a business normally go through these cycles strictly. Sometimes, an entrepreneur might be able to reignite change and reignite a product or service and can bring a new lease of life to it. The above can guide the entrepreneur the quantum of investments and pricing that is required at any particular stage. It can also guide the entrepreneur or management in reaching out to the market.

The P&L and balance sheet of any business thus depends on the four factors that were described above viz. market reach, product or service offered, pricing and trading investments. They are referred to as the **marketing mix**. They, in turn, define the quality of the P&L and balance sheet. **As I had mentioned in the introduction, an entrepreneur, people,**

place, and equipment are the quintessential elements of any business. But this needs to be properly blended to create a great product, which needs to be delivered to a wider market through creating awareness and at appropriate price to reap the benefits of higher value addition.

Proper capital expenditure has to be incurred to create assets that can deliver great products or services and these need to be optimally utilised. Optimal investments need to be made in the sales force and brand awareness or marketing investments to drive more customers or consumers. Care has to be taken to cover the costs of all these elements while being aware of the market reality and the value which the customer or consumer is willing to perceive for your product or service. This is what every investor or entrepreneur needs to look at. For investors, this forms the basis to ascribe a premium to a product or service or a company or business in which they are investing.

Having taken you through this, let me build a case study to take you through a strategic plan. A tactical plan is built on the same grounds, except that it is done at a quarterly or monthly level. These case studies will touch upon all operations carried out by the business in order to be successful. We'll build projections on P&L, balance sheet, and cash flow. We'll analyse the different elements that go into these projections, which become the controlling points for any business at a later stage. They set the stage for monitoring and controlling.

IV. Case Study

After considerable success with Nishka Toys, the entrepreneur decides to venture into creating a unique theme park for children in a piece of land spread over 15 acres on the outskirts of the city, which is 20 kms away from city centre. This theme park will have a picnic area, spread over 5 acres. There will be 2.5 acres for slides and other fun activities for children and adults. Lastly, the remaining 7.5 acres is utilised for creating an adventure park, which is getting a lot of interest especially from teenagers and young adults. The task looks daunting especially when there are multiple malls in the centre of the city offering play zones and each one is quite popular. However, getting good profits is a challenge for most of them. On the other hand, there are fewer parks near the city. Most of them are public parks and there is less willingness to accept private parks that charges fees but do not provide a good service and people do not see them contributing significantly to their overall experience. However, amidst this clutter, there is a possibility to create a unique space.

The entrepreneur is getting a proposal from its existing landlord to take his 15-acre land on rent for INR 300k per month which is on the outskirts of the city. The landlord is agreeing to give a long-term commitment and has no intention of selling it anytime soon. He agrees to give the land on rent for 10 year period, with a clause that rentals will be revised every 2 years. It is expected that typically there will be a 10% increase in rent after every 2 years. The land is somewhat fertile and could be used to develop a picnic spot which would be ideal for the city population. The entrepreneur decides to develop the land into two parts. One as a picnic spot and the other as an adventure park, which is equally distributed. A picnic spot will not attract too many people unless there is a play zone/area within this park. The entrepreneur decides to utilise 1/3rd of the land allocated for the picnic spot for developing a play area, with some exciting slides for children and a good gaming zone for teenagers and adults. The following is the proposed land allocation for the park.

	Year 1			
	Picnic Spot	Play Area	Adventure Park	Total
Acres	5	2.5	7.5	15

It acquires the land and within a year it's ready to start its operations. It has invested INR 35Mn in developing the whole area as a picnic spot cum play area. Also, the other part has been developed as an adventure park. The investments were made to develop a good lawn for the picnic spot. A lot of equipment was brought to develop the play area and adventure park. The total investments made has the following split. It is expected that these assets will have a useful life of 10 years. Thus, the amount that needs to be set aside every year for utilising these assets will be $1/10^{th}$ of the total asset cost value which will be referred to as depreciation.

	Picnic Spot	Play Area	Adventure Park	Total
Investments				
Assets Created (Amt in INRk)	2,500	20,000	12,500	35,000

To run the operations smoothly, the entrepreneur is estimating that it will require 20 people to run the park. Successful theme parks which have a lot of entertainment value can grow by nearly double every year. Given the fact that the park is outside the city perimeter, the entrepreneur expects that its operations will grow at the rate of 40% more or less every year, at least for 4 years. It is expecting to start on a small base and will then expand. With that in mind, it is expecting that the number of people required to run the operations will increase from 20 people in year 1 to 36 people in year 4.

Out of 20 people required in the 1st year, 2 will be supervisors taking care of the picnic area and the adventure park. The requirement for the supervisor will remain the same for the next 4 years. The person supervising the picnic area will also supervise the play area within the picnic area. His salary will get split between the picnic spot and the play area in the same proportion as the employees hired for each segment. Thus, in year 1, there are 2 people taking care of the picnic spot and 5 people taking care of the play area. The proportion of the supervisor's salary split between both these businesses will be 28.6% and 71.4% for the picnic spot and the play area respectively. This will be 20% and 80% for the 2nd year and so on.

For the adventure park, there's going to be just one supervisor taking care of it exclusively. So there's no need to split his salary.

The average cost of hiring each person will be INR 150k per annum and with an inflation of 5%, it is expecting that it will cost INR 174k by 4th year. Similarly, the supervisor's cost will be INR 300k per annum will rise to INR 347k by end of 4th year.

The following is the headcount split along with the cost of getting them for 4 years.

Amt in INRk

	Year 1				Year 2				Year 3				Year 4			
	Picnic Spot	Play Area	Adventure Park	Total	Picnic Spot	Play Area	Adventure Park	Total	Picnic Spot	Play Area	Adventure Park	Total	Picnic Spot	Play Area	Adventure Park	Total
Headcount																
People Required to Run Operations	2	5	11	18	2	8	15	25	2	10	18	30	2	12	20	34
Salary per Employee	150	150	150		158	158	158		165	165	165		174	174	174	
Total Salaries – Direct Staff	300	750	1,650	2,700	315	1,260	2,363	3,938	331	1,654	2,977	4,961	347	2,084	3,473	5,904
Supervisory Staff	1		1	2	1		1	2	1		1	2	1		1	2
Supervisor Cost Allocation- Picnic	28.6%	71.4%			20.0%	80.0%			16.7%	83.3%			14.3%	85.7%		
Salary per Employee		3,003	300			315	315			331	331			347	347	
Total Salaries – Supervisory Staff	86	214	300	600	63	252	315	630	55	276	331	662	50	298	347	695
Total Salaries	386	964	1,950	3,300	378	1,512	2,678	4,568	386	1,929	3,308	5,623	397	2,381	3,820	6,598

Maintaining these assets is another critical cost. The manufacturer of this equipment can provide AMC (annual maintenance contracts), where the rates will remain more or less the same for a certain number of visits. But with increased operations, the entrepreneur expects the frequency of visits to increase. Other maintenance costs are fixed but with increased operations there will be an increase in these costs as well. It is estimated that the maintenance costs will increase by 15% every year for 4 year period. The maintenance cost will be INR 1.6 Mn in the first year and it will increase to INR 2.43 Mn in the fourth year. The split of maintenance costs between the different businesses is given below.

Amt in INRk

	Year 1				Year 2				Year 3				Year 4			
	Picnic Spot	Play Area	Adventure Park	Total	Picnic Spot	Play Area	Adventure Park	Total	Picnic Spot	Play Area	Adventure Park	Total	Picnic Spot	Play Area	Adventure Park	Total
Maintenance Costs	100	1,000	500	1,600	115	1,150	575	1,840	132	1,323	661	2,116	152	1,521	760	2,433

Another important revenue expenditure will be electricity. Much of the electricity will be consumed by the play area, followed by the adventure park and then there will be some consumed by the picnic spot. Electricity is expected to rise in line with the growth in the number of guests. It's expected to be a variable cost. So every year, it is expected to grow by 40%. The following will be the split of electricity costs along with its allocation to different businesses.

Amt in INRk

| | Year 1 | | | | Year 2 | | | | Year 3 | | | | Year 4 | | | |
	Picnic Spot	Play Area	Adventure Park	Total	Picnic Spot	Play Area	Adventure Park	Total	Picnic Spot	Play Area	Adventure Park	Total	Picnic Spot	Play Area	Adventure Park	Total
Electricity Unit Allocation	10%	60%	30%		10%	60%	30%		10%	60%	30%		10%	60%	30%	
Electricity Costs	120	720	360	1,200	168	1,008	504	1,680	235	1,411	706	2,352	329	1,976	988	3,293

There are other costs associated with running the operations. These relate to insurance and other operating costs, which will be INR 1 Mn every year, and it is expected to rise by 10% every year to reflect the growth in operations. This will be allocated to the respective businesses based on the investments made for the respective businesses. Thus, a picnic spot will have the least allocation as the amount invested in the picnic spot is the least and the amount allocated to the play area will be the highest as most of the investments were made in the play area. Insurance and other operating costs are related directly to upkeep and protecting the assets. So their allocation should be done on the basis of investments made in these areas. Below is the allocation of other costs.

Amt in INRk

	Year 1				Year 2				Year 3				Year 4			
	Picnic Spot	Play Area	Adventure Park	Total	Picnic Spot	Play Area	Adventure Park	Total	Picnic Spot	Play Area	Adventure Park	Total	Picnic Spot	Play Area	Adventure Park	Total
Other Costs				1,000				1,100				1,210				1,331
Allocation Ratio (Based on Investments Made)	7.1%	57.1%	35.7%	100.0%	7.1%	57.1%	35.7%	100.0%	7.1%	57.1%	35.7%	100.0%	7.1%	57.1%	35.7%	100.0%
Other Costs	71	571	357	1,000	79	629	393	1,100	86	691	432	1,210	95	761	475	1,331

This leads us to putting down all the business activities that need to be done in order to get business at 40% growth for the next 4 years. This is an important step in business planning pertaining to resources. The monetary part is expressed in forecasted financial statements.

Amt in INRk

	Year 1				Year 2				Year 3				Year 4			
	Picnic Spot	Play Area	Adventure Park	Total	Picnic Spot	Play Area	Adventure Park	Total	Picnic Spot	Play Area	Adventure Park	Total	Picnic Spot	Play Area	Adventure Park	Total
Investments																
Assets	2,500	20,000	12,500	35,000												
Cash				17,500												
Land on Rent																
Acres	5	2.5	7.5	15												
Rent per Month				300												
Rent Allocation	33.3%	16.7%	50.0%	100.0%												
Yearly Rent Allocation	1,200	600	1,800	3,600	1,200	600	1,800	3,600	1,320	660	1,980	3,960	1,320	660	1,980	3,960
Headcount																
People Required to Run Operations	2	5	11	18	2	8	15	25	2	10	18	30	2	12	20	34
Salary per Employee	150	150	150		158	158	158		165	165	165		174	174	174	
Total Salaries – Direct	300	750	1,650	2,700	315	1,260	2,363	3,988	331	1,654	2,977	4,961	347	2,084	3,473	5,904
Staff																
Supervisory Staff	1		1	2	1		1	2	1		1	2	1		1	2
Supervisor Cost Allocation-Picnic	28.6%	71.4%			20.0%	80.0%			16.7%	83.3%			14.3%	85.7%		
Salary per Employee	300	300	300		315		315		331	331	331		347	347	347	

Total Salaries – Supervisory Staff	86	214	300	600	63	252	315	630	55	276	331	662	50	298	347	695
Total Salaries	386	964	1950	3300	378	1512	2678	4568	386	1929	3308	5623	397	2381	3820	6598
Electricity Unit Allocation	10%	60%	30%		10%	60%	30%		10%	60%	30%		10%	60%	30%	
Electricity Costs	120	720	360	1,200	168	1,008	504	1,680	235	1,411	706	2,352	329	1,976	988	3,293
Maintenance Costs	100	1,000	500	1,600	115	1,150	575	1,840	132	1,323	661	2,116	152	1,521	760	2,433
Other Costs				1,000				1,100				1,210				13,310
Allocation ratio (Based on Investments Made)	7.1%	57.1%	35.7%	100.0%	7.1%	57.1%	35.7%	100.0%	7.1%	57.1%	35.7%	100.0%	7.1%	57.1%	35.7%	100.0%
Other Costs	71	571	357	1,000	79	629	393	1,100	86	691	432	1,210	96	761	475	1,331
Depreciation	250	2,000	1,250	3,500	250	2,000	1,250	3,500	250	2,000	1,250	3,500	250	2,000	1,250	3,500
Total Cost of Operations	2,127	2,856	6,217	14,200	2,190	6,899	7,199	16,288	2,410	8,015	8,336	18,761	2,543	9,299	9,274	21,116

Electricity bills come 10 days after the month ends and a good credit period of 20 days is provided. Effectively, electricity is paid after a gap of one month. The rest of the costs are paid on time. The electricity cost is expected to be approximately the same every month.

The picnic spot is primarily built to attract people to come to a far-off place for recreation purposes. The price is kept very attractive. But the aim is to pull the crowd towards the play area, which will have state-of-the-art equipment. It is expected that 60% of the people that come for the picnic will also get attracted towards the play park. It is expected that, in the first year, the park will attract 2000 people per week. It is expected that people will normally spend 1.5 to 2 hours in the park.

The adventure park will have a different set of audience, which will include mostly teenagers and young adults, who have an appetite for adventure. It's expected that this category will attract 750 people on an average per week in the first year.

In both these businesses, there is 40% growth expected over the next 4 years and would be consistent year on year without much variation in any specific year. The following is the REACH expected in the next 4 years.

Amt in INRk

	Year 1				Year 2				Year 3				Year 4			
	Picnic Spot	Play Area	Adventure Park	Total	Picnic Spot	Play Area	Adventure Park	Total	Picnic Spot	Play Area	Adventure Park	Total	Picnic Spot	Play Area	Adventure Park	Total
No. of Guests Expected per Week	800	1,200	750		1,120	1,680	1,050		1,568	2,352	1,470		2,195	3,293	2,058	
No. of Guests Expected per Annum	41,600	62,400	39,000	1,43,000	58,240	87,360	54,600	2,00,200	81,536	1,22,304	76,440	2,80,280	1,14,150	1,71,226	1,07,016	3,92,392

The prices are kept at reasonable levels. As mentioned earlier, the price for the picnic spot is kept very attractive and will be INR 25 per guest. There are different coupons available for the play area for different types of games. It is expected that any guest will spend, on an average, INR 250 every time they enter the play area. Coupons of INR 100, INR 200, INR 500 and INR 1000 denominations are available. This spend will be over and above the INR 25 that they will anyway pay to enter the picnic spot. So, the average revenue per guest from the play areas will be INR 275 (INR 25 for the picnic spot+INR 250 average spend per customer). The price for the adventure park is kept at INR 450. This will cover a whole range of different adventurous activities like bungee jumping, walking on the rope, wall climbing, and many more.

To attract people to the park, the business has decided to take the help of the online event company, which will facilitate booking the tickets online. It is expected that most of the people coming to the park will take advantage of this facility. Nearly 80% of the guests are expected to book in advance through this online portal. The event company will get 8% upfront margins and 2% rebates, for providing this service. 20% of the people are still expected to come directly to the park and get the tickets from over the counter. The amount to be collected from the event company is expected to be settled after one month, once the month gets over. Revenues are expected to be more or less similar every month throughout the year. The amount from the snack bars is also expected to be settled through cheque after one month. The revenues on the snack bars is also expected to be more or less similar every month throughout the year.

With 40% growth for 4 years and the above scenario, the revenue estimates from the direct and online portal will appear as follows.

Amt in INRk

	Year 1				Year 2				Year 3				Year 4			
	Picnic Spot	Play Area	Adventure Park	Total	Picnic Spot	Play Area	Adventure Park	Total	Picnic Spot	Play Area	Adventure Park	Total	Picnic Spot	Play Area	Adventure Park	Total
Revenue Estimates																
Expected Earnings per Guest	25	275	450		25	275	450		25	275	450		25	275	450	
GST Taxes Applied at 18%				18%				18%				18%				18%
No. of Guests Expected per Week	800	1,200	750		1,120	1,680	1,050		1,568	2,352	1,470		2,195	3,298	2,058	
No. of Guests Expected per Annum	41,600	62,400	39,000	1,43,000	58,240	87,360	54,600	2,00,200	81,536	1,22,304	76,440	2,80,280	1,14,150	1,71,226	1,07,016	3,92,392
Route to Market																
Direct				20%				20%				20%				20%
No. of Guests (Expecting 20% of Total Guests Coming Directly)	8,320	12,480	7,800	28,600	11,648	17,472	10,920	40,040	16,307	24,461	15,288	56,056	22,830	34,245	21,403	78,478
Revenue Estimate (After Deducting GST)	171	2,814	2,878	5,863	239	3,940	4,029	8,208	334	5,516	5,641	11,491	468	7,722	7,898	16,088
Indirect – through online booking portal for events																
No. of Guests (Expecting 80% of Total Guests Coming through Online Portal)	33,280	49,920	31,200		46,592	69,888	43,680		65,229	97,843	61,152		91,320	1,36,980	85,613	
Upfront Margins and Rebates to Be Given to the Online Portal @ 10%				10%				10%				10%				10%
Revenue Estimate (After Deducting GST and Portal's Margins)	614	10,131	10,362	21,107	860	14,184	14,506	29,550	1,203	19,857	20,309	41,369	1,685	27,800	28,432	57,917
Total Revenue from Tickets	785	12,946	13,240	26,970	1,098	18,124	18,536	37,758	1,538	25,373	25,950	52,861	2,153	35,522	36,330	74,005

In order to cater to the food and beverages requirement, the park will have its own cafeterias, which will be given to the third parties who will be managing these snack bars. To start with, there will be 3 snack bars and the plan is to take it to 9 bars as the business grows. It is expected that 3 out of every 4 people will buy their snacks and beverages from these snack bars and the average spend per guest is expected to be INR 150 per guest net of all taxes.

It is agreed with the snack bars that the revenue will be shared with the park owner and themselves in a 2:3 ratio. It means the owner of the theme park will keep 40% of the total revenues. For the third party snack bars, it will still leave them with a strong profit of 25%-30%, which is lucrative for them. The revenues from these snack bars will be allocated based on the guests visiting picnic spot and the adventure park. The total revenues expected from the snack bars is as follows.

Amt in INRk

	Year 1				Year 2				Year 3				Year 4			
	Picnic Spot	Play Area	Adventure Park	Total	Picnic Spot	Play Area	Adventure Park	Total	Picnic Spot	Play Area	Adventure Park	Total	Picnic Spot	Play Area	Adventure Park	Total
No. of Snack Bars				3				5				7				9
No. of People Expected to Get into Snack Bar				107,250				150,150				210,210				294,294
Estimated Spend per Person				150				150				150				150
Gross Revenue Estimate from Snack Bar				16,088				22,523				31,532				44,144
Net Revenues from Snack Bars @40% Margins for Theme Park				6,435				9,009				12,613				17,658
Revenue Allocation to Snack Bars	1,872	2,808	1,755	6,435	2,621	3,931	2,457	9,009	3,669	5,504	3,440	12,613	5,137	7,705	4,816	17,658

The total revenue estimates for 4 years will appear as follows:

Amt in INRk

	Year 1				Year 2				Year 3				Year 4			
	Picnic Spot	Play Area	Adventure Park	Total	Picnic Spot	Play Area	Adventure Park	Total	Picnic Spot	Play Area	Adventure Park	Total	Picnic Spot	Play Area	Adventure Park	Total
Revenue Estimates																
Total Revenue from Tickets	785	12,946	13,240	26,970	1,098	18,124	18,536	37,758	1,538	25,373	25,950	52,861	2,153	35,522	36,330	74,005
Revenue Allocation to Snack Bars	1,872	2,808	1,755	6,435	2,621	3,931	2,457	9,009	3,669	5,504	3,440	12,613	5,137	7,705	4,816	17,658
Total Revenue Estimates	2,657	15,754	14,995	33,405	3,719	22,055	20,993	46,767	5,207	30,877	29,390	65,473	7,290	43,228	41,146	91,663

Having known all these facts, the first critical evaluation that needs to be done is the gross profits from each of the businesses. It helps in understanding how the product mix will shape overall profitability and it helps in assessing the trading investments the business can undertake to drive growth.

For assessing the profitability, we'll combine revenues and costs of the picnic spot and the play area into one single business or else the profitability of the picnic spot will always appear less and will be non-lucrative, which might paint a wrong picture. While the picnic spot is an important attraction, the entrepreneur wants people to visit the play area within the picnic spot. Thus the low fares charged for the picnic spot acts as an investment for the play area; therefore the picnic spot and the play area have to be considered a single business. Also, the profits have to be assessed together. The following will be the gross profits for the picnic spot (picnic spot + play area combined) and the adventure park.

Amt in INRk

	Year 1			Year 2			Year 3			Year 4		
	Picnic Spot	Adventure Park	Total	Picnic Spot	Adventure Park	Total	Picnic Spot	Adventure Park	Total	Picnic Spot	Adventure Park	Total
Revenues	18.4	15.0	33.4	25.8	21.0	46.8	36.1	29.4	65.5	50.5	41.1	91.7
Less:												
Operational Costs	8.0	6.2	14.2	9.1	7.2	16.3	10.4	8.3	18.8	11.8	9.3	21.1
Gross Profits	10.4	8.8	19.2	16.7	13.8	30.5	25.7	21.1	46.7	38.7	31.9	70.5
Gross Profit %	56.6%	58.5%	57.5%	64.7%	65.7%	65.2%	71.1%	71.6%	71.3%	76.6%	77.5%	77.0%

The gross profit % for both the businesses are more or less the same, except that the gross profit % on the adventure park is higher, but with higher volumes from the picnic spot, the amount earned from the picnic spot will always be higher. Also, with most of the costs being fixed, the gross profits will tend to increase year on year with increase in volumes. This implies that there will be higher **operating leverage**. At such a high operating leverage, the business will tend to have more space to invest in marketing, sales, and other support activities to drive growth.

The minimum marketing investment to be made to attract the local population and to ensure that the campaign is effective will be INR 15 Mn. The media campaigns will be done on the radio, through the press, and the internet. The media expenses expected in the 1st year will be INR 12.2 Mn. This was calculated based on the minimum air time, spots, and space required to catch people's attention. Also, promoters will be placed in different parts of the cities; they will be promoting about the park through different animations and leaflets. 14 promoters will be required to cover the different parts of the city and their yearly costs is expected to be INR 2.1 Mn. These investments will also cover the cost of people managing these campaigns. The costs were assessed after consulting a media agency. It was also advised to increase spends in line with the expected business growth.

Apart from these investments, there will be INR 2 Mn of minimum investments required for setting an IT infrastructure, including people required to maintain the IT set-up. Also, a general management, including a GM (General Manager) and a finance manager would be required to run the affairs. The other administration costs are expected to be INR 2 Mn.

These investments will not be covered fully from the gross profits in the first year as the volumes will be lower and the break-even point will not be met. From the second year, the volumes are expected to increase and the gross profits will cover the overall trade investments.

Below is the plan of trade investments that will be made.

				Amt in INRk
	Year 1	Year 2	Year 3	Year 4
	Total	Total	Total	Total
Marketing Costs				
Media Expenses	12,000	16,800	21,000	25,200
Promoters				
No. of Promoters	14	14	14	14
Cost of Each Promoter (Incl. Promo Materials)	150	150	175	175
Promoters costs	2,100	2,100	2,450	2,450
Salary of Marketing Personnel	900	990	1,089	1,198
Total Marketing Costs	15,000	19,890	24,539	28,848
Administration Costs				
IT Costs	1,500	2,000	2,250	2,500
IT Personnel Costs	600	600	600	600
Other Administration Costs	2,000	2,100	2,205	2,315
Administration Costs	**4,100**	**4,700**	**5,055**	**5,415**
Total Trade Investments	**19,100**	**24,590**	**29,594**	**34,263**

Media expenses will be paid after one month and are expected to be evenly spread throughout the year. IT vendors give one month credit but there will be no spends in the last quarter of any year. The rest of the spends will be paid on time, including the promoter's cost.

Out of the INR 35 Mn invested, INR 15 Mn was funded through a long-term loan from a financial institution. 1/10th of the loan must be paid every year and interest and fees for the same appear as follows.

				Amt in INRk
	Year 1	Year 2	Year 3	Year 4
	Total	Total	Total	Total
Financial Costs	1,500	1,350	1,200	1,050

The above gives a blueprint of how a business plan should be made. This forms the basis of creating a financial plan which then forms the basis for monitoring actuals. Having covered all the activities required to run the park, let's now put the same into a forecasted P&L and balance sheet.

Post that, we'll prepare a forecasted cash flow statement. This will cover the entire planning exercise.

Projected Financial Statements for 4 Years

We'll first start with the projected or forecasted or a plan P&L representation which covers all the impact of all the commercial activities that the entrepreneur wishes to undertake in financial terms.

Projected Profit and Loss (P&L) for 4 Years							
	INR Mn				YoY%		
	Year 1	Year 2	Year 3	Year 4	Y2 v/s Y1	Y3 v/s Y2	Y4 v/s Y3
Revenues	33.4	46.8	65.5	91.7	40%	40%	40%
Less:							
Operational Costs							
Salaries	3.3	4.6	5.6	6.6	38%	23%	17%
Rent	3.6	3.6	4.0	4.0	0%	10%	0%
Electricity	1.2	1.7	2.4	3.3	40%	40%	40%
Maintenance	1.6	1.8	2.1	2.4	15%	15%	15%
Other Costs	1.0	1.1	1.2	1.3	10%	10%	10%
Depreciation	3.5	3.5	3.5	3.5	0%	0%	0%
Cost of Operations	**14.2**	**16.3**	**18.8**	**21.1**	**15%**	**15%**	**13%**
Gross Profit	**19.2**	**30.5**	**46.7**	**70.5**	**59%**	**53%**	**51%**
Less:							
Marketing Costs	15.0	19.9	24.5	28.8	33%	23%	18%
General Administration Costs	4.1	4.7	5.1	5.4	15%	8%	7%
General Selling and Administration Costs (Trading Investments)	**19.1**	**24.6**	**29.6**	**34.3**	**29%**	**20%**	**16%**
Operating Income	**0.1**	**5.9**	**17.1**	**36.3**	**5519%**	**191%**	**112%**
Less: Financial Costs	1.5	1.4	1.2	1.1	-12%	-11%	-13%
Profit before Tax	**(1.4)**	**4.5**	**15.9**	**35.2**	**-416%**	**251%**	**121%**
Less: Tax @ 30%		1.4	4.8	10.6			121%
Profit after Tax	**(1.4)**	**3.2**	**11.1**	**24.7**	**-321%**	**251%**	**121%**
Cash Profit	**2.1**	**6.7**	**14.6**	**28.2**	**223%**	**119%**	**92%**

The P&L clearly suggests that there is an operating leverage. With most of the costs being fixed, any incremental revenues facilitate driving more profits. The product mix gives the same gross profits from the picnic spot and the adventure park. But even then, if there are higher volumes coming from the adventure park, they will drive even further an operating leverage.

Some costs are completely fixed like depreciation, but some costs are growing albeit at a slower rate than the revenue growth. Such costs can also be classified as semi-fixed costs. They are fixed and variable in nature. For example, in case of maintenance, upto certain visits, the costs will be same, but thereafter as the number of guests increase, the maintenance required will also increase and so the number of visits will also increase, which would entail higher maintenance costs. But since it's fixed up to a certain stage and will increase only after it reaches a threshold, the costs can't be classified as variable costs and similarly, since it will increase after a threshold, it cannot be classified as fixed. However, it has features of both the costs. So, it's classified as semi-fixed costs.

Another topic that I wish to cover is cash profit. Cash profit is arrived after deducting all activities which involve the utilisation of cash in either the present form or will be used in future. For example, if you incur certain expenses, you get a credit period. In the above example, the business gets credit for electricity and marketing costs. These are also considered while determining cash profits. From our case study, there's only one expense which is excluded and that is a provision made for depreciation, as it does not entail any cash outflow now or in future. This is not considered while assessing cash profit. Thus, a cash profit is nothing but profit after tax plus depreciation.

There is one more variation of cash profit which can be called operating cash profit. This will exclude financial costs along with depreciation.

The P&L is also a reflection of the product life cycle that I covered in the planning cycle. In order to keep things short, the inception phase is kept at just one year in our case study. In reality, a particular stage of a product life cycle can be much more than illustrated here. For example, it can take 2 to 3 years or even more to introduce a product or concept properly in the market. Thus, the break-even period might be more than 2 to 3 years or more, as against the first year in our case study. But I'm trying to keep things simple for my readers. Also, sometimes in the growth phase, more investments are required. In our case study, it's assumed that there will be an upper limit on what you might want to spend in marketing investments. Sometimes, in the case of intense competition, the marketing investments requirement could be huge. Businesses might find it difficult to make profits in this stage.

The first year in our case study is the year of inception, followed by growth. After 4 years, the business is expected to mature and thereafter it could decline. Of course, strategies by the company and external environment can play a big role in shifting the cycle.

Now let's try to understand what long-term investments were made, how much was borrowed from outside, and what value addition is expected in the next four years, and the working capital that will be required to cover the operations.. This will be derived from the forecasted balance sheet.

Projected Balance Sheet for 4 Years							
			INR Mn		YoY%		
	Year 1	Year 2	Year 3	Year 4	Y2 v/s Y1	Y3 v/s Y2	Y4 v/s Y3
Sources of Funds							
Entrepreneur's Capital							
Capital Introduced	20.0	20.0	20.0	20.0	0%	0%	0%
Add: Reserves (from P&L)	(1.4)	1.7	12.9	37.5	-221%	640%	191%
Less: Withdrawls							
Total Capital	**18.6**	**21.7**	**32.9**	**57.5**	**17%**	**51%**	**75%**
Borrowed Funds	**13.5**	**12.0**	**10.5**	**9.0**	**-11%**	**-13%**	**-14%**
Total Sources of Funds	**32.1**	**33.7**	**43.4**	**66.5**	**5%**	**29%**	**53%**
Application of Funds							
Fixed Assets	35.0	35.0	35.0	35.0	0%	0%	0%
Less: Provision for Depreciation	3.5	7.0	10.5	14.0	100%	50%	33%
Net Fixed Assets	**31.5**	**28.0**	**24.5**	**21.0**	**-11%**	**-13%**	**-14%**
Current Assets							
Cash	0.4	5.4	21.1	52.2	1369%	289%	147%
Debtors	2.3	3.2	4.5	6.3	40%	40%	40%
Less: Current Liabilities							
Creditors	1.1	1.5	1.9	2.4	40%	26%	22%
Bank Overdraft	1.0	-	-	-			

Tax Liability	-	1.4	4.8	10.6		251%	121%
Net Current Assets	**0.6**	**5.7**	**18.9**	**45.5**	**917%**	**229%**	**141%**
Total Application of Funds	**32.1**	**33.7**	**43.4**	**66.5**	**5%**	**29%**	**53%**

This is an important statement to analyse. It's a scorecard that helps a business to understand what capital was introduced initially and what value addition is expected to come in future. In the above example, a capital introduced of INR 20 Mn is likely to generate INR 37.5 Mn of cumulative profits at the end of the 4th year. Thus, INR 20 Mn invested will be almost 3 times value at end of 4 years and is expected to be INR 57.5 Mn at end of 4th year. Much of the profits will be in the form of cash. A progressive business might contest having such high value of cash in books, if it's not invested to drive further profits. But caution must be taken to ensure that the existing business is stable before driving any further investments.

To understand how debtors and creditors are calculated, let me provide you with their working notes which have gone into the planning exercise.

	Year 1	Year 2	Year 3	Year 4	
Calculation of Debtors					
Total Revenue from Portal	21.1	29.5	41.4	57.9	
1 Month revenue	1.8	2.5	3.4	4.8	a
Snack Bar Revenues	6.4	9.0	12.6	17.7	
1 Month Revenues	0.5	0.8	1.1	1.5	b
Total Outstanding Revenues	**2.3**	**3.2**	**4.5**	**6.3**	**a+ b**
	Year 1	Year 2	Year 3	Year 4	
Calculation of Creditors					
Electricity Cost	1.2	1.7	2.4	3.3	
1 Month Cost	0.1	0.1	0.2	0.3	a
Media Expenses	12.0	16.8	21.0	25.2	
1 Month Cost	1.0	1.4	1.8	2.1	b
Total Credit Available	**1.1**	**1.5**	**1.9**	**2.4**	

The last financial statement which is very critical for any business is the cash flow statement. As I had already called out earlier that 'Cash is King', it's equally more important to know how it flows during any financial period. It's important to know how much cash a business has been able to generate through its business operations and working capital program. It's important to know the investments that a business is making and how it's getting funded. The cash flow generated will always tie up with the cash/bank balance appearing in the balance sheet. Below is the projected cash flow statement of the business for 4 years.

Projected Cash Flow Statement for 4 Years							
	INR Mn				YoY%		
	Year 1	Year 2	Year 3	Year 4	Y2 v/s Y1	Y3 v/s Y2	Y4 v/s Y3
Cash from Operations							
Cash Profit (Incl. Depreciation)	2.1	6.7	14.6	28.2	223%	119%	92%
Add: Interest Payments	1.5	1.4	1.2	1.1	-12%	-11%	-13%
Add/(less) Creditors & Tax Liability	1.1	1.8	3.8	6.2	64%	112%	63%
Less:							
Add/(Less) Debtors	2.3	0.9	1.3	1.8	-60%	40%	40%
Cash from Operations	**2.4**	**8.9**	**18.4**	**33.6**	270%	106%	83%
Cash from Investing Activities							
Liquidation of Fixed Assets	-	-	-	-			
Less:							
Investment in Fixed Assets	35.0				-100%		
Cash from Investing Activities	**(35.0)**	-	-	-	**-100%**		
Cash from Financing Activities							
Capital Introduced	20.0				-100%		
Borrowings							
Long Term	15.0				-100%		
Short Term	1.0				-100%		
Less:							
Interest Payments	1.5	1.4	1.2	1.1	-12%	-11%	-13%
Repayment of Loan							
Long Term	1.5	1.5	1.5	1.5	0%	0%	0%
Short Term		1.0					
Cash from Financing Activities	**33.0**	**(3.9)**	**(2.7)**	**(2.6)**	**-112%**	**-30%**	**-6%**
Total Cash at Beginning of Year	-	0.4	5.4	21.1		1369%	289%
Total Cash Available at End of the Year	**0.4**	**5.4**	**21.1**	**52.2**	**1369%**	**289%**	**147%**

As it will be noticed, the cash flow statement basically has three parts. In a nutshell, cash flows into the business through operations, gets invested in different assets and investments and is sourced through multiple sources. Let's get into some details.

- **Cash from operations** suggests how the business was able to bring cash through its normal day-to-day transactions. It also tells us if money is stuck in certain current assets like debtors and evaluates the terms offered by creditors as can be seen in our case study above. A lower debtor and higher creditor could signal lower reliance on borrowed sources for working capital requirements.

- This cash can further be invested in creating fixed assets or other investments. This is reflected in **cash from investing activities**. If any assets are sold off, the same gets reflected here.

- Lastly, apart from the entrepreneurs or owners, cash can come from borrowed sources. Money coming and repaid to these borrowed sources or even money coming and going out from the Owners or shareholders is shown under **cash from financing activities.** In our case study, INR 20 Mn of entrepreneurs funds and INR 15 Mn of borrowed funds was utilised to create fixed assets worth INR 35 Mn. This was utilised to generate cash from normal day-to-day activities or operations worth INR 2.4 Mn in the first year and it is expected to grow to INR 33.6 Mn in the 4th year. These profits will help in repaying the borrowed funds and it is expected that the share of borrowed funds in the Balance Sheet will reduce from INR 15 Mn to INR 9 Mn by the end of the 4th year on the back of these strong operational profits. This is expected to help in reducing finance costs or interest costs every year. Apart from the above fixed assets, there is no other major commitment or investments for 4 years. This will result in cash availability increasing from INR 0.4 Mn in the first year to INR 52.2 Mn in the 4th year. If cash flow is so strong, the business can decide to repay the balance loan in one shot and save on some interest costs.

Now this tells a lot on how cash will be earned and will get utilised. A potential investor, owner and lender can use this to evaluate the impact of different business activities on cash. Such statements can guide an investor or lender in taking decisions related to investing or lending. The last thing that I wish to cover is DCF and IRR on the project. This will facilitate in evaluating the plan. We already covered it in the funds management section. Now it's time to assess the same in this case study. The cost of acquiring funds is kept at 10% to analyse the present value of future cash flows using the DCF method of valuation. Ideally this should cover all stages of the product life cycle till the product matures. This can help in assessing the feasibility of the investments.

	Year 0	Year 1	Year 2	Year 3	Year 4	Present Value of Future Cash Flows (DCF Valuation)	IRR
Cash Flows/Profits (in INR Mn)	(35.0)	2.1	6.7	14.6	28.2	2.4	12%

With this, I conclude the case study on planning. Planning forms the basis of proper controlling and that is what we'll see in the next section. A properly planned business will not find difficulty in addressing the variances which one comes across when monitoring it against the planned results.

Clarification on Calculating GST

GST is calculated as a mark-up to the selling price. However, in this case study, I have used the mark-down approach. This is only for the ease of readers to understand things in a simple way. But in reality, if you have the final selling price, GST should be calculated as a mark-up, as final selling price always has GST. Thus, if selling price is INR 25, then GST will be INR 25 divided by (1+18% GST rate) or 25/(1+18%), which will be INR 21.2. In our example, it's calculated as INR 20.5 as it was calculated directly on selling price of INR 25 which is (INR 25 multiplied by (1–18% GST rate) or INR25*82%.

V. Long-Term Planning for Individuals and Personal Branding

Operational elements related to controlling and recording earning and spends and cash flow projection are already covered in the accounting and funds management section. However, what's not covered is how to chart out a long-term plan that can facilitate building a personal brand and thereby helps in evaluating expected financial implications in the future. Personally speaking, this can be a good exercise for aspiring entrepreneurs and professionals. It can, however, be used by everyone to analyse where they stand and what needs to be done to achieve a particular financial objective.

Personal Branding

This is an important concept concerning individuals and could be of great value to any person trying to create a unique position about herself/himself. Personal branding is a practice used for marketing oneself and an individual's own career. However, I would like to caution my readers out here. It doesn't mean that a person with no good substance promoting herself/himself might fly down easily. It might give visibility for a short time but, in the long term, it will fizzle out.

Just like any marketing mix has a product, price, promotion, or advertising and a good supply chain through which the product or service is offered at multiple places, a strong personal brand should start with a strong individual. She/he must be a person of substance or have a strong expertise in any specific subject matter. While having substance is good, if it's not advertised or promoted, not many other individuals recognise it. Also, it shouldn't be confined within a specific boundary but an attempt should be made to increase its visibility by branding it across a wide geography as much as possible. All of this pays off in fetching a good compensation in the form of fees, salaries, profits, or any other mode of incentive.

This is a long-term exercise and a lot of investment could go into learning and studying different things. Ideally, a person's personal branding starts right from the time she/he leaves their school and enters a university or college or any other higher educational institution. It theoretically ends when a person retires or stops working but in practice, I feel it still continues. I would refrain from including schools as schools are the breeding grounds of gaining knowledge and knowledge has to be attained wholeheartedly without any consideration for competition. I'm not an expert in personal branding but I guess one needs to break their careers into different phases of their life and set a goal for themselves. This should then be properly monitored. Below is what I would call a guideline based on a random example that I picked up, which one can use (and make changes) to identify their goals. This should just be considered guidance and anyone is free to modify it as per their requirements. The accomplishment of these goals also translates into monetary rewards. The below exercise only considers the commercial aspect and that probably is also its drawback.

	Phase 1	Phase 2	Phase 3	Phase 4
Age Group	17–24 years	24–35 years	35 years – 58 years	58 – 60 years
Phase	Education phase	Learning and growth phase	Maturity phase	Winding up
Goals	Develop a career in Finance	Kickstarting and growing career	Stabilising and value addition or starting afresh with new venture	Transitioning things
Objective	Consider studying different professional courses in Accounting like CA/CMA or MBA in Finance	Take a job at a good organisation or institution (incl. educational) or start with a samll enterprise of own to learn trade/profession	Move to senior leadership roles in any organisation or institutions or become a leading force by starting a new venture	Mentor successors and people
Proposed Actions	Enrol for a course after evaluating different options	Find a good job/ start a small venture that suits your career interest	Aim to get a senior level leadership role or start a venture using the funds saved in phase 2	Guide people who could be potential successors and others who would be contributing to your activities

	Develop a working and expert knowledge on the subject	Continous learning the trade/profession and keep focus on it	Leverage learnings to drive more value addition to organisation or own venture	Create a learning ecosystem in which people can provide a healthy value addition
	Develop skills that might be required to kickstart the career through internship	Find avenues to grow career/venture on own merits	Learn or develop different things that impact your work	Impart skills required to do job and be an advisor
	Instil discipline to clear rigorous examinations	Contribute to society by giving back in some form	Try becoming a role model for others and contribute to society by giving back	Provide ideas that can help in contributing to society in creative different meaningful ways
Anticipated Result	Finish up with a certificate or master's	Continously move ahead and grow in your career/venture	Senior leader or businessperson/ professional	Retirement
Promotions Required	Building a personal profile on skills developed and knowledge gained	Creating a career profile and getting in touch with intermediaries like HR consultants, brokers, agents to create visibility	Networking more with people or undertaking a full fledged promotion just like any other business	not applicable
Geography	Not applicable	Local and country	Country and international	not applicable
Monetary Expectations	Not applicable	Growing salaries/ fees/profits or saving for a venture	Higher salaries or quest to earn bigger fees and profits	Security for future years through stable income in form of pension or investment income etc.

The format given above is an example of how a finance professional might create personal branding for herself/himself. As mentioned above, the format is not so relevant. One can create their own version. The definition of the age group might be completely different for different individuals. The example is just a guideline to help you create a systematic approach and measure results against your anticipated goals. However, one thing that I wish to stress is the fact that this process requires regular monitoring of your goals. If your plan requires a revision, the same should be incorporated. Priorities change many a times in an individual's course of life.

Section 5

Controlling

A sound business plan will materialise and provide value only when it's properly executed. The entrepreneur or management always endeavour to work as per the plans. In order to achieve the planned results, certain activities especially related to capital expenditure, asset acquisition, people hiring, marketing spends or procurement planning is done well in advance. Therefore, it becomes highly critical that one brings in the required set of revenues to achieve the plans. At the same time, in regular day-to-day activities, care must be taken that leakages are to the minimum, if they cannot be completely avoided. Also, as funds are arranged in advance to achieve the revenue plans, it's equally important to have a good control over internal and external sources of finance. If some changes are required, then they should be implemented. It's critical to have good control over the cash flow statement that we saw in the case study in the planning section. All this forms part of the controlling exercise. But before venturing any further, controls are not possible without an adequate monitoring or reporting process in place. Let's first touch upon reporting before we move any further with controlling.

I. Reporting

Imagine a cricket match where M.S. Dhoni is hitting sixes and fours and there is no one to tell how much the team has scored and how much Dhoni has scored in his personal capacity. Or imagine a tennis match where Roger Federer and Rafael Nadal are playing neck to neck, but no one knows the points scored by each of them. Will it be possible to assess the performance and decide a winner? The answer is a simple no. Just like you need scorecards to track the performance in sports, similarly, in business or in personal life, you need to have a monitoring mechanism or a scorecard that tracks how you're doing. This is fulfilled by the reporting exercise.

Individuals can refer to the tool that I have provided in the accounting section. If this is maintained and monitored on a regular basis, this will be more than enough to cover your needs. However, for businesses, this is not the case, including small businesses.

As I have been reiterating multiple times, a business enters into multiple transactions during a period. It's important to track these transactions. Accounting helps in serving that purpose. But it would be great if this can be summarised in a simple format and can be provided on a daily basis.

A lot of ERP systems available today help in serving this purpose. As soon as invoices are raised, they are visible inside the reporting tools, which are linked with these ERPs. This can happen instantly or maybe at a gap of a day. This depends on the data complexity and the type of tools the business employs.

Today, every business feels a need to track their performance on a daily basis. Before the end of day, they would be interested to know the revenues earned by them. This helps them to be more proactive and take appropriate decisions. Some of the reports that can be of great help to any business can be as follows:

1. Daily production/sales report
2. Product level/Customer level reports
3. Stock report
4. Business activity report (like customer trips done, marketing activities status, project progress report) monthly expense statement
5. Headcount report, especially for mid-size and large businesses

The list can be much more depending on the business requirements, but the above gives a gist of reports that a business can be looking at.

These reports would be more meaningful if they are properly summarised and key details are provided like how the growth is looking, where the growth is coming from, whether regular business activity levels have increased or dropped, and many more. These exercises would assess the performance using reports, analyse variances, suggest a course of action and monitor the actions taken. We've seen a lot of it in planning. We'll see the other part when we cover controlling.

Summarised below is how businesses typically tend to make intelligent use of data, which includes reporting as an integral part of it.

Now coming back to the controls, a controlling exercise can be broadly divided into three parts viz.

1. Transactional controls
2. Business controls
3. Funding controls

II. Transactional Controls

Every day, any business will enter into numerous transactions. All of this is not covered by the entrepreneur or the management who are entrusted with the task of running the business. It's delegated to different employees within the organisation or at times to an outsourcing agency. With limited resources at its disposal, it's critical that there is a track of these activities. These activities can be broadly related to procurement, hiring, or sales. While all these activities are always recorded in accounting, it's crucial that before the recording takes place, certain processes are followed to ensure that the activity occurs in a proper and transparent manner. If it is left loose, it is will only create chaos. The reconciliation process, which is normally followed between two different parties to settle accounts, might create a gridlock if things are not properly controlled at a transactional level. It can also result in frauds and leakages.

So let's understand the different types of transactional controls.

Procurement Controls

As called out in the planning section, a business does a tactical plan every year. Once this gets finalised, a budget is given to every department that is responsible to carry out the activities. For many of these departments, including the purchase department, they need to procure different things to carry out the planned activities. As mentioned earlier, the quantum of transactions can be huge. One can do a post mortem exercise to check if the purchasing activities are in line with what was expected and whether the requisite stock has arrived and has been consumed. But, at times, this might be too late if there are inefficient elements within the system. The damage might already have occurred by that time. Sometimes, it's not just the fraud or inefficiency, but miscommunication might also lead to over or under procurement of things, which might also be harmful for the organisation. However, if people responsible for the activities are subject to a specific set of controls and follow a proper process, much of these leakages and wastages can be avoided.

Organisations or businesses can have different approaches, but the basic principles on procurement should ideally be the same.

As mentioned earlier, every department, including those in charge of purchasing, are given a specific budget. The first thing that these departments need to adhere to is that their activities are aligned to these budgets. They need to remain within the budgets and the entrepreneur or management needs to track these activities. There should be some dedicated individual representing the interest of the business. This person acts as the custodian of the business and ensures the process is running smoothly. Ideally, this person should be part of the finance function. In case of small businesses, this can be the finance person in charge of the total business. There must be regular stock taking of the different procurement activities and it should be part of the reporting exercise. Proper communication needs to flow to the relevant individuals in charge of procurement to make them aware of how much they have spent against their budgets.

While maintaining a proper tracker related to all purchases is important, another critical area that needs to be managed is the procurement process. There must be a proper process or channel through which individuals responsible for procuring can commit their purchases of goods or services to third parties or vendors, on behalf of the business. There should be a written document through which such commitments are made. This can be called a **purchase order (PO)**.

This process of getting a PO should ideally start with a purchase request, which needs to be properly assessed and approved by different authorities within the business. There needs to be authority given to people to sign purchase requests of certain value.

For example, purchase requests of a small value can be created by the requestor directly with or without the financial controller's approval. Irrespective of whether the finance controller approves such small requests or not, they should still track these orders.

Similarly, purchase requests for a certain value, which are not big and not too small, relative to the size of the business, can be approved by the manager in charge of the division and finance controller. For high-value purchase requests, these requests should be approved by senior level management, controllers, and, at times, for large organisations the CFOs or finance directors.

There are many enterprise packages available which have the procurement process imbedded in their ERPs or suites. An organisation can utilise these services to develop their procurement process. Alternatively, a lot of cloud-based applications are available, which can be integrated into an organisation's system to develop such a process. An integrated process helps in simultaneous record keeping while conducting purchasing activities. This is ideally the practice followed by most of the business these days.

The creation of the purchase order is summarised below.

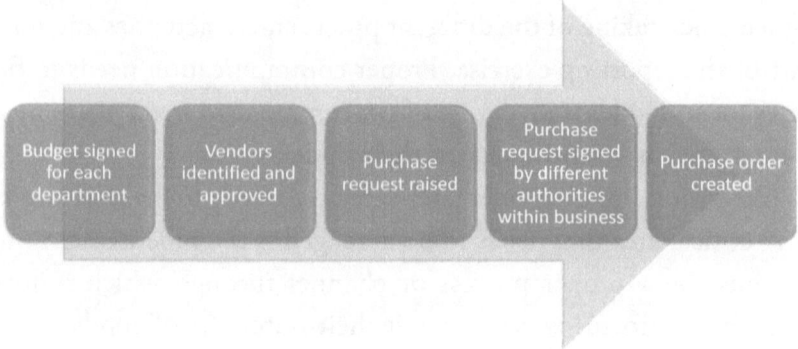

To facilitate the decision making by different authorities, it's also essential to understand whether buying the inventory for trading or production makes economic sense. The following guidelines should help in deciding to buy or not.

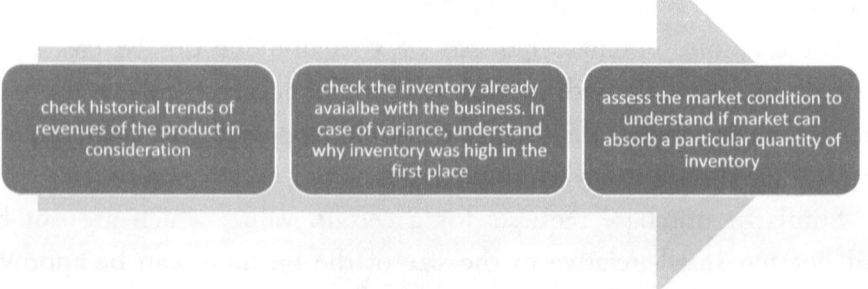

Once the PO is created, the process of procurement should begin. As soon as the goods arrive or services are performed, it should be properly receipted by the person in charge of procuring. Whenever, goods or services are received by the business, it creates a liability of the business to pay money. Remember the principle of accounting that mentions that every transaction has two elements. The time at which the goods or services are received should be the time when it's considered that the terms are met by the supplier and the same should be recorded in the accounting systems as an expense. Most of the enterprise packages or applications would directly treat such receipts of goods or services as an expense. Care should be taken to ensure that all goods and services related to a period are properly received in the system so that all expenses related to the period can be recorded. Where it's not possible to make a receipt of services as some documentation wasn't available, then proper accruals need to be created for such expenses. If goods are to be returned due to some issues, proper debit notes need to be raised by the business to the vendors.

The following guidelines enunciate the process that needs to be carried out after a purchase order is created.

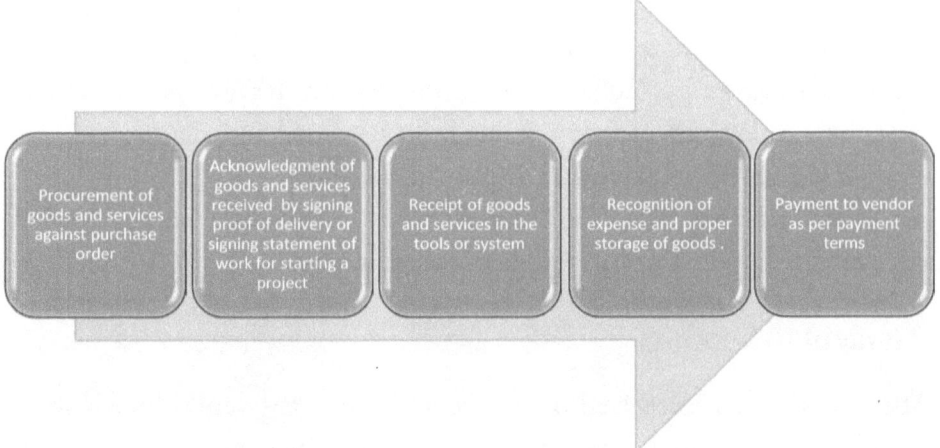

Documents to prove that delivery was made of goods or services:

Proof of Delivery

When goods are received, the customer should sign that they have received the goods. This is proof that the goods are delivered.

Statement of Work (SOW)

A document used in project management that defines the scope of the project, timelines, pricing and other conditions associated with the project and is binding on the vendor and the customer to deliver and pay for services or goods according to the terms agreed in the SOW.

Proper care must be taken to audit or check these receipts on a regular basis to ensure that the business has benefitted from those goods or services.

There must be proper documentation on receipt of goods or services that is agreed upon by both the vendor and the customer. At times, the physical verification of goods available as stocks in the warehouse must be done. In the case of projects or service contracts, the milestones must be agreed in the SOW by both the vendor and the customer. Let's take an example. Let's assume a business enters into an agreement with a vendor to develop a mobile application. Project milestones are defined with the vendor. As per one of the milestones, if the vendor and the customer agree that the product is ready to be tested, than 50% of the project will be considered as complete. If the project reaches this stage and both agree, then it becomes a liability for the business to pay 50% of the agreed amount. It's always advisable to have these milestones properly defined, documented and signed or agreed by both the parties to avoid any dispute in future.

Sometimes there are some other evidences to showcase that the services were received like a **third party verification report.**

Payment to Vendors

After the goods are received or services delivered, the vendor needs to be paid. Normally, as mentioned earlier, there are credit terms agreed with most of the vendors. Care should be taken to pay as per the agreed terms. This is important for working capital management. Care should also be taken to pay on time as the trust on which these terms were offered will remain intact only if the money is paid properly on time. This, ideally, should be the responsibility of the people within the accounting department who are responsible for these cash flow related activities and its recording. However, proper coordination needs to be done with the procurement function while making such payments.

In the case of the procurement related to goods for either trading or manufacturing or as spares, it must be ensured that proper controls are maintained for the same. This is also referred to as **inventory control** but I would classify it under the broad area of procurement controls.

Proper records need to be maintained when the goods come into the warehouse and when they leave the warehouse. There must be records maintained for receipts and the issue of goods.

All goods once brought in, whether they are raw materials, spares or finished goods, should be properly stored. There must be a proper physical facility to take care of the same; this is called a warehouse. There must be a proper layout in which the goods are stored. The arrangement should be such that when the goods are stored, ideally, it should be easy to pull them out of the inventory when required by the business. This depends on the approach the business wishes to take with respect to the storage of inventory. A business may follow an approach where it will utilise first those goods which come in first. This is called the first in first out (FIFO) approach. On the contrary, at times the business may decide to utilise the goods coming last to be utilised first. This is called the last in first out (LIFO) approach.

Typically, most of the business use the FIFO approach of maintaining stock or at least try to practice a FIFO approach. To follow any specific approach, the people or the entrepreneur maintaining such stock should maintain a good discipline. Inspite of this, at times, it's not possible to maintain a specific approach on stock keeping, maybe due to lack of funds or shortage of resources or the sheer size which makes it humanly possible.

In such cases, a proper physical count needs to be maintained on regular basis. If required, proper rectification needs to be done. In the process, any loss identified should be provided in the books of accounts as a loss. Either the entrepreneur or someone delegated needs to maintain this process on a regular basis.

Personally, I think FIFO is one of the best ways of managing stocks, but in certain industries it might be important to follow LIFO. But inspite of FIFO or LIFO, maintaining stocks is a painstaking task, and many times, inspite of all care, it might just be practically not possible to have a specific approach that can be followed. I therefore always suggest that a weighted average method of assessing the costs should be used if you do not have a robust mechanism for maintaining stocks using the FIFO or the

LIFO approach. But this is my personal opinion and one has to apply their diligence before deciding on a specific approach.

Reconciliation of Procurement with Consumption

The last part of this exercise relates to the reconciliation of procurement with consumption. At the end of every month or quarter, a reconciliation of physical inventory needs to be done with consumption. This can go a long way in reducing any possible leakages. This is applicable to all businesses that buy some or the other goods for trading, manufacturing or as spares. This also helps in identifying process efficiencies or leakages.

	Units
Opening Stock (of Raw Material/Finished Goods/WIP/Spares)	xx
Add: Purchases	xx
Less: Issues (For Production or Sales or Other Use)	xx
Available or Closing Stock	**xx**

People Controls

While procurement control deals with third parties, people controls deal with an internal set of people or employees of the organisation. The process will be the same principally. Like procurement, it should start with the budgeting process. At the time of planning, an assessment must be made about the people required to carry out the activities in different functions. Once this is agreed, the entrepreneur should start the hiring process in the case of small businesses. However, in large organisations, a process like procurement is followed. A request must be made by the person who needs people. This should be reviewed by human resources (HR) and a finance manager/controller and only after approval should the recruiting process start. In the case of people, HR and finance is typically the custodian of hiring and budget controls. In the case of high profile jobs, the entrepreneur or management is directly involved.

An arm of HR function which deals with engaging and getting the talent for the organisation will get involved in identifying people who could be better suited for the job. After a short selection, the pay scale must be decided. Ideally, there needs to be controls in place which outline the salary scale for different type of levels in the organisation. The level at which an employee will be recruited depends on the complexity of the job and the role of the employee, along with her/his experience. Budgeting and actual pay need to be aligned to this scale. Thus, there will be a pay scale for entry level employees and a different pay for junior officers, middle management, and top management. Care should be taken to finalise a candidate's salary as per the requisite scale. Care also should be taken to select candidates at the same level, which was provided in the budgeting, unless compelled to act otherwise to tap a potentially strong talent, which again should be subject to an exceptional approval process.

Sometimes organisations offer perquisites in the form of joining bonuses or they take care of your relocation expenses. In those cases, one should ensure that the perquisites are properly budgeted.

Certain salaries are variable in nature and depend on the revenues generated. These are typically sales function related assignments. Here, it becomes critical to ensure that proper targets are given in line with the business plans and it should be ensured that revenues are credited to respective individuals in line with their actual performance. For large organisations, a special compensation function operates to take care of these requirements.

As a control point, the regular assessment of employees needs to be done by their managers along with HR mostly on a yearly or a half-yearly basis. Also, the entrepreneur or management or their delegation needs to review the overall headcount performance regularly. In case of changing market dynamics, which present higher opportunities, care should be taken to invest or vice versa.

The overall hiring and review process can be summarised as below.

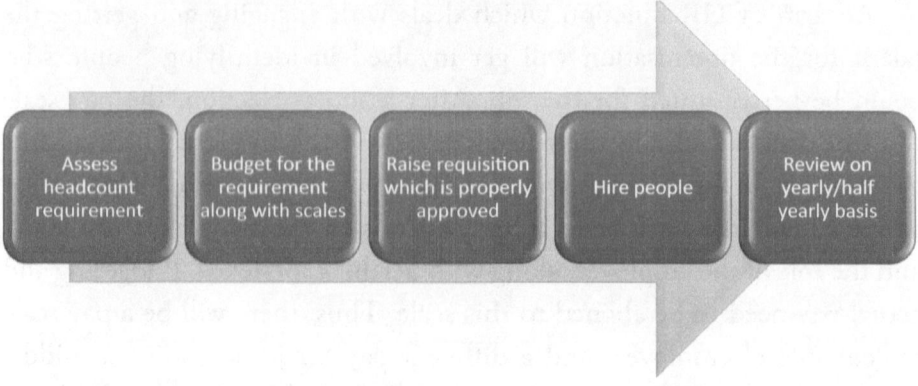

At the end of every month or bimonthly in some countries, pay needs to be paid to the employee's bank account or through a cheque. Care must be taken to calculate the pay properly. Before paying off the final salary, proper checks need to be performed to ensure that the right pay is going to the right employee. Also, it needs to be ensured that the employee is working for the company. The leave that an employee is eligible must be properly factored into the salary. In case the employee is leaving, a proper final settlement needs to be calculated and the pay ideally should be held for a temporary short period till the final settlement is worked out. There could be instances when an employee might have taken advances and in the final settlement, those have to be taken out, or sometimes if the advances are huge, then the employee might have to pay the company, which needs to be recovered. Care must be taken that the employee gets the salary on the agreed date, which typically is the end of the month. A delay can create panic, or the employee might lose trust, leading to the loss of potentially good people.

In case of a bonus payment, incentives or rewards, care should be taken to pay employees who were eligible to receive them. The payment should be in line with the terms agreed either in the beginning or as revised for employees from time to time, or at times in line with the guidelines which are set by the organisation.

Retirement benefits should be properly credited to the employee's account. Proper provisioning needs to be done for different retirement benefits that the employee is eligible to receive at the time of their retirement. Much of these require actuarial valuation and need to be correctly assessed.

To attract talent, the salary structures are designed to give either flexibility in terms of what pay the employee wants to allocate for a specific part of her/his salary. For example, an employer can give an option to the employee to decide on the house rent allowance component of his/her salary, subject to a certain limit. Similarly, an employee can be given an option to decide on the leave travel allowance component that they wish to define for each year. While giving these benefits, an employer needs to collect requisite proof of the house rent paid by the employee, a quantum of the house loan paid by the employee or the amount incurred on travelling along with the proper receipts for the purpose of taxation applicable in a particular country. A proper system needs to be put in place to collect such documentation on time and care should be taken to store and record it for future purposes. Statutorily, records must be maintained for a specific period of time by law and proper provisioning needs to be there to store them.

Tax needs to be properly deducted as per the provisions laid down in the income tax or direct laws of the country and the same needs to be deposited to the government on time. A delay in paying these amounts could result in penalties, which could be an unwarranted cost for the business.

Proper pay slips need to be dispatched to the employees at the end of each month. This should clearly provide all the details of salary like the base salary, house rent allowance, other perquisites, tax deducted, retirement benefits deducted, and the number of days for which the salary was calculated.

The above is ideally the responsibility of the payroll function in a mid or large-size organisation. The same can be summarised as below.

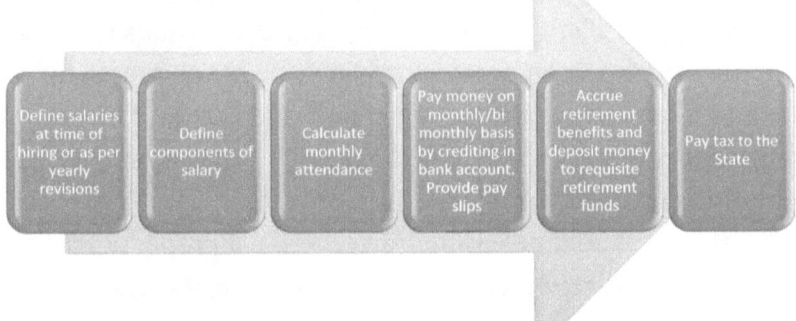

Define salaries at time of hiring or as per yearly revisions → Define components of salary → Calculate monthly attendance → Pay money on monthly/bi monthly basis by crediting in bank account. Provide pay slips → Accrue retirement benefits and deposit money to requisite retirement funds → Pay tax to the State

A pay slip could have the following format.

Nishka Toys				
Plot no. 10, Vasant Vihar, Surat, Gujarat				
Name of the Employee	XXXX	Employee Provident Fund A/c No.		Xxxxx
Employee Number	XXXX	Employee PAN no.		Xxxxx
Period	1ˢᵗ Sep to 30 Sep 2017			
No. of Days Attended	30			
	Amount INR			Amount INR
Receipts		Deductions		
Basic Salary	10,000	Provident Fund		1,200
House Rent Allowance	5,000	Income Tax Paid		–
Medical Reimbursement	1,250	Other Deductions		–
Others	1,250			
Leave Travel Allowance				
Bonus/Incentives	2,500			
Rewards				
Gross Total	20,000			1,200
Net Pay	INR 18,800 (Rupees Eighteen Thousand Eight Hundered Only)			
Prepared by		Signed by		

A proper headcount needs to be done in a timely manner and assessed against the budgets. This helps in keeping a track of the people working with the organisation.

Sales Control

A transaction on sales should be recorded and recognised only when a transfer in ownership of goods moves from the seller to the buyer. This basically means that significant risks in ownership of goods or services are transferred to the buyer in return for a consideration, especially money, which is agreed upon mutually between both the parties. The price of the goods or services plays a key role in determining the amount that can be realised from sales.

Before that, it should be ensured that there is a proper purchase order or acknowledgement received by the business from the customer, which provides an agreement or commitment on the part of the customer to buy a certain amount of goods or services, at a certain price which is agreed by both the parties. An incomplete acknowledgement or commitment can be a risk and the process of sales should not start in such cases or it might create unnecessary risks for the business.

Also, there must be a reasonable assurance that the payment for the same can be received from the customer. If the amount of money from a sale is not expected to come, then the transaction cannot be considered a sale. These transactions could be subject to fraud and should not be recognised as revenue in the books of accounts. If at all anything is credited, the same should be reversed. This could entail a loss if goods or services have already moved out from the business. There should be proper due diligence in the form of fraud controls or credit checks to ensure that the amount can be realised from potential sales transactions. These controls can be in any form, but it's important that they are put in place.

As mentioned above, price plays a key role in determining the value of the sales transaction. Care must be taken to ensure that the right price is communicated to the buyer. Once a price is communicated and accepted by the buyer, it is then legally binding on the business to sell to the buyer at that price. It's an essence of a contract of sale. It means that if someone proposes to sell something at a particular price, which is agreed by the buyer, then a contract comes in place. Proper terms need to be defined in the standard terms and conditions

The price at which sales happens is therefore very important and only a few entrusted people within the organisation should have the authority to make changes to it. They too should be subject to checks and balances. In modern times, prices for goods or services are determined by the management or by the entrepreneur and are locked in ERP. At the time of the invoicing process or the quoting process, the system picks up that particular price while providing a quote to the customer. Proper systemic checks must be in place to ensure that invoices pick up the correct prices. An ideal way would be to check random orders of the previous day on daily basis to see if transactions are occurring at proper prices. This can help in avoiding any potentially big leakage. This is very true for modern e-commerce businesses.

In order to remain competitive and win large orders, businesses might have to offer an aggressive price, which might be much lower than the approved price. This should be subject to a proper proposal, which should be assessed financially by either the management, the entrepreneur or a finance delegate of the management, and only after their approval, it should be communicated as a quote to the customer.

In the case of sales to intermediaries like distributors, retailers and resellers, proper checks should be done to ensure that the prices remain sacrosanct and in line with the terms agreed with such distributors, resellers or retailers. For example, if a business is selling a consumer product which is sold through a retail channel, there should be internal audits to ensure that the distributor or wholesaler through whom it passes to the retail channel is selling at agreed terms. In case they must pass some benefits like additional rebates, it must be ensured that it's been passed properly.

Many times, additional incentives in the form of rebates, concessions or discounts are offered after the invoicing happens, which in most cases are settled by credit notes or sometimes by payment to the customers. A **credit note** is a document which acknowledges a liability to pay something as agreed by the business mostly to its customers. It is settled by reducing the outstanding amount from the respective customer. The credit note is the document that gives the authorisation to reduce the outstanding amount.

The calculation of rebates, concessions or discounts should be done in line with the agreed terms. The volumes against which such rebates are offered should be properly checked and should be in line with the orders invoiced by the business. After proper assessment, the same needs to be recorded in the debtors ledger. This will go to reduce the amount which the debtors are supposed to pay to the business. Much of these rebates or concessions go to the intermediaries. Most of the business operates with intermediaries. Sometimes, when the business deals with the customers or consumers directly, at times, it can offer such discounts to its high-profile customers, who are like loyal customers and buy regularly. Proper care must be taken to assess the value of such rebates at the end of the period and should be provided properly in the form of provisions or accruals in the books of accounts. After all, calculations are done, and after the agreed period, the rebates should be either paid out or a credit note should be made that reduces the outstanding amount from the customer.

Like the procurement process, a business would offer credit terms to the customer. After the end of the credit terms, money needs to be collected from the business on time. This has a direct impact on cash flow. If the amount is received late, a business might have to borrow working capital funds and this could entail additional costs for them. A diligent process should be there to collect the amount in time. For large organisations, this would also mean putting people to collect money. Similarly, they would have separate people doing credit assessment of their customers. For small organisations the accountant and the entrepreneur might be carrying out this exercise. A proper review should be done every month ideally to assess the amount pending from debtors and the quantum of money which is held for long time. If it requires addressing some concerns of the customers, proper steps need to be taken to take care of the same.

For small organisations, proper control can be kept, by either the entrepreneur or his entrusted accountant taking care of pricing, conducting checks on invoicing and collection. But in the case of large organisations, there needs to be a proper delegation of responsibilities. The pricing should be proposed by the marketing organisation which needs to be approved by the finance function and only then it should be locked into the invoicing tools. Accounts receivable and rebate calculation should be done separately. There has to be a controlling mechanism through which there can be an assurance that the contract of sale has taken place. For large organisations dealing in complex products or services, there should be a separate revenue assurance function taking care of the timing of revenue recognition.

Sometimes, goods sold must be returned due to some quality or compatibility issue which was not possible to assess at the time of sale. In such a case, returns should be properly authorized before taking them back. Again, for small businesses, this is straightforward, but this needs to be approved by the management's delegate, who is a finance controller. Proper credit note or refund should thereafter be dispatched to the customer. In some cases, it's not possible to assess the returns as the business is legally obliged to take returns. The nature of the business is such that it must accept goods returned by customer. In such cases, taking the historical records, a provision which is an estimate of the likely impact because of returns needs to be made in the books of accounts. When the final impact comes, the estimate is dropped down against the actual value. This will ensure that the impact is taken in the period in which the sales took pace. This should be reviewed on a regular basis to consider the changing dynamics of the business.

As mentioned above, many times, the business sells to intermediaries. These intermediaries will thereafter sell to the end customer or consumer. In such a situation, it is important to note the quantum of stocks available at these intermediaries. Sometimes, in the quest to record high sales volume, there could be more invoicing done to a few or select intermediaries which might not have the capability to push it forward to end customers or consumers. As their money is locked up in such inventory, they might not buy in the near future or even worse, they might stop paying money to the business. Here it's very critical to measure the inventory at these intermediaries and proper review should be done on a periodic basis, maybe a monthly basis, to check the inventory built up. Every intermediary would sell a certain stock on a daily basis or weekly basis. The average sales of a particular period should be considered to express inventory in terms of no. (number) of days of sales or no. of weeks of sales.

Keeping certain days of inventory is considered normal. If the inventory is lower or exceeds these levels, the same should be replenished by invoicing to these intermediaries or, if needed, at times, pulling out the inventory of stocks which are not considered or expected to be sold at these intermediaries. Over selling to intermediaries will put financial strain on the intermediary and it will stop doing business with you in the future.

The intermediaries normally sell to the end consumers or customers. They are critical for the success for most businesses. Proper help needs to be given to them whenever required to push sales to end customers/consumers.

Average daily sales= (Total sales for say 3 months/6 months) / (3 months/6 months)

No. of days of stock = Total stock at intermediaries / Average daily sales to that intermediary

It's always advisable to do a special audit of such intermediaries to check the situation at the ground level against what appears in records. Significant variation should be brought to notice, and actions need to be taken wherever required. For example: An intermediary might have sufficient inventory, but most of it is getting expired. Typically, the margins offered to the intermediary should cover such losses, but sometimes, a few stocks are dumped to such an intermediary which looks quite impossible to sell. In such cases, care should be taken to pull out such stocks back from these intermediaries. There is always a chance that if not done, such an intermediary might not take the risk again to build up stock of new products. However, the business needs to apply proper diligence before taking any action.

The tracker below can help in assessing stocks at intermediaries. This is done on a monthly basis. This can be done for quarter or year as well.

Monthly Inventory Control at Distributor ABC Company						
	A	B	C	D=B+A-C	E=C/30 days	F=D/E
	Invoiced by the Business	Opening Stock at Intermediary	Sold by the Intermediary	Closing Stock at Intermediary	Average Daily Sales by Intermediary	Stock (In No. of Days)
Product A						
Product B						
Total						

The chart below describes the sales process.

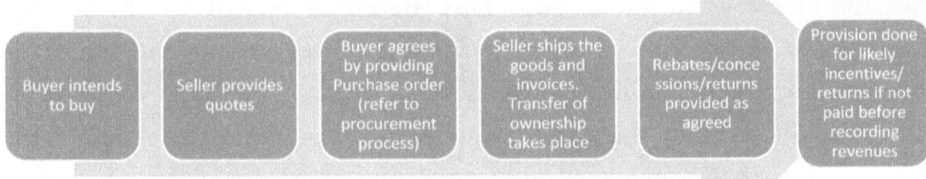

III. Business Controls

The transactional controls primarily help in protecting the assets of the company. They are the basic controls which any business needs to have. They help in avoiding leakages and ensure that transactions happen in a transparent manner. While transactional controls are important, it's also critical to ensure that the business is running efficiently as per the business plan set across by it. It's important to analyse if the assets are being productively utilised and driving sufficient revenues and profits. There are many resources already committed in advance to meet a specific business objective. It therefore becomes important that plans are properly reviewed and monitored on a regular basis. Proper variance analysis need to be done and wherever required corrective actions need to be taken. The broad areas where such monitoring and controls are required, relates to production of goods or services, sales and overall operating expenses. Controls around these areas are referred to as **business controls**.

Production or Service Delivery Related Controls

In case of manufacturing, capital expenditure needs to be incurred to procure an asset which can be in the form of a factory, a plant or machinery. Sometimes a company can decide to go with outsourcing partners as well. This depends on the volume which the business plans to offer in the market. If the volumes are such that it makes more sense to incur capital expenditure, it's important to ensure that the production coming from these assets are driving the respective volume of goods, which are required to meet the potential demand. It's always advisable that a proper report is made of the daily production. This should be monitored against the expected or planned production. If the daily production trend indicates that production is behind, proper actions need to be taken to bring it on track. Sometimes, the actual volumes driven from an asset might be much less than the expected volumes from such assets. Proper checks and maintenance need to be put in place to facilitate driving towards expected volumes. Sometimes, it might not be possible to get requisite volumes inspite of all actions taken to drive volumes. In such cases, the contracts with vendors ideally should provide for replacement of such assets with new ones. Not having such kind of guarantee can expose a business to a considerable risk.

Related to the above risk is the topic of insurance. Sometimes the asset procured could be vulnerable to fire, accidents, theft or a natural calamity. Adequate insurance needs to be taken to cover these risks so that a business does not get into a cash flow problem in case of unforeseen circumstances.

There must be proper control of the man-hours spent on operating assets. This can also go in explaining variances. While obtaining asset is one thing, care must be taken that adequate infrastructure is in place for operation of those assets. This can be in the form of electricity or maintenance. It must be ensured that proper supply of electricity is always available. Sometimes, this could entail setting an additional asset in the form of a captive power plant to meet the power requirements. This should also be subject to the same review as any other asset.

The asset requires raw materials to get the production of finished goods. The raw materials are processed inside the machine and finally the finished product comes into existence. Thus, two important elements to recognise out here are raw materials and processing activities. There are costs associated with raw material procurement and processing. Let's touch upon these costs.

Raw Material Costs

The materials that are required to produce the finished products are procured typically from a third party vendor. A lot of money is spent or invested to get the materials, which are then transformed to a different form. The quantum of material required is based on the planned sales and inventory policy that the business wishes to maintain. Each finished unit would require different materials in different proportion to get in final shape.

Let's take a simple example of tea. It requires water, tea powder, sugar, ginger and milk in certain proportions to make a cup of tea. The same goes for production of goods. Of course this will be much more complex than making tea. But one needs to understand the principle. The quantum of material required to produce one unit of product needs to be properly assessed and accordingly materials should be procured.

The quantum of raw material consumed against the estimated consumption needs to be properly evaluated. This is critical as it helps in understanding the variance. Typically, the variance could occur due to higher or lower consumption than planned. This can be further explained by higher or lower production or it can be due to better efficiencies which can be a result of better utilisation of raw material, lesser leakages and wastages. This should be assessed in a certain format which I call input output analysis. The following would be the components of input output analysis.

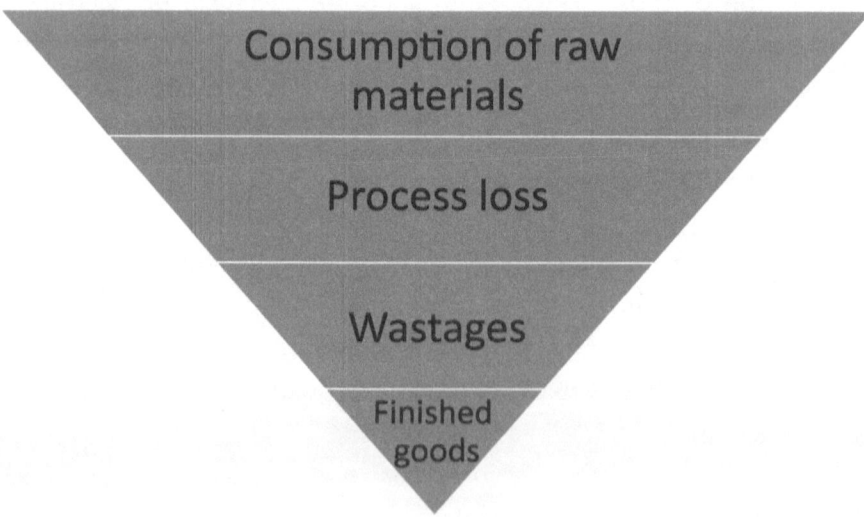

The elements of input output analysis that needs to be assessed a daily, monthly or quarterly basis should be as follows:

- **Consumption of raw materials** – In order to manufacture a unit of finished goods, certain raw materials in different quantity are required. As against the actual units of production, the consumption needs to be assessed against the standard consumption or estimated consumption. Thus, if in order to manufacture say a unit of toy, you need cotton, dyes and cloth in certain proportion; then in order to manufacture say 100 toys you would require 100 times of those quantities. Now this estimated quantity should be measured against the actual consumption.

— **Process loss** – During the process of manufacturing, certain losses occur as some material has to be discarded or some material gets lost due to its natural form. For example, petrol starts evaporating once it starts getting exposed to air. It must be assessed how much of raw material gets converted into finished goods. Example: in order to manufacture a toy 300 gms of raw material might go in, but in the end 250 grams of finished goods eventually would come out. This process loss can be different for different kinds of business. The complexities could be different for each business.

— **Wastages** – During the manufacture, certain unwanted products get manufactured. There is always a possibility of human error or unforeseen errors. There should be a proper assessment of this based on some studies or experience and the same should be provided for. This should be assessed against actual faulty production.

The above kind of analysis lays the groundwork for understanding the monetary impact which is also referred to as cost variance. There are two parts in cost variance. In the first part, we try to assess the efficiency with which the material was used. In the second part we try to understand the effectiveness in procuring through understanding the actual rate at which it was procured versus the estimated rate.

Let's take an example to understand this.

During the month, Nishka Toys manufactured 1000 units of soft toys. To manufacture one unit, it anticipated utilising 500 g of cotton and estimated to buy at INR 80 per kg. The actual consumption was 490 kg of cotton. The bills related to the same amounted to INR 39,690.

In this case, the business was expecting to consume 500 kg (500g*1000 units) of cotton and was expecting total cost to be INR 40 k (500kg*80 per kg). However, actual costs came to INR 39,690 which represents a savings of INR 310. This is a positive variance and very much welcome. But let's try to understand where the saving is coming from. The savings can be coming due to efficiencies in producing toys or it could be because of an effective way of managing procurement costs.

The rate at which the cotton was purchased was INR 81 per kg (INR 39690 divided by 490 kg). Thus, it's clear that it was the efficiency in production that helped in driving savings. This can be further explained in the following way.

	Usage (kgs)	Rate per kg	Total cost	
Estimated Costs	500	80	40000	
Actual Costs	490	81	39690	
Difference			310	
Now, Let's Analyse the Savings Due to Usage				
Savings in Usage (in kgs)	10			
Let's analyse the monetary savings due to lesser usage, if it was brought at estimated rate				
Savings Due to Usage	10	80	**800**	A
Let's Now Analyse the Additional Costs Due to Procurement at Higher Rates				
Actual Units Consumed	490			
Estimated Rate Minus Actual Rate		-1		
Additional costs incurred due to procurement at higher rate				
Dis-Savings Due to Rate	490	-1	**-490**	B
Net Savings			**310**	(A+B)

As you'll notice, the net savings of INR 310 is the same as the difference between estimated costs and actual costs. This approach helps us in analysing variances in a much better way and paves the way for taking corrective action. Here the corrective action could be to evaluate the procurement rates.

In the above example, if someone wants to assess things technically, then the input output analysis can help in understanding the reason for the efficiency. It can be due to lower process loss or less wastages.

Processing Costs

While monitoring raw materials used in production is one part, it is equally important to assess the costs of running the assets, which ultimately facilitates in getting the final product. On either a monthly or quarterly basis, these costs need to be assimilated and reviewed. These costs can be related to running the assets. Costs associated with running assets need to be properly assimilated and reviewed. To run the asset, you need power or fuel. Similarly, there are people employed in running these machines. Their productivity in terms of man-hours available and production generated needs to be measured. An asset requires regular maintenance to ensure that it has a long life. All these costs can be referred to as processing costs and are related to the cost of manufacturing a specific product. This should be measured against the planned costs or estimated costs and variance should be assessed.

Certain costs are associated with manufacturing of multiple goods at same time. These costs should be allocated to the products on a certain basis. For example, there could be a single supervisor managing production line of product A and B. The manpower required for both these products are different. Product A requires more manpower than product B. In such case, the cost of supervisor needs to be allocated more to product A than B.

All of what has been mentioned above should be assessed against the estimated or standard costs and variance should be analysed. These variances help in measuring the efficiencies of production and effectiveness of procuring. When this is done at the overall level and product level, it helps the entrepreneur or management to understand productivity.

A manufacturing controlling statement would look like something given on the next page. Sometimes the scale is very huge. In such cases, each line of costs should be assessed separately in depth.

	Esimates			Actuals			Variance		
Units Manufactured	**0**			**0**			**0**		
	Units	Rate	Costs	Units	Rate	Costs	Units	Rate	Costs
Raw Materials Consumed									
Material A	0	0	0	0	0	0	0	0	0
Material B	0	0	0	0	0	0	0	0	0
Material C	0	0	0	0	0	0	0	0	0
Material D	0	0	0	0	0	0	0	0	0
Material Consumption	**0**			**0**			**0**		
Salaries and Wages									
Labour Costs	0			0			0		
No. of Employees	0			0			0		
Cost per Employee	0			0			0		
Management Costs	0			0			0		
No. of Employees	0			0			0		
Cost per Employee	0			0			0		
Total Salaries and Wages	**0**			**0**			**0**		
Cost per Employee	**0**			**0**			**0**		
Power and Fuel	0								
Depreciation	0								
Maintenance	0								
Total Costs	**0**			**0**			**0**		
Total Cost per Unit (Total Costs/Units Manufactured)									

The above kind of analysis is quite comprehensive and could be one of the best ways to assess productivity of manufacturing operations. The cost per unit is one of the most powerful indicator out here. It can provide avenues to do cost control exercises. The above can be replicated at the product level. This can go a long way in improving profitability.

The above helps in assessing the overall health of manufacturing operations. But the operations are made of multiple production lines related to different types of products. It's important to have a good control over product costs which can come from a product cost sheet. This will be on similar lines as we saw above. Let's look at a format of a product costs sheet.

	Esimates			Actuals			Variance		
Units Manufactured		**0**			**0**			**0**	
	Units	Rate	Costs	Units	Rate	Costs	Units	Rate	Costs
Direct Costs									
Raw Materials Consumed									
Material A	0	0	0	0	0	0	0	0	0
Material B	0	0	0	0	0	0	0	0	0
Material C	0	0	0	0	0	0	0	0	0
Material D	0	0	0	0	0	0	0	0	0
Material Consumption		**0**			**0**			**0**	
Direct Labour Costs		0			0			0	
Direct Supervisory Costs		0			0			0	
Other Direct Expenses									
Depreciation Related to Specific Asset		0			0			0	
Running Costs Related to Asset									
Maintenance of Specific Asset		0			0			0	
Total Direct Costs		**0**			**0**			**0**	
Indirect Costs									
Indirect Labour Costs		0			0			0	
Supervisory Costs		0			0			0	
Depreciation		0			0			0	
Maintenance		0			0			0	
Power and Fuel		0			0			0	
Total Indirect Costs		0			0			0	
Total Costs		**0**			**0**			**0**	

The above analysis brings to light one more point, which relates to allocation of costs. The indirect costs are allocated on a certain basis. For example, supervisory costs will be allocated on the basis of number of employees managed. Depreciation and maintenance can be based on usage of assets by different types of products. Power and fuel can be based on power consumption. An incorrect allocation can result in taking some misinformed decisions. Each cost could have a different basis for allocation. For large organisations, there needs to be cost specialists or cost accountants who should be carrying out such tasks.

It's also important to have a technical manufacturing process map in place. This too can help in proper allocation but the use of manufacturing process map is much more than just facilitating allocation.

Example of manufacturing process:

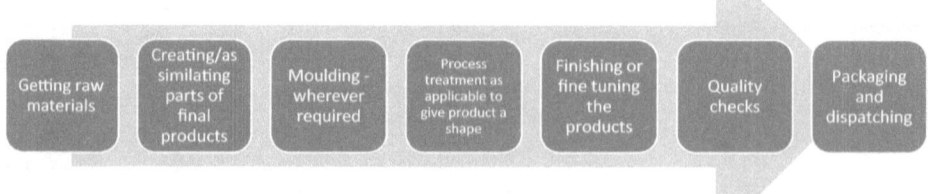

Depending on the complexities and nature of products manufactured, the process maps can be different, but the above provides a guideline on how a manufacturing process should look like. Such process maps give a bird's eye view of the entire production and can further facilitate in controlling things that imply controlling costs.

Service Delivery Costs

Unlike manufacturing costs, the costs associated in delivering services are different. A service delivery model doesn't require raw materials.

In some services, spares are required at times which facilitate in delivering the service. For example, in the car servicing industry or pathological laboratories some reagents or other chemical compounds are required as spares to run the business. The quantum of assets required might be different. There might be more costs associated with technology. However, the structure of assessing costs will be more or less the same as manufacturing costs.

Two important costs which can be key business drivers in a service delivery model are employee costs and technology costs. Most of the costs will be fixed in nature. The efficiency depends on more revenue generation using a specific set of assets.

Employees are the assets of any business. For most of the service delivery business they directly influence fee generation or revenue generation. It's very important that the right set of people are recruited to generate the services that provide the fees or revenues. It's important to monitor the talent pool available every time and care should be taken to have a proper bench in case of attritions. At times, the employees need to be provided regular training to keep them abreast of the market. It's important to assess the training needs and measure the cost impact. Also, alternatives need to be considered in order to drive cost optimisation in this space.

Similarly, for technology related business, the technology developed by the business is a critical asset and it's important to analyse how effectively such assets can be used to drive revenues. Such technology would require maintenance on a regular basis. It might have to be scaled as operations are expanded. Different dimensions and improvement need to be incorporated on a regular basis to keep such technology alive in the market.

In case of manufacturing operations too, technology plays a key role. There too, this cost needs to be assessed on a regular basis and allocated to the product line.

A sample is provided which helps in understanding how service costs need to be assessed.

Service delivery costs assessment			
	Esimate	Actuals	Variance
Salaries and Wages			
Employee Costs	0	0	0
No. of Employees	0	0	0
Cost per Employee	0	0	0
Management Costs Associated Directly with Managing Services	0	0	0
No. of Employees	0	0	0
Cost per Employee	0	0	0
Total Salaries and Wages	**0**	**0**	**0**
Cost per Employee	**0**	0	0
Training Costs			
In House			
Outsourced			
Depreciation on Training Assets			
Total Training Costs	**0**	**0**	**0**
Spares Consumed	0	0	0
Technology Costs Hardware Costs	0	0	0
Manpower Costs	0	0	0
Software Development /R&D Costs	0	0	0
Depreciation	0	0	0
Total Technology Costs	**0**	**0**	**0**
Depreciation on Other Assets	0	0	0
Power Costs	0	0	0
Rent/Maintenance/Others	0	0	0
Cost of Delivering Service	**0**	**0**	**0**

The **cost of delivering a service** needs to be deducted from the revenues to get the gross contribution or gross margins. It's similar to the cost of manufacturing. Normally, in the service business, the costs should be assessed directly against the revenues, because the services directly result in getting the fees. It doesn't result in creating an inventory which is then converted to cash. These costs also facilitate in assessing the pricing.

The following is a process map that can help in identifying the cost components associated with delivering a service. There are numerous service related industries. Their process maps will be different from each other, but the idea is to give you a flavour of how to map a process and identify the costs associated with the same.

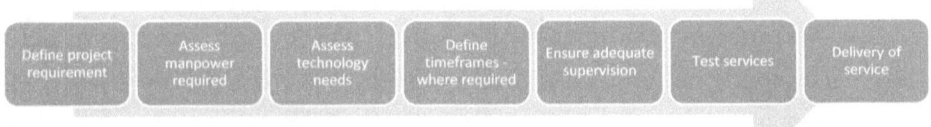

Revenue Generation Controls

While the production and service related controls facilitate in controlling the costs of the products, one of the most important elements of any business is revenue generation. Any business needs to tap into customers directly or through intermediaries. There are costs associated in maintaining these intermediaries and big customers. Similarly, there are marketing costs incurred to create a presence of the product in the market. Any of these activities will fail if the price is not properly determined. Prices are determined by market forces, but care must be taken to ensure that they cover all the relevant costs.

Let's try and understand the different types of revenue generation controls that need to be put in place.

1. **Pricing** – This is the most important of all the controls. While there is a transactional element to this, which is already covered earlier, but sometimes, special pricing has to be offered in order to tap the market and drive incremental profits or cater to big projects. Normally, cases of special pricing contain a lot of aggression. The company invests through pricing to tap more market share and intends to recover them in future once relationship and trust with customer is built through better customer service or at times by driving more sales volume. Sometimes, the supply in the market is such that special pricing is the only option available to drive sales volumes. Profits are recovered through other products or services. Sometimes, in case of special pricing, it is not possible

to recover all the costs, but one needs to know the nature of costs. Certain costs are fixed, while others are variable. It is always be advisable to have a mechanism to have variable and fixed costs assessed separately. Fixed costs would have to be incurred irrespective of whether the business has lower volumes or higher volumes of production or sales. However, if the pricing is able to cover variable costs, then in such cases, the business tends to get some incremental profits, which help in covering the fixed costs to some extent. Let's recollect the example that I had shared in the planning section related to the cost of manufacturing of two products viz. Product A and Product B. Let's bring back the cost sheet of Product B to understand the above concept.

	Expense Type	Product B
Units Manufactured		10000
Raw Materials Consumption	**Variable**	**800,000**
Labour Cost	**Fixed**	
No. of Labourers		4
Cost per Employee per Quarter		45000
Total Cost of Labourers		**180000**
Depreciation	**Fixed**	
Machine Value		2,000,000
Useful Life (In Years)		10
Depreciation for the Year		200,000
Depreciation for the Quarter		**50000**
Maintenance Costs	**Fixed**	**20000**
Electricity Costs	**Variable**	**20000**
Total Direct Costs		**1,070,000**
Direct Cost per Unit		**107**
Indirect Costs		
Rent	Fixed	60000
Supervisor	Fixed	40000
Total Indirect Costs		**100000**
Cost of Production or to Bring Goods to Saleable Form		**1,170,000**
Cost of Production per Unit		**117**

In the above case, the total variable costs amount to INR 820 k. This means that the variable cost per unit is INR 82 per unit on 10k of production. The cost of production is INR 117 and if you recollect from the example as given in the planning section, the freight costs is INR 10 per unit. INR 92 per unit (INR 82 variable cost + INR 10 as freight) will be incurred with every additional unit manufactured.

Now, let's assume that there is a proposal given by a customer to purchase 1k units at INR 110 per unit of Product B and there is spare capacity to manufacture Product B.

One might be tempted to reject the proposal outright to sell the product at INR 110 as it does not cover the cost of production, which is INR 117. However, one needs to remember that out of this INR 117, INR 92 is variable costs. The rest is fixed costs. In such case, the variable cost that is applicable for each unit is INR 92 per unit. Every unit sold will have these costs. If pricing is below INR 92, business must bear the costs and it does not result in any value addition. In the above case the value addition is INR 110-INR 92 or INR 18 per unit. At INR 18 per unit, the business makes an incremental profit of INR 18k. Remember the fixed costs are anyway there. They have to be incurred whether you produce one unit or 10k units, as long as there's spare capacity to produce additional units. So, if there's some spare capacity, the INR 18k will help in recovering a part of fixed costs.

Thus, in the above scenario, even if the price is too aggressive, it makes sense to offer special pricing if it's able to cover a part of fixed costs. In management accounting terms, this is referred to as **marginal costing**.

2. **Product mix or Product profitability**– Apart from pricing, another important element that needs to be controlled is product mix. Normally a business might offer different products and services to different customers and intermediaries. There is always a possibility that business can achieve its revenue plan, but it might miss its profit plans. One reason could be that it wasn't driving enough of margin-rich products. Not all products have the same profitability.

The profits coming from certain product lines are significantly higher than the other products. Similarly, the volume of sales for certain products are higher than others. In a product mix, one tries to assess the volumes sold of different products and the net contribution coming from different product lines, after considering all costs and investments done. One of the best ways to control this is by doing a product level profitability analysis, upto a point called net contribution. Below is a sample explaining the same.

	Product A	Product B	Total
Selling Price per Unit	300.0	220.0	255.6
Units Sold	8,000	10,000	18,000
Revenues	2,400,000	2,200,000	4,600,000
Cost of Production per Unit	142.7	117.0	128.4
Cost of Production	1,141,600	1,170,000	2,311,600
Freight Costs per Unit	10.0	10.0	10.0
Freight Costs	80,000	100,000	180,000
Cost of Goods Sold	1,221,600	1,270,000	2,491,600
Cost of Goods Sold per Unit	152.7	127.0	138.4
Gross Profits per Unit	147.3	93.0	117.1
Gross Profits %	49.10%	42.27%	45.83%
Gross Profits	1,178,400	930,000	2,108,400
Direct Marketing Costs	500,000	300,000	800,000
Direct Selling Expenses	100,000	70,000	170,000
Net Margins/Contribution	578,400	560,000	1,138,400
Net Margin/Contribution %	24.10%	25.45%	24.75%

From the above you can see that Product A has a higher gross profit % than Product B and it makes more sense to drive more of Product A. However, the action taken by the business to boost demand of Product A through marketing and selling efforts isn't paying off so well as the volumes are not helping it to drive higher net margin or net contribution from Product A. Inspite of having a stronger gross profits, the net margin or net contribution is more or less same for Product A and B.

Such kind of analysis can provide insights with respect to the returns that can be expected from marketing and sales investments. This should be reviewed on a periodic basis, maybe a monthly, quarterly or yearly, to make a judicious call on future investments in certain product lines. It's always better to compare them versus plan and variances should be measured. However, this should be used along with other factors to see if this investment is sustainable in the long term or corrective action needs to be taken now to bring back better profitability of Product A. Sometimes, current investment takes time to get the right level of volumes. However, one must be really careful and objective while making decisions on continuing or curtailing some of the investments. This is more of an art than science and requires a lot of prudent thinking.

A typical format that can be used to measure product profitability will be as follows.

Product A Profitability			
	Plan	Actuals	Variance
Gross Revenues	0	0	0
Rebates/Discounts	0	0	0
Net Revenues	0	0	0
Cost of Goods Sold	0	0	0
Gross Contribution	0	0	0
Gross Contribuiton %	0%	0%	0%
Direct Marketing Costs	0	0	0
Direct Sales Costs	0	0	0
Net Contribution	0	0	0
Net Contribution %	0%	0%	0%

3. **Marketing costs/Selling costs** – While the above gives a good understanding of the product profitability, it's also important to assess the efficacy of the marketing and sales investments on a regular basis. This can be done by evaluating the marketing costs in further details to see the marketing vehicles used to drive revenue generating activities. Also, it's important to see how sales force has sold different lines of products or services. Similarly, rebates are given to different lines of products. It should be seen how different rebates or concessions are facilitating in driving business of specific products. The productivity of spends should be assessed.

Wherever required, necessary changes should be done to drive the optimal results. This should be reflected in the plan and should be measured against the same on a periodic basis. For example: if advertising is done on large scale for a much higher duration of time, but volumes are more or less the same, call should be taken to curtail or reduce such spends. Similarly if more rebates are given to a product that has high gross margins, but doesn't have enough sales volumes, the same should be analysed properly and proper actions need to be taken to drive better volumes and if it's still not possible to drive good sales volumes, decisions on rebate investments should be made regarding continuing with such investment or cutting it down.

This sample format might help in assessing marketing spends and sales spends. This should be assessed against the planned spends. This format can be expanded further to incorporate more details. For example, if one wishes to know in which media the advertising costs are incurred, then a split of TV, internet, newspaper etc. should be provided. Similarly if there different type of rebates offered, the same should be reflected if some of them are strategic in nature.

	Product A	Product B	Common	Total
Revenues				
Advertising Costs				
Media Costs				
Fees Paid				
Total Advertising Costs				
Promotions				
Other Marketing Expenses				
Total Marketing Expenses				
Marketing Expense % to Revenue				
Rebates & Concessions				
Sales Costs				
Salaries				
Other Selling Costs				
Total Selling Expenses				
Selling Expenses % to Revenue				

Similarly, headcount productivity should be assessed to understand how efficiently sales force is being deployed.

	Product A	Product B	Common	Total	
Revenues					A
Gross Margins					B
No. of Employees					C
Revenues per Employee					D=A/C
Gross Margin per Employee					E=B/C

4. **Customer level profitability/Reach** – While product level profitability is important, it's also important to assess customer level profitability or route to market level (RTM) profitability. Certain route to markets might be more profitable than others. Care should be taken to nurture and drive more volumes from that route to market. This is the essence of driving profitability in the omni channel set up. Like route to market, customer profitability can facilitate in understanding the profitability from the top revenue contributing customers. This can go further in negotiating better terms with the customers, if required.

Also, this exercise might help in assessing the growth of customers or growth of route to market, which can be quarter over quarter, year over year or month over month. Many a times this facilitates in pricing decisions as well.

Customer/Route to Market (RTM) Profitability Analysis			
	Customer A / RTM A	Customer B / RTM B	Total
Gross Revenues	0	0	0
Rebates/discounts	0	0	0
Net Revenues	0	0	0
Cost of goods sold	0	0	0
Gross contribution	0	0	0
Gross contribuiton %	0%	0%	0%
Direct Marketing costs	0	0	0

Direct Sales Costs	0	0	0
Net Contribution	**0**	**0**	**0**
Net Contribution %	**0%**	**0%**	**0%**

While the above can be of great help, it's important to dissect the growth in revenues coming from the total number of customers which can be end customers, consumers or intermediaries catered by the business. This can be done at the product level and separately for each RTM. Growth in revenues can come from increasing spends from existing buyers or it can be from increased account penetration. It's always advisable to assess revenue growth on these lines. The format below can help you understand the same.

A	B	C	D	E	F	G=A-D	H=C-F	I=B-E	J=G*F	K=H*A
Current Year			Last year/Forecast			Variance				
No. of customers	Revenue	Spend per customer	No. of customers	Revenue	Spend per customer	No. of customers	Spend per customer	Revenues	Account penetration	Share of wallet
100	1000000	10000	120	960000	8000	-20	2000	**40000**	-160000	200000

The above is a powerful tool to assess how you are performing in terms of getting more customers or increasing spends from existing customers. **It's a tool to assess REACH.** Not only that, it also helps at times to **assess the elasticity of prices** if done at the product level. Share of wallet can be replaced by price realisation and no. of customers can be replaced by sales volume to assess elasticity of prices.

In the above case, revenues of a RTM for the current year was measured against last year. This can be done against forecast as well if you're building such forecast.

We assessed that the number of additional customers penetrated was less than last year. So it was shown as -20. Spend per customer was higher than last year by INR 2k per customer. Revenue difference between current year and last year was INR 40k.

As we saw, the no. of customers that gave business was less than last year and spend per customer had increased. So one can deduce that spend per customer was the driving force for revenue increase. However, it's important to assess the impact of this on revenue growth. So we calculated growth coming due to account penetration and share of wallet. The sum of both of them will be same as revenue growth between two years.

Growth coming from share of wallet was INR 200k higher than last year. This is measured by assessing the increase in spends viz. INR 2k versus last year and measuring it against or multiplying it with the current year's customer base, which is 100 in our case. Thus on 100 customers, we managed to increase spend per customer of INR 2k which gave us INR 200k higher revenues.

The no. of accounts got reduced from last year by 20. This has an impact on growth coming from account penetration. In fact there was degrowth due to account penetration of INR 160k. This was measured by assessing the increase or decrease in no. of customers viz. 20 less customers in current year or – 20, with the base spend per customer. The base spend for us is last year's spends which is INR 8k. Thus, on 20 reduced customers, we had earned INR 160k last year with an average spend of INR 8k per customer, but we missed earning it this year.

Thus, the above analysis tells you that maybe the price offered in trade was not lucrative to tap more customers or there was more reliance on less customer base in the current year, which could be a real concern. Accordingly, it facilitates in taking appropriate decisions which could be tapping more markets or becoming a bit more aggressive with pricing.

Opex Controls

Opex controls would tend to cover all the administrative costs that facilitate in running the business. These typically consist of maintaining staff to do general management of the business which can include general management costs, support level costs like HR costs and finance costs.

This can also include the cost of facility and costs required to maintain the facility.

These costs are fixed in nature. Care must be taken to see that these costs do not run beyond a certain threshold. One simple way, though not perfect, to see this is to assess it as a percentage of sales viz. opex cost/revenues.

Also, care should be taken that, as business expands, proper investments are made here to provide relevant support to the business. A proper assessment of headcount should be done to assess the number of people supporting the business. Sometimes, business is called to take some tough decisions like rationalisation of costs. In such instances, proper care should be taken to analyse headcount and call should be taken to reduce those costs which have least impact. This requires an in-depth analysis of work stream, which is carried by different people.

Business P&L

Every month, quarter or year, a business P&L, management P&L or business operations P&L should be reviewed. This should be assessed against the plan and previous years or quarter. Business P&L is the result of all transaction and business controls that were put in place. It also reflects the efficiency of the planning process. It reflects how well each activity was managed. So this P&L should be reviewed in conjunction with all the above elements we had covered in the controlling section so far to get a holistic view of the business operations. A business P&L gives a bird's eye view of the total operating income of the business and is an indicator of how strong the operating leverage of the business is. A typical business P&L can look as follows. It will not cover finance costs as it's related to funding controls and business P&L is more about operational controls.

	Current Year			Current Year – 1		Current Year – 2	
	Actuals	Plan	Variance	Actuals	YoY%	Actuals	YoY%
Profit and Loss Statement							
Gross Sales							
Rebates/Discounts							
Net Sales							
Cost of Goods Sold							
cost of Manufacturing							
Freight							
Other Costs							
Total Cost of Goods Sold							

Gross Contribution/Gross Margin								
Gross mgn %								
Marketing Costs								
Advertising								
Promotions								
Others								
Marketing Staff Salaries								
Marketing Costs								
Marketing Cost %								
Selling Costs								
Sales Force Salaries								
Other Expenses								
Selling Costs								
Selling Costs %								
Administrative and General Expenses								
Operating Profit								

With this we have covered all aspects of business controls that one needs to maintain to improve productivity and thereby create more value addition. This can act as an indicator to the entrepreneur to drive more business and expand in size. It can also facilitate in better profit management due to identifying efficiency and economies in different parts of business. Ideally management needs to do a critical review of business P&L on a regular periodic basis.

IV. Funding Controls

The short-term and long-term fund requirements of a business can be met by internal or external sources. Irrespective of how the business obtains its funds, it is important to have a control over them. There should be a mechanism to evaluate all the funding options before choosing the appropriate one. It is very important to ensure that the cash conversion cycle is intact and moving seamlessly. The policies revolving around working capital should be properly monitored. There has to be a robust credit and collections process in place. The repayment of loans or any other external source should be done on time to avoid late fees or penalties. All this is part of having a proper control over funds which is the lifeline of the business. Let's understand what factors need to be evaluated to have a better control over funds.

Evaluate All Funding Options Before Choosing The Appropriate One

A business can obtain funds from various sources. If it wishes to take less risk, it can try to pull like-minded minds to join its business and obtain funds from them. It can be in the form of partnership or in case of companies it can be through issuing additional shares. These funds are typically required for long-term purpose. In such a case, the entrepreneur or existing shareholders will have to reduce their stake and therefore will have a less share of profits. But this funding option makes more sense especially when the gestation period or the period by which the business starts making profit takes more time. It's important to understand the break-even period of any business.

But not everyone will be willing to part with their funds in a business which has such a high gestation period. Sometimes, it makes more sense to get venture capitalists or other investors who have a higher appetite to take more risks to fund the business. Such a business needs tight monetary controls to ensure that they are investing properly and leakages are kept at minimum. It is always advisable to work towards getting profits at the earliest. Many of today's online businesses are funded in this manner. The gestation period of such businesses is very high.

In the case of internal source of funds, it's always advisable to assess the proportion of ownership that you're willing to let go in return of funds which you require to run your business. The providers of funds will always negotiate for a larger share in business. It's up to the entrepreneur to showcase the kind of value addition that they are capable of driving and build a case for a maximum amount it can let go as its ownership. Ideally, it's always advisable to get back the ownership from financial investors who are interested in their capital appreciation, after the business turns profitable. Care should be taken to ensure that the proportion of stake that is diluted is at comfortable levels; otherwise the entrepreneur or promoters might lose interest or will have less incentive to drive more value-added growth.

External source of funds should ideally be resorted to for short-term requirements or where the visibility on earnings is high. Sometimes, it's not possible to obtain funds from an internal source and so one has to rely on external source. In such cases, care should be taken to ensure that there is no huge strain while making payment of loan and it is not resulting in a debt trap. Proper interest rates should be negotiated after consulting different banks and financial institutions. This is like taking a loan for a house or a car on an individual basis. In such cases, we would refer to different banks to fund our requirement. However, unlike a bank loan for a car or a house, which is easy to obtain if you have a fixed salary, in case of business, it's a bit difficult as earnings are not fixed. It's therefore important to demonstrate the earning capability by providing a proper audited P&L statement and showcasing the ability of the business to generate such kind of profits in future. For a new business, the plan should be very detailed and critically evaluated before presenting to bankers for loan. Also, it's important to remember that a bank may charge higher interest rates if it perceives risk. Sometimes other alternatives could be available which do not require higher funding. Alternative options like outsourcing should be considered if higher capital commitment doesn't make sense.

Cash Conversion Controls

The cash conversion controls are typically related to managing debtors or accounts receivables. It's important to get money on time from debtors to reduce dependence on other sources to fund a business. Similarly, inventory should be kept at a minimum or optimal level so that much of cash doesn't get blocked in inventory. The key is to have a proper control over debtors and inventory. The controls related to debtors and inventory were already reflected in transactional controls and business controls. Apart from this, it's also important that the asset is turning around quickly and generating benefits or revenues for the business. This is covered under business controls. These controls directly impact and facilitate the conversion of cash back into cash.

I definitely suggest readers to use cash flow extensively to analyse how cash is generated over different time periods, how it's being utilised and where it's coming from. **Please refer to the case study in the planning section for more details on cash flow statement.** Cash flow analysis should be done on a regular basis and compared with the planned cash flow projections. The variances can help in maintaining best practices and taking corrective actions wherever needed.